The Glazer Gatekeeper

Six years' speaking for Manchester United's silent owners

Tehsin Nayani

First published in 2015 by TH Media, Derbyshire, United Kingdom.

ISBN 978-0-9928398-3-3

Cover concept by Tehsin Nayani. Design by Andrew Swainson.

Printed by Digital Print Media, Cambridgeshire, United Kingdom

www.theglazergatekeeper.com

"The natural state of the football fan is bitter disappointment, no matter what the score"

Nick Hornby, *Fever Pitch*

Contents

Foreword

Better the Red Devil You Know?

The Glazers may not be the ideal owners of Manchester United.

The publicity-shy Americans will never know what it's like to be a true local supporter living within spitting distance of Old Trafford. Their American accents, should they ever voice them in public, will always jar with those who resent the loss of *their* club to global commercial forces. And then there's the debt…

When Roman Abramovich was contemplating a purchase of an English football club, he asked his advisors to draw up a feasibility study of prospective teams. According to Abramovich's lawyer Bruce Buck – who would go on to become chairman of Chelsea – the study adjudged that Manchester United "would be expensive and the fans would go crazy"[1].

When the Glazers sought to buy Manchester United many of its fans did indeed go crazy; some still are.

This book reflects on a riveting time to be at the business end of a game when stories relating to football clubs' off-the-pitch affairs would at times eclipse the on-the-pitch action. This, of course, was especially so for Manchester United, where every nugget of information would carry enormous resonance in the media and beyond, and whose owners, the Glazer family, courted such suspicion and controversy that it was often difficult to look beyond the customised portrayal of them as sinister cartoon bogeymen.

---

[1] Chelsea owner Roman Abramovich is a football anorak, reveals chairman Bruce Buck, *The Daily Telegraph*, 21 September 2011

I hope *The Glazer Gatekeeper* will provide a unique glimpse into the considerable off-pitch activity of a top club like Manchester United and how it engages, not always happily, with the world's media.

Also, I would be pleased if this book can contribute to the debate about football ownership, especially in light of the Glazers' own reluctance to engage publicly. However, I appreciate it is unlikely to assuage the deep-rooted resentment of their presence at Old Trafford among some United fans.

Finally, I am writing this book to shine a light on this very special time of my life and career. Throughout a momentous six-year period I felt extremely proud and privileged to serve Manchester United. I hope the book offers up some very human insight and colour into the unique journey I made working for the owners of an illustrious football club at the peak of its global powers.

Part One
The Takeover

The Green and Gold Poster Boy

'*We want Glazer out, we want Glazer out*', and '*Love United, hate Glazer*' chants reverberated loudly around the stadium. The highly-charged atmosphere at Old Trafford that cold March night was a culmination of months of fans' escalated anger and was like nothing I had experienced before. The supporters' joy at the prospect of Manchester United sweeping past AC Milan to reach the quarter finals of the Champions League quickly transformed into mutinous dissent that seemed to permeate every snaking row of the Theatre of Dreams' 75,000 strong crowd. Huge swathes of home fans – maybe as many as half of them – brandished their vivid green-and-gold scarves, which had come to symbolise their open defiance of the club's owners, the Glazer family.

I was perched inside Old Trafford's press box and the club's co-chairman, Avie Glazer, was in view across from me in the cordoned-off directors' area. To the left of us, fans had draped two large 'Love United Hate Glazer' banners from the Stretford End stand, almost like a makeshift altar to illustrate the accumulated years of resentment towards the club's owners. Already 3-0 up on the night, 6-2 on aggregate, I'd had enough as well; the fans' anger and animosity towards my employers was just too toxic for me, and was something from which I was happy to make a premature exit.

Minutes later, and safely back in my central Manchester Malmaison hotel room, I switched the television to ITV's live coverage of the match. With the game nearly over, United were 4-0 up and through to the next round, leaving their fellow football aristocrats AC Milan utterly humiliated. And yet the anti-Glazer chants and scarf-twirling seemed, if anything, to have intensified. Tiring of the dead-rubber status of the match, the television cameras dutifully panned to the vociferous supporter protest, beaming it live to the millions watching worldwide.

Following the final whistle, the chants turned to *'There's only one David Beckham'* as the Milan substitute and erstwhile United idol acknowledged his generous homecoming from the Old Trafford crowd and made a slow, emotional exit. As he neared the players' tunnel, Beckham briefly stooped in front of the Stretford End and picked up a green-and-gold scarf that had been thrown down to him on to the pitch side. He put the scarf around his neck and raised his arms in grateful applause to an ecstatic home crowd. A pivotal moment? My adrenaline pumping, I immediately grabbed my BlackBerry, scrolled through my address book to 'JG' and pressed the green icon, dialling up United's other co-chairman Joel Glazer, Avie's brother, who was over in the States.

"Joel, are you watching what I am watching?"

"Yes I am Tes, what's your take?"

"Well, the green-and-gold movement have just found their poster boy. That's big news likely to go around the world…"

"Uh-huh, sure, but is that so bad?"

"Well, it'll give the fans opposed to your ownership even greater publicity, on a worldwide level. And David Beckham's a good catch for the protesters."

"I get that, but we don't know Beckham's motives for putting on the scarf. Also I'm not sure the publicity is necessarily bad."

"But Beckham's gesture is likely to be construed as a negative."

"Sure, but let's strip this back. What I mean to say is that football is a passionate business. Won't it blow over? It's always blown over in the past. Anyway, what's your advice? What do we do next?"

"There's likely to be loads of coverage tomorrow. You heard the chants at the game. I've never seen anything like it. It might be an idea to not react to it. Certainly my instinct would be to not comment on the Beckham incident; anything we say will merely give the story even further oxygen."

"Agreed. Remember Tes, you're in the eye of the storm over there. Sure, some fans are angry and protesting inside Old Trafford. But from where I'm sitting there are many millions of fans who are just happy the team are through to the next round. They're supporters of Manchester United too. I get that some fans don't like us, but to *hate* us, it's such a strong word. To hate us when the club has been so successful, it's extraordinary."

"Football's an emotionally-charged affair Joel. That's what you've always told me."

"Sure Tes. Anyway, let's think on, we don't need to make any decisions right now. Let's check in tomorrow."

Barbarian at the Gate

Some five-and-a-half years earlier, in late 2004, I was finishing off my ritual Sunday evening ironing in the humid kitchen of my rented flat in north London. As usual, the radio was humming in the background and I was half-listening to Jeff Randall's *Weekend Business* show on BBC Radio 5 Live. Up for discussion was an American, Malcolm Glazer, whose bid to buy Manchester United looked doomed after a fractious annual general meeting of shareholders. Even that weekend's *Financial Times*, still unread and plonked on the glass top of my Ikea kitchen table, screamed "Glazer scores own goal over Man Utd". A universally vilified Glazer, with his bid rebuffed, had vindictively voted off three board members, only to see his furious bankers and PR representatives resign in protest. The consensus was that the club's board had succeeded in beating off the barbarian Glazer at the gate.

Well, that's how it appeared to most at the time.

Of course, it never occurred to me then that within a few months I would be intimately involved, plotting the Glazer family's takeover of the world's most iconic sporting institution, not least because the Glazers seemed to me – like most outsiders – to be an undesirable busted flush.

With the 2005 New Year just a few weeks' old I was occupied with bread and butter financial public relations work, researching the possible flotation of a small company on London's booming AIM stock market. At the end of what felt just like another humdrum day, with the cold office already shrouded in a Dickensian winter gloom, my agency's managing director, John Antcliffe, impishly invited me into his office, which he liked to line with mementoes and tombstone trophies of the publicity campaigns he had worked on while at the front end of Margaret Thatcher's privatisation revolution.

Barely disguising his excitement, John said he would like me to join him on a new account involving football, which he knew I was keenly interested in: the takeover of Manchester United. Immediately I felt seized with a torn ambivalence; while the prospect of working on such a high-profile account thrilled me, it was tempered by the anxiety of representing such a reviled – and seemingly doomed – client.

There hadn't been the usual beauty parade of potential PR agencies pitching their wares to the Glazer family. My agency, Smithfield (which shared its moniker with London's neighbouring meat market) had been referred to the Glazer family by one of its long-term clients, namely the illustrious merchant bank – by now rebranded 'investment' bank – NM Rothschild, which had been recruited by the Glazers for advice on a fresh takeover attempt.

John's response, which seemed rehearsed, was considered and convincing. Rothschild, John's previous employer and longstanding Smithfield client, stood 100 per cent behind the Glazers and did not back losers. What about the Glazers' hostile raid on the venerable Manchester United, I mused. Rothschild, John explained, had cherished historical links with Manchester. Its eponymous founder, Nathan Mayer, had settled in the city and had established himself in the British Empire's booming industrial engine room, making a fortune from finance and textile trading. Two centuries on, the bank would not support the Glazers if it had any suspicions of their wealth and good intentions.

So the following day, on Wednesday 19 January, with my doubts soothed and the plan cloaked in complete secrecy (even among agency colleagues) our team of four found ourselves at Rothschild's headquarters. An imposing City mansion, the building was a stone's throw away from the Bank of England and was decorated inside with the restrained sophisticated chic reminiscent of a first class airport departure lounge. Rothschild's team was headed by the bank's managing director, Robert Leitao. Leitao embodied the as yet unchallenged perception of banker as master of the universe: super-confident and resplendent in his expensively tailored lounge suit, yet beguilingly blunt and thoroughly engaging. Leitao's colleague was Majid Ishaq: twinkly-eyed, down to earth and a Manchester United season ticket holder in the Stretford End who, significantly, was satisfied by the Glazers' provenance, too. Both had recently returned from a post-Christmas trip to Florida where they had spent time with Malcolm's son, Joel Glazer, meeting him over a sun-drenched lunch at the Mar-a-Lago resort in West Palm Beach.

The briefing meeting was a long one. It detailed the complexity of the challenge at hand, namely how the Glazers might be able to go over the heads of a recalcitrant Manchester United board and efficiently hoover up the publicly traded shares available on the open market. During the meeting we also gleaned insights into the main players in Florida and Manchester, including the club's distinguished and long-serving manager Sir Alex Ferguson, and their likely next moves.

One important issue Rothschild had already divined was the other major shareholding block, approximately equivalent in size to the Glazers' 29 per cent (just below the 30 per cent level which would automatically trigger a takeover attempt). The so called 'Cubic Expression', owned by Irish racing tycoons John Magnier and JP McManus, would be willing to sell at the right price, probably at 300 pence per share, enabling the Glazers to secure majority ownership regardless of the United board. Significantly, too, we learned that JP Morgan had been charged with syndicating the debt to help fund the takeover; a twist in events given that JP Morgan had been seen to angrily resign its advisory role to the Glazers at the stormy annual general meeting of shareholders (AGM) that took place in Manchester in November 2004. It would transpire that JP Morgan, whose company policy was to not support hostile takeover bids, had indeed forfeited their role but, in cahoots with the Glazers, had pre-agreed to work behind the scenes on any future takeover bid.

The main document circulated that night was a letter drafted by

Rothschild and the lawyers Allen & Overy, which had already been checked over by the Glazers. It outlined a provisional takeover bid including a proposal to reduce the level of debt from their previous 2004 offer by including a quasi-equity instrument provided by hedge funds; a Payment-in-Kind (PIK) note. The plan was to lodge the letter with Manchester United chairman Sir Roy Gardner at some point in the near future, subject to tentative talks with the club's board, the hope being that it would fire the starting pistol on the American family's renewed takeover attempt.

Project Hampstead

We left the meeting into the cold dark evening, reasonably sure that the Glazers, contrary to perceived wisdom, would succeed buying Manchester United, although not certain about any likely timeframe. Indeed, the months between our furtive January visit to Rothschild and the takeover in the warm long daylight of mid-May proved to be relatively low key, marked by continuing stealth and secrecy. The project, to maintain a semblance of confidentiality, was incongruously entitled 'Hampstead'. The prospective acquirers were self-styled 'Red Football' and Manchester United was code named 'Mercury'.

The first half of 2005 saw me continuing to serve my other clients, while keeping a watching brief on Red Football. Speculation of a revived Glazer bid was rife against a backdrop of supporter ire, whipped up by continuing media interest. Indeed, a late January lunchtime meeting with a Scottish broadsheet business editor proved to be particularly illuminating. Already tiring of discussing my Scottish telecoms client, he drew closer to me and said in hushed tones: "The only story in town is Manchester United". And we were sitting in Edinburgh. Not for the first or last time, I would keep my counsel, satisfied with the pleasure of being trusted with such a tantalising secret.

Towards the end of January, news broke in the London *Evening Standard* that Rothschild had been hired by the Glazer family. This report of a concrete development, the first since that notorious AGM two months previously, was to fuel speculation that a Glazer move was imminent. The *Standard's* story would prompt a further wave of virulent supporter anger. Rothschild was forced to take down its website which had hitherto hosted contact details of its key staff. Mindful of reports that the Glazers' previous PR agency, Brunswick, had been subjected to a barrage of unsolicited pizza deliveries, black ink faxes and website attacks, Smithfield commissioned a review of security at the agency's cramped offices which culminated in a new set of locks, an upgraded alarm system and the website being replaced with a disingenuous 'currently under redevelopment' message.

In truth, while we were to be deluged with emails (half of them somewhat abusive and deranged, the remainder polite and business-like, pleading us to stop working for the Glazers) we did not receive anything too menacing. However, as a director of the agency I was allowed the privilege of not having my personal details lodged on public record at Companies House, a prerogative normally accorded to those involved in the security services or in animal testing!

6th of February

An early example under my watch of how the Glazers would forever be cast as the villain of the piece occurred in early February. The sixth of February marked the anniversary of the Munich air disaster, a date that carries a deeply sad resonance among all those who care for the city of Manchester and its football. Newspapers cried foul[2] that the Glazers had the callous insensitivity to launch their bid around this most emotionally charged of days; fans' groups jumped on the bandwagon cementing the myth that the Glazers had no scruples whatsoever.

The accusation was absurd. The leak seemed designed to pre-empt another takeover bid by causing irreparable damage to the Glazers' reputation. Indeed, it did serve to further poison relations among some

---

[2] United bid opens old wounds, *The Times*, 7 February 2005

already sceptical fans, goaded by a frustrated media seemingly all square against the Glazers.

So sensitive were the discussions underway, that it was paramount that secrecy had to be upheld, not least to comply with draconian stock market rules policed by the UK Takeover Panel. But by early February the widening circulation (among a multitude of advisors) of the Glazers' letter to the Manchester United board meant it was perhaps inevitable an undesired leak could and would occur.

Sources Close to Magnier and McManus

Throughout spring 2005, press speculation was rife that a hostile takeover would be attempted, although there was no consensus as to whether Cubic Expression would sell its 30 per cent stake in Manchester United. Many reputable newspapers claimed that 'sources close to Magnier and McManus' were adamant they would *not* sell their shares. But, in the previous November, the Glazers had already established that Cubic would be willing sellers, but only at the right price. Rather than an 'own goal' as was widely reported, the Glazers' proxy vote by their legal representatives to boot off the three non-executives from the board during the heated AGM in Manchester had succeeded in smoking out Cubic, who conspicuously did not come to the board's rescue to countervote the Glazers. It might not have been obvious then, but the Glazers and their advisors had established that Cubic, who had very publicly fallen out with United's manager Sir Alex Ferguson over the ownership of the racehorse Rock of Gibraltar, had no loyal ties to the PLC board.

This vital piece of intelligence would clear the way in 2005 for a revised approach to the Manchester United board. While the Glazers would continue to seek a constructive dialogue with the club's board, they felt confident they could resort to a Plan B of dealing directly with Cubic Expression.

Behind closed doors the Glazers and the Manchester United board, together with their respective advisors, were locked in frequent (and often fraught) negotiations, interrupted for a spell when Joel Glazer fell ill. As I was not present in these meetings I will not elaborate on them, although Mihir Bose's book *Manchester Disunited*[3] which relies on many interviews with the advisors who attended, provides a reliable chronicle of events.

Communications remained reactive and discreet to avoid the wrath of the Takeover Panel, and to adhere to everyone's wish to keep a lid on expectations of a bid. John Antcliffe took responsibility for providing understated and unattributable briefings to the media, carefully guiding journalists along the lines of the original letter drafted by advisors. Eventually signed by a convalesced Joel Glazer, this letter was sent to the Manchester United board and detailed the rationale and credentials for a takeover.

Put up or Shut up

By late April, press speculation was mounting that a 300p per share offer for the Club was imminent, especially in light of the Takeover Panel's decision to impose a 17 May 'put up or shut up' deadline on a bid.

So much had been written and commented on in the media – much of it wide of the mark and hostile to the prospect of a Glazer bid – that, by early May, John Antcliffe and I mused that once the takeover was launched the story might very well settle down quickly, and may perhaps be over in two to three days. It was a classic case of us being so immersed in the story that we couldn't see the wood for the trees.

On the eve of the takeover – Wednesday 11 May – we were called into Rothschild's office to attend a meeting that had been postponed from the previous day. We were informed by a preoccupied but calm-headed Majid Ishaq that the amber light had been given to the takeover for the following day, contingent on the Irish pair Magnier and McManus getting their money in time: a same day transfer of some £235million in cash, apparently, would require some organising.

---

[3] Manchester Disunited, Mihir Bose, Aurum Press Ltd 2006

Accustomed to sitting on bigger value merger and acquisition deals which would often have a large impact on shareholders and employees, I wasn't especially excited. Indeed, I was rather relieved that after four months of cat and mouse with the media, we would finally be able to go public with the much-anticipated takeover.

Leaving Rothschild we headed back to the agency's offices and furiously finished off the communications materials ready for the next day. Late into the night, UK time, we sat in on a couple of transatlantic conference calls with the Glazers to discuss communications options.

This was the first time I had heard the Glazer brothers' voices, although the father, Malcolm, was not in attendance, despite having worked for them for four months. This may seem odd, even proof of their perceived reclusiveness; rather it was simply because proactive communications had hitherto not been an issue. The lawyers had unequivocally advised from the outset that, as significant shareholders in Manchester United, the Glazers had started to amass shares in the PLC in early 2003 and could not say anything in public that may have an effect on the club's share price. Period.

The fact that the Glazers did not go public in the run-up to the takeover understandably infuriated the media. Normally a suitor to a football club would seek to discreetly whisper in the ears of influential journalists to ensure their position was understood and reflected in favourable newspaper coverage.

While the Glazers were suitors to not just a publicly listed company but one that was so forensically scrutinised as Manchester United, it made complete sense to us that they should play by the book and keep their counsel, lest they could be accused of seeking to manipulate the share price; with a personal stake of more than £200 million that would have been hard to contest. Even after the takeover was launched, we knew that strict rules would significantly constrain them from speaking until they owned the vast majority of shares. Such an approach would usually not raise an eyebrow in any other industry… except football, that is, where a rabid desire for information by the media trumps the legal niceties of doing business, especially when it pertained to Manchester United.

The club's board, led by Sir Roy Gardner and aided by its London PR agency, Finsbury, would take full advantage of the Glazers' months of legally tied silence by making frequent overtures to the press, championing their hostility to the Americans, delivering PR coup after coup versus the 'secretive' and 'hostile' bidders.

During the conference calls the Glazers – led by the brothers Joel and Avie – seemed, of course, energised at the prospect of reaching the finishing line. I was struck by their sharp-mindedness, softened by an easy-going informality that is often attributed to American business people. Suffice to say that when it was mooted that Joel would be needed to sign off a technical issue at around 5am Florida time, Joel immediately shot back, "Of course, call me anytime…I doubt I'll be getting much sleep tonight!"

In truth, the communications discussion was tellingly short. Any media engagement would still be strictly governed by Takeover Panel rules, restricting any guidance to the dense financial jargon in the 74 page Offer Document, a highly legalised tome petitioning shareholders to offload their shares. So discussion was confined to confirmation that no on-the-record statements could be made, as well as whom the Glazers would courtesy call just before the takeover went live. Joel and Avie insisted that David Gill and Sir Alex Ferguson were top of their list; their respect for them was clear as was their avowed desire to get them on side as soon as was practicable. No such courtesy would be extended to the soon-to-be superfluous chairman of the PLC board, Sir Roy Gardner.

After a very late night it was another early morning back in the office, ensuring that all the i's and t's were dotted and crossed respectively. Experience with working for other clients meant there would always be an element of uncertainty right until the moment the button was pushed on a transaction, just as anyone who nervously looks to exchange contracts on buying a house will testify. So, that morning was marked by the constant checking of incoming emails, the tentative picking up of the telephone for news, and the careful monitoring of the wires for any impromptu developments.

2:33pm, Thursday 12 May 2005

When the news did go live (at 2:33pm British summer time, the arbitrary time reflecting the frenzied and delayed efforts to get the cash transferred to the Irish to buy their shares) the afternoon of Thursday 12 May 2005 was no damp squib, no anti-climax. The revelations that the Glazers had succeeded in buying out Cubic Expression, and thereby becoming majority owners of Manchester United, felt seismic after so many months of uncertainty. Indeed, returning to the house-buying analogy, there had been a sufficient number of glitches in the process to ensure that the actual moment of purchase would provide real cathartic relief.

However, I vividly remember the trance-like calm before the storm; the short hiatus as the world's media grappled with the decisive news. The office was eerily quiet. Perhaps it wasn't a big deal after all, I wondered. Had it already been all priced in?

And then the telephones started to ring. Initially the calls came in a trickle, sufficient for the agency's managing director John Antcliffe – who could now look forward to an astronomical 'success' fee – to deal with. But as the news spread, there came a deluge of enquiries from an unpredictably wide range of worldwide media outlets, which required all hands to the pump from our team of four. While we had the Offer Document to hand, the fact that it was still a working draft with blacked out passages meant we were tightly restricted as to what we could say. Most calls centred on whether it was a done deal (most probably); the debt finance (yes, there was debt, but a huge cash down payment too) and the poorly-understood Payment-in-Kind (PIK) notes (which we struggled in vain to explain). We also could provide some background on the Glazers' sporting pedigree, including their success with the Tampa Bay Buccaneers who had recently won American football's premium prize, the 2003 NFL Superbowl.

At around 6pm, after having fielded around 30 telephone calls (my left ear was by now numb from the moulding of the plastic receiver) John Antcliffe asked me to accompany him to the Rothschild offices where Robert Leitao was to provide further press briefings. Leitao, like us, seemed fuelled on adrenalin, flushed with the success of managing and engineering what had been quite an audacious takeover. We sat around the circular conference table in another of Rothschild's many upmarket meeting rooms, witnessing Leitao leaning over a landline speaker-phone as well as his constantly vibrating mobile. Leitao, like us previously, found himself confined to the script of the Offer Document, although he could flesh out some colour around the takeover to journalists from the main national UK newspaper titles – mainly their M&A correspondents – who had conscientiously followed the story for a considerable period of time. Outside it was already dark but by then I had lost all sense of time; hours had swept past as they always tend to do when consumed with something so enthralling and challenging.

Later, back inside Smithfield's office, telephone calls continued to come through, in particular from journalists in the US who were still embroiled in their working day. Towards 10pm, with the national TV news bulletins about to broadcast, I remember frantically briefing correspondents who minutes later would repeat my carefully crafted words verbatim on air. The working day continued early into the following Friday morning, with 'taking stock' conference calls to the Glazers and their Stateside advisors. These centred on discussions surrounding the contents of a draft letter to supporters assuring them of the Glazers' promise to respect the club's traditions and their commitment to future investment in the team. Alas, this letter would never see the light of day.

I have no idea when I got back home, probably around 2am, only that when I did alight from the taxi I managed to momentarily forget where I lived. I spent a good while searching for the front door on what suddenly seemed my eternally long residential street in north London, clearly addled by fatigue and surviving on the last remnants of adrenalin from the preceding 48 hours. However, getting to sleep wasn't helped by my workaholic insistence at monitoring early morning coverage on the rolling TV news and radio channels. Back in 2005 I didn't yet have the luxury of a home Internet connection or a BlackBerry, otherwise I would have never got any shuteye.

Friday the 13ᵗʰ

A few hours later the early morning taxi was waiting to whisk me back to the office. Here, a colleague and I shared the task of making sense of the newspaper coverage, and dissecting the first verdicts on the takeover less than 24 hours after it had gone live. During the previous four months we had become accustomed to spending an hour or so summarising the steady flow of news coverage each morning. But, that morning of Friday the 13ᵗʰ, there was a staggering amount of reportage, analysis and comment splashed across most newspapers' home, business and sports pages. These were strewn like a colourful mosaic upon every spare inch of the tatty carpet tiles around our desks, the tabloid images of raging fans and archive photos of a beaming Malcolm Glazer vividly staring up at us.

Protests by supporter groups – which threatened to disrupt the following weekend's FA Cup Final involving Manchester United versus Arsenal – were widely reported. The *Daily Telegraph's* Henry Winter, one of the most erudite and elegant of sports writers, raged with a call to arms[4]: "The battle is over, but the resistance begins. As the Theatre of Dreams becomes Sold Trafford, Manchester United's irate fans will rally to defy the American carpetbagger, Malcolm Glazer... Glazer is a predator that all of English football must resist. This man will damage our national game."

Some football journalists continued to speculate over the future of Sir Alex Ferguson, one claiming Sir Alex was "repulsed by the prospect of a takeover"[5], and others suggesting it could bring his near 19 year-old tenure to an abrupt end. Some even speculated that the team's stars would have to be sold off to fund the debt.

More dispassionate business journalists, more inured to the prospect of another foreign takeover of a UK household name, questioned the level of debt and seized on the questionable logic behind spending a record £790million for a Premier League club,

---

[4] *The Daily Telegraph*, 13 May 2005
[5] *The Guardian*, Daniel Taylor: 'Deal could spell the end of Ferguson' 13 May 2005

especially one that was perceived to be on the wane and was seemingly cowed by the riches of Roman Abramovich's Chelsea (a team that had just clinched its first top-flight league title in half a century). Speculation tended towards the sensational and cynical: the Glazers would seek to break up the Premier League's collective TV rights agreement and would negotiate unilaterally to boost revenues; Old Trafford would have its naming rights sold.

In fairness, some coverage was more measured, and from unlikely quarters too, with the *Sun* even eschewing much of the anti-foreign takeover sentiment, mooting in its leader column[6]: "Glazer is an entrepreneur who knows how to run a sports club... Man U fans should ask themselves this: Has Abramovich been bad for Chelsea?"

But the story was also a strongly visual one. Images of groups of disgruntled fans outside the Theatre of Dreams, bearing placards featuring unflattering caricatures of Malcolm Glazer, or burning effigies of him, were compelling and characterised the (global) news agenda, especially in the continued absence of any interview with Mr Glazer or his sons. To my mind some of the newspaper cartoons bore an unhealthy resemblance to the caricatures of Nazi propaganda; the *Daily Mirror* carried a drawing of Malcolm Glazer with an exaggerated hooked nose and sharpened teeth raiding the safe of Manchester United.[7] When the London-based *Jewish Chronicle* called me to ask whether I thought there was an anti-Semitic element to the coverage I paused and thought for a few seconds before replying curtly "No". I was absolutely determined *not* to generate a new angle to an already highly-charged and volatile situation.

Equally, the nation's airwaves were jammed by a tirade of angry callers to talk radio stations, most of whom despaired that Manchester United was now in the clutches of the reviled Malcolm Glazer. One participant to a radio phone-in particularly struck me; he represented Shareholders United, which spoke on behalf of the disparate group of small shareholders when Manchester United was a listed public

---

[6] The Sun Says: 'Money Man' *The Sun*, 13 May 2005
[7] 'Greedy Glazer set to make Roman look like football's Robin Hood', 11 June 2005

company. He was angry; so angry that he called for the "Glazer leech to be bled away from the club". Strong words, but more disturbingly so when the interviewer challenged him, asking whether this meant he wanted the club he claimed to love to fail under the Glazers – even losing on the pitch – if it meant precipitating the Americans' exit. "Yes," he replied. I was shocked that *any* football fan would contemplate sacrificing his team's success for his avowed hatred of the new owners. Yes, he was angry, but for this to translate into a perverse scorched earth approach to the club he purported to love indicated the depth of emotion that the Glazers' takeover had triggered among some of its supporters.

I found myself to be on a steep learning curve.

The morning after the takeover announcement, and before I could even start to digest the ensuing press coverage, the phone calls began to pour in again. This time, one day on, it seemed that media interest, if anything, was intensifying as reporters were seeking every possible angle to stretch the news cycle and satisfy their readers for the Saturday and Sunday editions. With our guidance that Sir Alex and the equally respected chief executive, David Gill, were to remain in situ, press focus understandably switched to what plans the Glazers had for their new acquisition. We would counter with the key message 'business as usual'; a prosaic and genuine response which, however, did nothing to quench journalists' mounting cynical curiosity.

As the Glazers' representatives we were to receive countless requests from the media for an interview with a member of the family, in particular Malcolm. This included every broadcast news strand under the sun, all of whom were ready to arrange to send a film crew and satellite truck to his Palm Beach home at a drop of a hat. Indeed, we had drawn up a detailed proposal for a large list of potential journalists to fly out to Tampa and meet the Glazers at their NFL team's stadium, including flight itineraries and costings. However, it was by now increasingly evident that the Glazers did not want to engage. So our stock response, "Not for the time being, thank you," predictably prompted universal frustration and not a little opprobrium.

Tampa

By Friday evening, still in the office and still swamped by media telephone calls, Majid Ishaq from Rothschild emailed to suggest someone get out to Tampa as soon as possible, as the press office of the Glazer family's other sports team, the Tampa Bay Buccaneers, was also being deluged with international media enquiries. John Antcliffe asked me whether I would like to go; I jumped at what was to be a pivotal opportunity and was thrilled at the prospect of the adventure, although not quite sure what I would be doing when I got there.

I spent the next day alone in recovery mode having absorbed the morning's back pages, most of which were still saturated with negative sentiment surrounding United's new owners. With my flight booked to Tampa for the following morning, my body and mind started to succumb to the exhaustion from the previous days' relentless activity, my head abuzz with probably a hundred or so telephone calls that I had fielded. I was determined to have as much down time as possible, although this was punctuated by a protracted panic attack when I frenziedly tried to find my passport. One of the few telephone calls I did make that day, something I had looked forward to making for many months, was to one of my best friends from school, a diehard Liverpool Football Club fan who had ended up moving from London to live near Anfield. I delighted at the anticipation of his likely shock to find out that his friend of 25 years was now working for the enemy! His response, however, was surprisingly stoic and forgiving; he recognised the merit of United having new owners, suggesting that at least some of our temperate key messages may have made it through the media storm. The call ended with him revealing his despairing impatience with how his club was being run, and him pleading for some new blood on the Anfield board. He was to learn to be careful what he wished for.

The flight to Tampa was scheduled for the Sunday morning. I arrived early at Heathrow airport, weighed down by a stack of newspapers, their content dominated by the week's biggest business and sport story. Probably the biggest corporate story of the year, I reckoned.

Snugly aboard the aeroplane in British Airways' Club Class, my complimentary post-9/11 plastic flute of orange juice in one hand and nibbling on a small bag of pretzels with the other, I was to experience the first of many occasions where a passing reference to my role in a friendly chat with the passenger adjacent to me would spark incredible interest and initiate hours of animated conversation. This was usually regardless of the other person's gender or nationality, such was the international resonance of Manchester United everywhere I went.

Arriving in a hot and humid Tampa, I felt well and truly jet lagged. However, my departure from the UK (where the Manchester United story had ruled the news agenda) and my subsequent arrival in the US provided me with a useful reality check. On the other side of the Atlantic Ocean the takeover did not seem to merit any national news coverage at all. Notably, though, there was one high-profile Brit that had aroused the attention of America's media: George Galloway, the controversial UK Member of Parliament, appeared on the nation's news networks enthralling Congress with his powerful testimony on the Iraq War.

That said, the Glazers' latest acquisition did seem to command significant interest among the local Florida media, more specifically how it might impact on their NFL team, the Tampa Bay Buccaneers. I was generously hosted by many of the city's prominent sportswriters, all clamouring to glean as much insight as they could, especially as they had rarely – if at all – engaged with members of the Glazer family. I wasn't the only Englishman chatting soccer to the attendant US sports writers, though. James Fletcher, an enterprising reporter from the *News of the World*, was also in town attempting to track down the Glazers, and I found myself trying to chaperone him, desperately trying to deter access to my clients. This bizarre episode of cat and mouse had sitcom potential, I reckoned.

It was also my first encounter with American football, at a time when Tampa Bay were about to commence their many months of pre-season training. It was remarkable how cordial, even symbiotic, relations between the team and the press seemed (in stark contrast, I would soon learn, with the media's relations with Manchester United). While Tampa Bay had scaled the heights of gridiron by winning the

Super Bowl XXXVII two years previously, the franchise did not enjoy the recognition of a Dallas Cowboys or Washington Redskins, say. Yet the facilities were extremely impressive, with a gleaming new stadium (controversially funded by the local taxpayer rather than the Glazers themselves) and new training facility under construction. The fact that, in 1996, the Glazers had bought a near bankrupt team (and one so accustomed to losing that it had broken the NFL record for 'futility') and had transformed it into a rich Super Bowl-winning side spoke volumes to me. It was also evidence of the Glazers' sports pedigree and their likely sensible stewardship of Manchester United. This is how local Tampa Bay media saw it too; while many were weary of the family's aloofness, no one I spoke with doubted their credentials and flair for running a sports enterprise.

The Glazers' sports pedigree, the written summary of which I had read and proofed countless times in the draft Offer Document, was made immediately tangible to me when I was given a tour of Tampa's Raymond James Stadium, home to the Buccaneers. The stadium, which was built some seven years previously, boasted a capacity of around 67,000, thus matching Old Trafford's. The stadium bowl was surrounded by a multitude of fast food and merchandise outlets; there was even a mock pirate ship from which, I was told, a cannon would blast when a home touchdown was made. Behind the scenes the scale of every aspect of the stadium was superlative, reflecting its modernity as well as the ambitions of the Glazers. From vast atriums with huge glass frontages to sumptuously decorated suites (all using top end materials and built to impress), everything appeared state–of-the-art. This extended to the luxurious wood-panelled VIP lounge, the pristine locker rooms and a press box and lounge so vast that it seemed to dwarf Old Trafford's many times over.

The Glazers were understandably proud of what they had achieved in Tampa, and during their early days of owning Manchester United often suggested that I invited UK journalists over to view the facilities for themselves. Unfortunately, while most reporters would have jumped at the chance, the Glazer family imposed a caveat which meant that no one took up the offer: no interview opportunity with them would be forthcoming.

For much of the time I based myself at a makeshift desk in the Buccaneers' cramped and unglamorous press office – housed inside a large temporary Portakabin – with my borrowed local clamshell phone stuck to my ear as I took calls from ever-curious UK journalists searching for any scrap of information to move their stories forward. Sat in the privacy of Joel's spacious office at Tampa Bay, which was festooned with a treasure trove of Buccaneers and NFL memorabilia, I was involved in frequent conference calls with the Glazer brothers and their advisors to address our future communications strategy. With the FA Cup final imminent – the first game Manchester United would play under new ownership – discussion centred on whether any missive to fans would be appropriate. However, as the Glazers did not yet technically own Manchester United outright (Rothschild were still in the process of ensuring that PLC shares were being hoovered up), the default 'not for the time being' response would prevail.

Hi Joel

By mid-afternoon in Tampa, and due to the minus five-hour time difference, media enquiries from the UK would slow down, meaning that I could afford to relax and learn more about the Glazers in the USA by spending time with correspondents from the local Florida press. On my way to dinner, while being driven by Bill Ward, a seasoned sportswriter with the *Tampa Tribune*, my phone rang, causing me to ask him to stop on the hard shoulder of the freeway so that I could jump out. Amid the noisy hum of cars speeding past me, I had the first of countless private telephone conversations with Joel Glazer. As he had consistently taken part in the conference calls, I recognised Joel's friendly laid-back voice which would unfailingly project a sunny optimism. He immediately struck me as a particularly measured listener and, over the years, when I sought to provide the Glazer family with advice and opinion, I would often do so very self consciously, realising that Joel would carefully hang onto every word I proffered.

After quickly introducing myself I remember cutting to the chase and asking Joel "Just how much do you like football and care for

Manchester United?" On reflection, it might have seemed a rather impertinent question to pose to one's client, who was effectively my boss. But it was a fundamental issue I needed to hear Joel Glazer's opinion of. Especially as I, like everyone else, had been fed for months on end with the usual diet of xenophobia dished out by an often vicious UK media, implying that an American could neither care about football, nor understand the nuances of a club as revered as Manchester United.

Joel responded candidly and sincerely. "Of course I love football," he replied, my noting his 'correct' use of the term for the English game; never 'soccer'. "I've followed the game for as long as I can remember," Joel continued. "I got into the Premier League when I roomed with an English friend at college. He may have loved Tottenham but for me it was all about Manchester United and Fergie. Sure it's been quite an amazing few days, but we're all truly pleased to now own such a fabulous football club."

I was convinced of Joel's sincerity; his love for football had originated alongside his brothers as young children and had intensified as he'd grown older. I thought it appropriate to 'confess' to Joel my allegiance to Liverpool Football Club by saying, rather tritely, "I may pray in a different church, but at least it's to the same God". Joel's response was generous, "As long as you love football, Tes, that's good enough for me." The small talk dispensed with, over several calls that week we moved on to discussing various communication issues and ideas now that the takeover's completion was in sight.

During my week in Tampa I was able to learn more about the Glazer family; 'outsiders' from affluent Rochester in upstate New York who had built up a considerable business network in the sunshine state. Their influence was evident in the city's bid to host the 2010 Super Bowl when Bryan Glazer – who was representing the family's interest – had arrived for a well-attended press conference in one of the gleaming atriums at the Raymond James Stadium. Bryan was the first Glazer I would meet in person and, as with my previous conversations with his younger brother Joel, I was impressed with his courteous and down to earth manner. From the outset it was made clear that Bryan would not be taking questions on his family's purchase of Manchester

United. Although there were legions of local reporters covering the event, none would 'doorstep' Bryan about this most topical of issues, so accustomed – or resigned – they seemed to be in dealing with the Glazers' reluctance to engage with the media. Another observation, which seemed to capture the contrasting sports cultures in the USA with the UK's, occurred when the Mayor of Tampa, Pam Iorio, sought to talk up the city's appeal to the NFL's billionaire club of owners who would determine the venue of the 2010 Super Bowl. Iorio's winding-up comments were predicated not on Tampa's great facilities for fans (although that seemed to be so) but rather on its excellent yachting moorings and private jet terminal. Tampa went on to win the bid, and many of my local media contacts told me that Bryan Glazer and his family, ever discreetly behind closed doors, were crucial in the city's successful Super Bowl quest, countering widespread expectations that it would be awarded to another candidate city.

Marathon not a Sprint

With my many conversations with Joel Glazer ringing in my ears I flew back to London, sketching out a communications plan during the overnight flight. I arrived back home on Saturday 21st May, in good time to watch on television Manchester United versus Arsenal in the FA Cup final at Cardiff's Millennium Stadium. Despite comfortably outplaying the Gunners, Sir Alex's team lost; an inauspicious start to the Glazers' era in charge. There had been a threat of a mass protest, but it was the football that stole the headlines, although during the decisive penalty shoot-out, a large 'Die Glazer' placard was hoisted loftily by a section of Manchester United supporters behind the goal, clearly visible to the tens of thousands in the stadium and the many millions of viewers around the globe. Ironically it was the Arsenal fans that, like every opposition support would go on to do, would goad the United end, chanting "USA, USA!" Probably the most arresting off-the-pitch image, widely circulated in the media the following day (and consequently achieving iconic status) depicted three *Arsenal* fans sporting grinning Malcolm Glazer face masks, one of whom was flaunting a mock one million dollar bill.

One dubious personal milestone: the FA Cup final marked the first time I had *ever* wanted Manchester United to win, implicitly challenging my increasingly compromised support for Liverpool FC which, just four days later, was to reach its apotheosis in Istanbul.

Back in the London office, media calls were beginning to subside, giving me time to prepare for any possible communications for the period once the takeover offer to buy shares had expired, and the Glazers were in full control of the club. I spent a lot of my energies hooking up with the journalists that I had previously briefed on the telephone. In PR, as in other walks of life, breaking bread over a longish lunch was the best way to forge trust and understanding with reporters. Lunches represented a great opportunity to trade gossip, since conversations were tacitly (and mutually) agreed to be unattributable and off-the-record.

Armed with my insights from Tampa, as well as the kudos of having spoken directly with Joel Glazer, these meetings were the nearest that most journalists would get to this notoriously elusive family. Alas, I do not have any tales of long and debauched liquid lunches; by the new millennium those days had already been confined to Fleet Street mythology, with bottled water and tight afternoon copy deadlines giving most press lunches a professionally brisk and orderly air. Indeed, I always suspected that my policy to abstain from alcohol proved to be a virtue as I sought to maintain discretion for my very private clients.

My preferred restaurants were not particularly renowned for their cuisine, rather for their lively atmosphere. Bustling eateries like the Coq d'Argent or One Lombard Street – which served as canteens to the generous expense-accounted bankers, corporate lawyers and financial PR operators in the area – were stalwarts. The subsequently defunct Bank restaurant in the West End's Aldwych was also a favourite, its large open white space with its long signal red banquettes attracting a more media-savvy clientele. Often, restaurants required reservations weeks in advance, reflecting the boom time that the UK economy – especially London's – was enjoying at the time. An abiding memory was the feeling of entitlement among diners to perpetual boom; this was akin, with hindsight, to the Lawson boom euphoria of the mid-eighties. While I always enjoyed lunching – I considered it a real perk of my job – it was remarkably easy for the law of diminishing returns to kick in and to have too much of a good thing. Three posh lunches in a row and I would find myself craving a simple sandwich at my desk by the fourth.

Some journalists were still bemused as to why the Glazers would fork out close to £800 million for a leveraged buyout (i.e. using debt) of Manchester United if they were not planning to break away from the Premier League's collective TV agreement. Many speculated that, to finance the takeover, the Glazers would need to securitise (i.e. remortgage) Old Trafford or at least sell its naming rights. There had even been claims that the Glazers were mooting a change to the club crest or even a shift away from the traditional red kit; two months after April Fool's day. When I responded with a simple: "It's very much business as usual, a marathon not a sprint", it appeared that this most innocuous of points would actually compound journalists' suspicion that the Glazers must have had a secret – and decidedly more sinister – agenda up their sleeves.

One of the most acute examples of this relentless negative media speculation – heralded as news – focused on the continuing role of club legend Sir Bobby Charlton. In early June 2005, there was an official Stock Exchange announcement confirming changes to the executive board, effectively the grouping responsible for the business end of the club. Joel and Avram Glazer would become joint chairmen, while their brother Bryan would join them alongside chief executive David Gill and commercial director Andy Anson. The football club board was left unchanged.

Two days later the *Daily Mirror* screamed[8]: "Sir Bobby gets the boot... Sir Bobby Charlton is set to become a victim of Malcolm Glazer's ruthless overhaul of Manchester United... The revelation will infuriate United fans opposed to Glazer's takeover and also anger boss Sir Alex Ferguson, for whom Sir Bobby has become a close confidante during his 18-year reign in charge".

---

[8] Sir Bobby Gets the Boot, *Daily Mirror*, 9 June 2005

One thing about the media's pervasive influence is that, even when I knew better, there could be a moment of doubt when the written word would force a double-take, perhaps a reflection of my own impressionability.

While this *Mirror* headline struck me as being completely at odds with my understanding of the Glazers' rationale, before I set out phoning reporters to rebut it I needed to check first. I put a transatlantic call into Joel as early as possible, during which I heard his anger, albeit muted, for the first of only two occasions during our six years of dealings. He immediately rubbished any speculation over Sir Bobby's future at the club, and was clearly hurt that a newspaper would stoop so low in order to fit its anti-Glazer agenda. "Sir Bobby's got a job for life at the club," Joel exhorted. "He is like royalty, he *is* Manchester United." I immediately put in calls to refute the story, mindful that its damage had been long done, especially among those whose resentment of the Glazers was so visceral and by then probably irreparable.

Nothing is Set in Stone

Although one month had passed since the takeover, media interest was showing little sign of waning. To be honest, I loved being immersed in such an interesting and unpredictable news story. It felt satisfying, too, as it presented me with such a steep learning curve and allowed me to while away many an hour in the office reading about football! With the *Mirror* story dispensed with, I received a call that afternoon from Ashling O'Connor of the *Times*, purporting to possess a leaked business plan containing highly sensitive information. My response was one of relief. Aware that a series of financial presentations had been in circulation for several months among potential debt holders, it had been a complete mystery to me that they hadn't arrived in the public domain earlier. I put a quick call into Joel Glazer (who mirrored my sanguine reaction) before getting back to Ashling, feeling pleased that at least it was an outlet with the stature of the *Times* that had the scoop. My only comment to her – not knowing precisely which presentation she had to hand since she had refused to fax it – was to bear in mind that any business plan would be completely notional. Now that the Glazers' full ownership was imminent nothing was set in stone, especially in a business as fluid and as unpredictable as football.

The *Times'* sensationalist treatment the next day of the business plan took me by surprise[9]. The story was splashed on the front page alongside a none too flattering archive photograph of Malcolm Glazer awkwardly clutching an American football, and there was additional coverage in the business and sports pages. On the other hand, the publication of the investor presentation had indicated how measured the Glazers would likely be towards their ownership of Manchester United, contrasting with the rumbling myth that they would be asset-stripping United as soon as they had got the keys to the stadium. My off the cuff 'nothing is set in stone' remark ended up being picked over in the *Times'* eminent editorial the next day, the column understandably adjudging that the real issue going forward lay in the Glazers' 'poor communications rather than any malign intentions'[10].

As the *Times* had presciently mooted, the following weeks would present a narrow window of opportunity to table and discuss communication plans before the closure of the Glazers' offer to purchase all outstanding shares, at which point they would in effect be the outright owners and the Stock Exchange's takeover rules (which had imposed the Glazers' purdah) would cease to be in effect.

After months of wondering what the Manchester United board might have been thinking – and now that the club was effectively owned by the Glazer family – on Joel's request I put a call into Phil Townsend, United's director of communications. Phil arranged to come down to Smithfield's office in mid-June to meet our team for the first time. The meeting felt pivotal and I was nervous, worried at the prospect of not getting on with him, which didn't seem that far-fetched given how bad a rap the Glazer family had received from the United PLC board. On the other hand, I had heard that Phil, who had

---

[9] Revealed: Glazer's plan for Manchester United, *The Times*, 10 June 2005
[10] Glazer and stones, *The Times*, 11 June 2005

previously worked as a civil service spokesman for the government's Department of Culture, Media and Sport, was an easy-going chap who had sought to keep a diplomatic distance from any mud flinging. I greeted Phil in the reception. He was dressed in his customary black suit and crisp white open-neck club shirt, and had just taken a call about United's newest signing that day, the South Korean Ji-Sung Park. I took Phil upstairs to Smithfield's boardroom, a beautiful sun-drenched space, dominated by a large boardroom table that faced the trendy warehouse apartments of Clerkenwell.

Fortunately, Phil and I did hit it off and I immediately warmed to his down to earth manner and dry sense of humour. Our first meeting was mostly a listening exercise as Phil outlined the club's complex relationships with the media, enabling us both to scope out a draft communications plan over a long lunch at a nearby French brasserie. Among the useful information that I gleaned from Phil was the fact that Manchester United could be abbreviated to 'Man United' or 'United', but never 'Man U' which its core local supporters hated. I blushed, aware that I had referred to 'Man U' in all the confidential documents I had drafted hitherto.

With the financial takeover mechanism about to come to an end, Phil Townsend's experience of serving under Labour ministers Tessa Jowell and Richard Caborn also gave valuable insight into the increasingly politicised conflict between the Glazer family and the various Manchester United supporter groups.

Manchester Bound

A few days later I found myself at Old Trafford, undertaking my first visit to the stadium for nearly 20 years. It being the close season, the stadium and surrounding streets were relatively quiet, save for the steady trickle of visitors to the club's megastore and museum.

I'd travelled north with an agency colleague on the much vaunted Virgin Pendolino tilting train which, in just two hours, had transported us from the brutal sixties' gloom of London Euston to the airy splendour of Manchester Piccadilly. Over the next six years I would never tire of Virgin's First Class service, particularly when I travelled off-peak and qualified for amazingly cheap 'value advance' fares, often having a carriage to myself. In the early days I recall being served a decent meal with cutlery, with the service including free newspapers and personal headphones. However, by 2011 I noticed that, while fares had inexorably risen, the meals had been downgraded to plastic sealed sandwiches, although passengers continued to be treated to huge pots of freshly brewed tea and coffee.

My previous visit to Old Trafford had taken place in early 1988, when I'd watched United lose at home to Southampton. Back then football seemed a parochial, often hooligan-infested pastime that had yet to be affected by Gazza's Italia '90 tears and the Premier League's television riches. On a positive note, however, in those days it was commonplace for supporters to casually stroll up and buy a ticket on a Saturday afternoon.

Even in the late 1980s I remember being awestruck by Old Trafford, which felt more modern and imposing compared to the grounds I was more familiar with, like Anfield, Highbury and Upton Park. However, when Phil showed me around the 2005 version of Old Trafford – which had been substantially extended since my previous visit – it felt grander still, while offering an intense intimacy. It being mid-June, there were no goal posts or markings as the pitch was receiving its annual close season makeover, overseen meticulously by the small band of dedicated ground staff. I was surprised to see that the pitch was elevated above ground level which, I imagined, must have made it seem even more intimidating to visiting teams. During my six years' of visits to the ground I would occasionally come pitch side – particularly for new sponsor photo calls – but I knew better than to ever step onto the hallowed turf. Somehow it did not feel appropriate and it was, in any case, an entitlement above my pay scale.

To be honest, on such a tranquil day I found it difficult to imagine a 67,000-plus crowd screaming out their passionate fervour. And as I had no idea whether I would be retained by the Glazers beyond the end of June (when their takeover would be sealed) and as someone who naturally veered towards pessimism, I never assumed that I would be back one day to sample an actual game.

The stadium itself was massive and, during 2006, was due to be further expanded with two imposing Quadrant corner complexes. The stadium interior comprised countless suites and executive boxes, as well as the many kitchens that would artfully serve the club's growing legion of corporate supporters who, in the booming Manchester economy, demanded much more than a humble prawn sandwich.

Inside, the multitude of corridors were lined with hundreds of largely contemporary action photographs of the players, and were interspersed with a series of fire protective doors, creating a maze-like thoroughfare. It was only when I managed to peep through the door of an executive box that I could regain my bearings, my gaze instantly being drawn to the gleaming baize of the Manchester United pitch.

Old Trafford also housed the club's office complex which had burgeoned over the years as the club's corporate stature mushroomed and the legal, financial, hospitality and marketing functions were bolted on. The area I would most frequent was the marketing floor, where Phil Townsend's communications department's offices were located. Operating alongside him were the staff responsible for servicing the club's sponsors and commercial partners, their desks clustered in quadrangles making for a chatty and convivial atmosphere.

These offices, situated in the East Stand, overlooked the front aspect of Old Trafford, just behind the statue of Sir Matt Busby, which towers above every visitor to the stadium arriving on his eponymous road. An enormous green-tinted glass panel spanned the entire height and length of the floor and was sometimes used by the club to hang huge translucent hoardings outside, making the office environment particularly spacious and pleasant. The piles of autographed shirts and merchandise contained within – most of it awaiting secure dispatch to sponsors and supporters – gave this inner sanctum the air of an Aladdin's Cave.

Phil Townsend's narrow office overlooked the marketing floor, and I would often perch around his small conference table, competing for elbow space as I perused the daily heap of local and national newspapers.

It was during my first trip to see Phil, after lunch at a nearby eatery, that he and I signed off the communications strategy, effectively marking the first moments when the club would fall under the complete ownership of the Glazers. This also included plans for the Glazer brothers' meetings with the country's football regulators and politicians, which would be supervised by Phil. Returning to the London office, I excitedly put the finishing touches to the plan which I then forwarded to Joel Glazer for his and his family's careful consideration.

That week I made another quick visit to Manchester, again hooking up with Phil who introduced me to two important locally based journalists, with whom I was to form a valuable working relationship. Stuart Mathieson was the *Manchester Evening News* reporter dedicated to the red side of his city. Equally, Simon Stone from the Press Association news agency seemed to devote his waking hours to all things United, and whose reportage carried enormous global weight as online readership grew exponentially.

A Done Deal

By the last week of June, expectation was mounting that the Glazers would be visiting the UK and would be attending Old Trafford as its new owners, the final act after six months (and more) of intriguing takeover talk and intense media interest.

On June 28th an official announcement was published to confirm that the takeover process was officially over. Red Football had secured a 98 per cent share of Manchester United, which was enough to force a compulsory purchase of any outstanding shares. However, the Glazers sensibly sought to avoid any prospect of confrontation with recalcitrant shareholders by keeping the offer open to the remaining two per cent that hadn't yet sold their shares. This rump wouldn't be worth too much consideration in any case, as it was likely to include only a handful of individuals unaware of their holding or perhaps people who were now deceased.

On the day of the announcement the Glazers had completed the first half of the communications plan by meeting and greeting the heads of the Premier League and the Football Association. Together with Manchester United chief executive David Gill, they also dined at the Houses of Parliament with Minister of Sport Richard Caborn, whom Phil Townsend had served prior to his role at Old Trafford.

The following morning, Manchester United's new owners hooked up with executives from the club's main commercial partners, Nike and Vodafone. That afternoon I was back on the Manchester-bound Virgin Pendolino, feeling excited about rolling out the next leg of the communications plan, but experiencing the same self-doubt that had plagued me on my way to Tampa. That doubt probably stemmed from my somewhat undefined role; unlike the majority of my clients who liked to establish how an external communications advisor would operate within their organisation, the Glazers were always so undemanding, and were more than happy for me to use my initiative to get on with the job. While this blank canvas was a covetable opportunity, it was not without stress or challenge particularly given my lack of previous sports-oriented experience.

Any time for self-doubt was quickly dissipated within minutes of the train's departure from Euston, however, as I was deluged with a torrent of press calls enquiring after the Glazers. An abiding bugbear would be the frustration encountered trying to make and take calls on the Pendolino; the train's 100mph-plus speed was nausea-inducing enough, but even more infuriating was the amount of calls that would be interrupted, and then dropped, as the train tilted its way through middle England's countryside. On the other hand, this could sometimes be a boon, especially when it felt more appropriate to say very little. On this occasion, I must confess to having been economical with the truth to some journalists who called me, declining to give any information on the Americans' whereabouts. As it stood, I wasn't sure myself; indeed, when I called Joel on a crackly line he warned me that their people carrier was delayed, and was inching its way northwards through motorway rush-hour traffic.

Upon my arrival in Manchester I headed towards my usual hotel, the Radisson Edwardian, a handsome building in the city's regenerated Deansgate district that was becoming something of a second home to me. I shoved my crumpled trousers into the Corby trouser press, had a shower and then switched on Sky Sports News to catch up with the increasingly febrile coverage of the Glazers' movements. A little later I called Phil Townsend to arrange a meeting at Old Trafford.

I never wearied of the taxi ride through Manchester to the 'Theatre of Dreams', which totally dominated the cityscape as I journeyed along Bridgewater Way. It always reminded me, rather unimaginatively, of a large shiny spaceship stranded on a dreary industrial estate. Sir Matt Busby Way felt much busier than a week before, with people milling around on the pavement expanse outside the megastore, the general hubbub heightened by the growing legion of press and their satellite trucks camped in the car park opposite.

Inside his Old Trafford office, Phil Townsend and I rehearsed that evening's and the next day's communication plan, which included a recce of MUTV's studio and a walk around the pitch. We then moved to the VIP lounge in the South Stand, which hosted the club directors' matchday guests. The Directors' Box commanded a magnificent central view of the pitch, and was home to the most exclusive – and luxuriously padded – seats inside the stadium, many of which carried small silver name plaques. One conspicuous absence among the seats, however, was Sir Roy Gardner, who had automatically resigned as club chairman shortly after the takeover was completed. Tellingly, his name plaque had already been removed.

The VIP Lounge

Just like an elite golf club, Manchester United had strict rules and protocols governing access to its VIP areas, and to ensure that they retained an exclusive highfalutin' atmosphere. As such, they were only accessible to the club's current directors as well as an invited retinue of the great and the good.

The impressive VIP lounge, which had been recently refurbished, was accessed via a grand entrance in the South Stand tunnel. Narrow stairs led into a large white space with a high, arched ceiling embellished with tastefully discreet silver club logos. Despite being windowless, it felt airy, conveying a chic, modern corporate feel. On a match day, especially if it was a high-profile midweek Champions

League game, the lounge could become very busy, populated by a veritable who's who of the football world and the Manchester celebrity scene, all abuzz at the honour of being there.

The lounge was divided into two levels; the lower area had mostly standing room and offered light snacks as well as a free bar to its guests, who tended to comprise the away team's entourage, other scouting managers and football agents.

The upper level, which would be guarded by a smartly-blazered United employee, resembled a well-appointed restaurant, with plush United-red carpet and lacquered wood panelling on the wall. This is where directors and their guests, alongside ex-directors, family members, VIPs and the occasional celebrity, would sit down to be treated to first class hospitality, expertly-prepared three course meals and carefully selected wines.

Located just off the upper level was the club's inner sanctum. In contrast to the glitzy lounge, this room had a very traditional, stuffy feel to it, reminiscent of an old-fashioned club house with Manchester United's many successes recorded on the walls for posterity. This room had very restricted access and, partly due to it being windowless – had an unappealing, austere gloom to it. This was the part of Old Trafford in which the owners, chief executive and club dignitaries like Sir Bobby Charlton would gather and dine, in addition to their high-flying executive counterparts from the visiting team. When the then Prime Minister Gordon Brown visited, he was hosted in this room.

Old Trafford's New Guard

Standing inside the VIP lounge waiting for the Glazers to enter, while sipping at a Coca-Cola, felt as awkward as the anticipation of a blind date. Of course, I already had a good description of them, but having not met them in the flesh (with the brief exception of Bryan) I did feel a slight trepidation meeting my clients face-to-face for the first time. Avie, Joel and Bryan were accompanied by their long-time friend and legal advisor Mitch Nusbaum. Mitch had been closely involved in the takeover and bore a striking resemblance to the Glazer siblings, resulting in the media automatically assuming that he was a fourth brother. It was also the first time I got to meet the chief executive David Gill, who was as elegantly attired as always, and whose imposing towering frame was offset by a friendly, no-nonsense demeanour.

I introduced myself to each brother – all expensively groomed and sporting hand-tailored suits – before switching easily into small talk with Joel Glazer who, like the others in his party, was suffering with slight jet lag. Thankfully, Joel was as personable as he had seemed on the telephone. His capacity to listen and concentrate on every word I uttered, while clasping his hands tightly together, felt as slightly disconcerting as on the phone. While the entourage was being guided outside towards the directors' box, I swiftly exited the lounge ahead of them and moved down to the pitch, ready for their entrance into the stadium. This footage would be captured by an MUTV cameraman and an in-house club photographer before being disseminated to the media and to the Glazer family themselves.

A few moments later the Glazer brothers made their first tentative steps inside Old Trafford's arena as owners. Walking down to the pitch, they dwelled to inspect United's hallowed turf – their pay scale did indeed merit such access – where further footage and photographs were taken (I recall reminding Avie to take the flap out of his jacket pocket for an unsullied picture). I wondered what the Glazers might have been thinking at that moment; only they would know how it felt to possess something of this magnitude with such an illustrious history, but I suspected they, like anyone else, might have struggled to absorb it all.

As it happened they kept their counsel, but I was curious to know how they would have felt stepping into this awe-inspiring 'cathedral' of world football while at the same time knowing that, like any new owners, they would be ringing in the changes. I suppose it was akin to a new US President and his First Lady stepping into the White House on inauguration day, with half a mind to change the furniture and curtains. Indeed the Glazers' ownership would initiate sweeping cosmetic changes to inside Old Trafford – all for the better in my view – such as cleaner and simpler advertising boards inside the stadium perimeter, as well as a programme to modernise and redevelop the stadium's many tired interiors.

While the brothers were having their souvenir photographs taken, my phone rang and I stepped away towards the players' tunnel where the teams' changing rooms are located. Situated at the end of the tunnel are huge iron gates, large enough for the team coach to drive through. I could just make out an intermittent din of chanting fans coming through from the other side, with the gates occasionally thundering as people appeared to batter their fists against them. There was no time to ponder the significance of what might be happening outside, as we were whisked off on a whistle-stop tour of the stadium accompanied by David Gill and finance director Nick Humby. This included a visit to the club museum to behold the well-stocked trophy cabinets, the presence of the Americans, I noticed, prompting some curiosity among the attending staff.

What struck me then about the Glazers was their sometimes awkward and unassuming body language. This was reinforced by their quietly spoken manner and their unfailingly polite demeanour towards their new employees, a mode of engagement that I had often seen in Americans.

One of my responsibilities that evening was to ensure that the first footage of the Glazer brothers was made available to broadcasters for two reasons: firstly, the obvious news value of their visit and, secondly, to relay the key message that it was largely Joel, Avie and Bryan who would be responsible for the family's ownership rather than their father, Malcolm, who'd had little direct involvement in the takeover and was not in attendance. Whenever journalists would query Malcolm's role, I would explain that, while he did not participate actively in the takeover, his status as family patriarch would have been decisive in all business affairs. But I felt the media's persistent insistence that Malcolm Glazer was owner – usually accompanied with an unkind caricature of him as a leprechaun – was misleading and served to underestimate the family's incredible cohesion and their undoubted business acumen.

I Predict a Riot

As dusk approached, and with the Glazers moving on to an executives' dinner at Old Trafford, I needed to leave the stadium and make my way to MUTV's central Manchester edit suite to fine-tune the exclusive footage. By this time, however, it was evident that Old Trafford appeared to be under siege by a mass of noisy protesters. I went up to the stadium's security headquarters, a large control room housed in the corner of the East and South Stands, where I could see the bank of CCTV screens displaying grainy black and white images of chanting demonstrators.

On security's advice I was escorted through a warren of corridors which took me to the North Stand, whereupon I sneaked out into the relative quiet darkness clutching the video tapes. I recall walking up towards Sir Matt Busby Way, witnessing to my right a large police presence and by then hundreds of people outside the East Stand, noisily jostling their way through the South Stand tunnel. 'If only they knew who I worked for…' I pondered.

Jumping into a taxi, within minutes I was enjoying the relative calm of the MUTV edit suite, discreetly located in a modern office block just off Deansgate. There I supervised the cutting of short clips of the Glazers' first tentative steps inside Old Trafford as well as footage of them visiting the club museum. These were then sent via satellite link to the UK's main broadcasting outlets, namely BBC, ITN and Sky, for immediate use in that night's bulletins.

I returned to my hotel and rushed into my room, switching on the rolling TV news coverage, thrilled to see this widely-anticipated video footage. Although every news channel seemed to broadcast pictures of the Glazers surveying their new acquisition, as the hours unfolded these images would be superseded by fresh, vibrant footage of the disturbances outside Old Trafford. Hundreds of angry protestors (surrounded by a heavy police presence) were filmed chanting 'Die Glazer, Die!' thus creating some of the most enduring images of the Glazers' first days of ownership. A police van, apparently containing the three brothers, was shown struggling to exit the stadium they had just bought amid what could best be termed a riot; macabre and chaotic scenes straight out of a Tom Sharpe novel.

While it seemed as though our best laid plans had come undone I felt strangely stoic, not least because I felt hopeful that we had an ace up our sleeve to move the news cycle on.

Business as Usual

I awoke early the next morning, trawling through newspaper coverage which, as expected, focused on the Glazers' fraught exit from Old Trafford. Still, I was pleased that some newspapers had also referred to the owners' more business-like London meetings of the previous day.

By the time I'd headed back to Old Trafford there was little trace of the riot, apart from some bemused onlookers and a growing number of media reporters. Inside the stadium, Phil Townsend and I swapped notes before joining up with the Glazers. They seemed completely unruffled by the preceding night's events, and I accompanied them through the stadium concourse to reach the International Lounge, a huge area normally reserved for match hospitality but which could also accommodate the hundreds of non-playing staff who worked for the club.

Bryan, Avie, Joel and David Gill took their seats behind a rectangular table at the front of the room. The commotion inside quickly switched into expectant silence as the headmasterly chief executive formally introduced the brothers, before handing the floor to Joel Glazer. Joel stood up to deliver a rehearsed, measured 10-minute talk to the employees. Humble in tone, and with his hands tightly clasped across his buttoned-up blue blazer, he reassured them of their respect for United's traditions and their conservative, 'business as usual' ethos as owners. Joel's speech was received very positively, and served to diffuse much of the tension in the air. This was some achievement, given how many staff members had been fed a diet of hostile press coverage and were, perhaps understandably, wary of their new paymasters. Still, an offer by Joel to take questions from the floor received a muted response, reflecting, I thought, the apprehension still prevalent among these loyal employees.

The town hall-style meeting then came to a close with the Glazers sensibly remaining in the room to mingle with their staff, many of whom clustered around the brothers to ask questions in privacy. I felt the meeting went as well as could be expected; the Glazers had shown themselves to be human, even reasonable. A straw poll of staff I took later that day drew a positive response, although they made clear to me that they wanted to return to the club's core activity: football.

I accompanied the Glazer brothers to Manchester United's boardroom where we regrouped for a few minutes. The glass-walled room was a typically corporate affair, with comfy (albeit dated) green leather chairs arranged around a long wooden table. I couldn't help thinking that, only a few months earlier, many of Sir Roy Gardner's meetings with his advisors would have been held here, as the PLC sought to vehemently block the Glazers' takeover.

On the dot, and as planned, Sir Bobby Charlton entered and met the Glazers for the very first time. I sat in while formalities and pleasantries were swapped, and it was immediately clear how Sir Bobby was revered by the Glazers. They hung on every word the football legend had to say as he eulogised about the club he had served with distinction for the best part of half a century. About ten minutes in, and aware of the intimate significance of this meeting, I decided to leave the four club VIPs to themselves and quietly crept out of the room. It was one of those moments that, as an external consultant, I had to make an instinctive judgement call without any cue from the Glazers. By staying, I could risk crossing the line by intruding on intimate club business as Sir Bobby spent time with the new guard of his cherished club.

Leaving the boardroom, I spent a few quiet moments on the other side of the closed door, reflecting how privileged I was to have witnessed such a significant meeting. I gazed across the landing and looked through the atrium down onto those gathered outside the East Stand reception entrance, most of whom were peering into the Old Trafford fishbowl, avidly tracking the ins and outs of this momentous and historical day.

For me, it also brought home a truth that would pervade my whole time with Manchester United. Beneath the glamour and excitement associated with being privy to the club's inner workings, the reality of off-the-pitch business was always more straightforward, even mundane. People are people, and the more I dealt with them, the more they would become, in my mind, stripped of status or fame.

'Tie or No Tie?'

Back in Phil Townsend's office it was time to finish preparations for an interview, which included my meeting Steve Bower, the MUTV anchor who was assigned the task of interviewing Joel Glazer, who had cut short his convalescence and who still had one leg in a plaster cast.

Then it was back onto the Old Trafford pitch for the Glazers to have their formal pictures taken with Sir Bobby; images that would be the first of a select collection of official pictures of the owners to be distributed among the media. As the photo-shoot took place, a stadium tour group stopped and stared, completely dumb-struck, as they found themselves metres away from their Manchester United idol, Bobby Charlton. After the initial shock, they proceeded to take photographs with Sir Bobby duly obliging. The fact that the tour group completely ignored the Glazers was a healthy juxtaposition to the preceding takeover furore; as far as they were concerned, it was the football they cared about and the thrill of seeing and meeting Sir Bobby eclipsed everything else.

The decision by Joel Glazer to give an exclusive interview to MUTV was, of course, going to antagonise the members of the media who had relentlessly sought access to the new United owners. The in-house TV station had already earned the sobriquet 'Pravda' among the press, reflecting the widespread cynicism over its perceived editorial subjugation to the club. Admittedly, David Gill, Phil Townsend and I had considered advising Joel to sit down with some print and broadcast journalists, but we finally plumped for the MUTV option for two reasons. Firstly, the main aim of the interview was to reassure the club's concerned supporters, and the subscription-based MUTV viewers were adjudged to be our prime target audience. Secondly, and bearing in mind our time constraints, we wanted to avoid alienating editors and reporters by choosing one media organisation over another. It seemed fairer, therefore, to allow everyone equal access to the MUTV interview rather than favouring any particular news outlet.

I returned to the boardroom where the Glazers continued to hold court. While Avie and Bryan were nervously pacing around the room, Joel remained seated and was, I thought, unusually composed for someone about to give a television interview. I felt sure his cordial meeting with Sir Bobby had provided a fillip. We went over a few likely questions and answers, but the most memorable thing Joel asked me was, 'Tie or no tie?' It was the classic 'no right answer' question; I advised him to continue wearing his tie as it projected a business-like image, mindful that an open collar could invoke comment, even castigation. The nuances of PR!

Leaving Avie and Bryan behind, Joel and I made the short walk to MUTV's studio, located within a converted corner executive box that commanded a great view of the pitch. The soundproofed studio accentuated the calmness that I felt ahead of the Glazers' first (and, unbeknownst to me, last) direct communication as owners of Manchester United. Steve Bower introduced himself to Joel and they exchanged small talk before the interview, in a single take, began in earnest. I remained inside the studio along with the camera operators, excited that an interview was finally in progress and frantically taking notes of each answer Joel gave, fearful that my switched-off mobile phone might suddenly ring.

The interview proved far reaching, with Steve Bower's conversational style putting Joel immediately at ease. Joel was keen to use the opportunity to respond to the charge sheet that had built up in recent months; he placed his family's support wholly behind Sir Alex Ferguson, promising 'resources to compete on the field at the highest possible level'. Not only that, accusations that Sir Bobby would be removed from the board, that United would ditch the Premier League's collective TV agreement, that the club crest would be changed and that Old Trafford would be sold and leased were duly debunked. While Joel admitted that ticket prices could rise, he stressed that they would not out-price supporters, emphasising his family's respect for the club's traditions and even apologising for the turmoil that the takeover had created.

Retail Therapy

I felt a huge sense of relief once the interview was over. Having only recently met Joel for the first time, I could not have been more pleased with his assured TV performance. I even quipped to him afterwards that he should consider going into politics. With the Glazers' trip to Old Trafford nearly over, there was just enough time for some shopping at Manchester United's gleaming Megastore. As they stepped inside, it was clear how much reverence the brothers had for Manchester United, so mesmerised they seemed by the array of branded merchandise. They settled on gifts for their friends and children, including replica tops and t-shirts, thus providing an instant boost to club revenues. Not for the first time I was struck by their unassuming demeanour, which I would often find incongruous with their ownership of football's jewel in the crown.

I chatted further with the Glazer trio as they made their way to the people carriers awaiting them in the North Stand. This time, however, they were surveyed by a phalanx of curious onlookers rather than the baying crowd of the previous night. In order to complete their whistle-stop tour of the club, the Glazers were to be whisked to their private plane in time to be introduced to Sir Alex Ferguson at the squad's training camp on the Algarve.

When Joel joked about the frenetic nature of the previous two days, my genuine reaction was to smile and say, 'I love it, it's great fun,' remaining hopeful that his family would be retaining my PR services going forward. 'As long as you're having fun, that's the main thing, Tes,' Joel assured me.

Joel, Avie and Bryan allowed me full control of the MUTV interview and my instinct, as a former TV producer, was to condense it from 40 minutes to 30 minutes. I consulted Phil Townsend who immediately advised it would be better to broadcast the interview uncut, so as to dispel any accusation that 'Pravda TV' had sought to censor it. I immediately demurred, also relieved at the prospect of not having to laboriously edit the footage. And, now that the Glazers were on their way to Portugal, I finally had the chance to relax for the first time in 48 hours.

Stepping out into the East Stand concourse that humid summer afternoon felt like walking into a North African bazaar, bustling with onlookers and opportunists hawking counterfeit goods. The atmosphere was largely good-natured, in contrast with the menace of the previous night. There still lingered a significant number of media reporters and camera crews, scavenging for any insights to sate their rolling news audiences. I spotted Sir Bobby Charlton leaving the East Stand reception, surrounded by a throng of supporters and TV camera lenses. His calm, impassioned and supportive comments following his meeting with the Glazer brothers would prove pivotal especially given how emotionally raw the mood had been.

'Candid, Passionate and Uncut'

Later that afternoon I was back inside Old Trafford, sitting at a vacant desk in the marketing department and looking out at the dissipating crowd on the East Stand concourse. I proceeded to take calls from newspaper journalists clamouring for any information on Joel Glazer's MUTV interview, which was to be screened at 6pm the following day. Phil Townsend and I had decided against providing any specific guidance, as we were keen for the broadcast to be as fresh and as exclusive as possible, and were mindful that any leak would greatly reduce the interview's impact.

Still, I was keen to trail the USP for Joel's interview; the fact it would be unexpurgated, and my sound bite describing the interview as 'candid, passionate and uncut' was widely reported. Equally, reporters were desperate to get any colour they could about the Glazers' brief visit. Inside the Megastore I had suggested to Joel that he buy his twin daughters pink 'I love Manchester United t-shirts' which he duly did. I went on to casually mention the t-shirt purchase to one journalist, a trifling detail I thought. The following day saw this snippet of information being mentioned in a number of newspapers, reflecting the hunt-in-a-pack nature of football journalism.

The next morning's media coverage focused on Sir Bobby Charlton's meeting with the Glazers and his pacifying comments, illustrated with the pitch-side photos of the quartet. The press, while conceding that the Glazers had not cut and run after the riot, remained largely hostile, the debt issue being a residual anathema to all. Again, the influential Henry Winter of the *Daily Telegraph* repeated his call to arms[11]: 'Manchester United supporters demonstrating outside Old Trafford have every right to make life uncomfortable for the profiteers from Florida who have taken over their beloved club.'

That morning I made the short walk from my hotel to MUTV's production office to review and transcribe the entire interview; a painstaking, time-consuming process. With the broadcast due later that day there was a lot of anticipation surrounding Joel Glazer's comments – as well as the prospect of a media leak – so I could not risk anyone other than Phil Townsend and the tight group of MUTV employees knowing precisely what Joel had said. With the transcript finished, Phil and I chose the soundbites we would provide to a local Manchester radio station and the national TV news broadcasters – BBC, ITN and Sky – to ensure blanket coverage on the early evening news as soon as the interview went live.

An Anonymous Spokesman

While the crowds had all but gone, there were still a few broadcast vans camped outside Old Trafford, as television reporters sought to maintain news momentum ahead of the interview with live hourly updates. I spent a lot of time providing background briefings to the journalists, attempting to give some balance to their interest in this 'riot stricken' football club. An ITN correspondent asked why I didn't appear live on air to offer my well-versed defence of the Glazers' ownership – echoing Joel's comments to MUTV – to his lunchtime audience. Certainly I felt skilled at doing so, having served as an on-screen correspondent for many years with CNBC, and would have enjoyed the catharsis of speaking my mind. However, while the merits

---

[11] 'A wound that will never heal', *The Daily Telegraph*, 1 July 2005

of putting my head above the parapet had never been discussed with the Glazers, I instinctively knew to mirror my clients and maintain a very low profile, something that I would preserve throughout my association with the club.

This curiosity of being an anonymous spokesman is not unusual in public relations. The royal family and 10 Downing Street, for example, have a time-honoured tradition of briefing the media through an unnamed spokesperson. For me it felt appropriate to stay in the wings, reflecting what I knew to be the owners' own desire for a low profile. It also served to avoid any political risk of intruding upon Phil Townsend's role as the club's official spokesman. Also, as Manchester United aroused such fervour I realised that I did not speak with the same tongue as its core supporters. I was not a lifelong supporter of the club, would not have been able to list United's 1968 European Cup final start-up, and would frequently half-joke with Phil that my public school-honed London accent might, in any case, not help the Glazers' cause.

Come 6pm and there was heightening interest in Joel Glazer's interview, with MUTV likely to achieve a record viewing audience. I watched the now familiar broadcast with Phil Townsend in his office at Old Trafford, switching between channels as the BBC, ITN and Sky also filed their own packaged reports using excerpts that we had provided earlier. After emailing the transcript to all my journalist contacts, there was a profound sense of calm. Job done. There were no further emails or telephone calls from reporters that evening; now that the press pack had finally got something substantial from the Glazer camp to feed on, it seemed that the media frenzy had well and truly abated.

That evening Phil and I had dinner together, already ruminating – and seeing the funny side – at what had been a surreal 72 hours, and also celebrating the strong working relationship that we had forged. While Phil could look forward to United's tour of Asia, my immediate future wasn't so certain; now that the takeover communications strategy, so meticulously formulated, had been enacted, I was unsure whether my mandate with the owners and club was to continue.

'A Wound that Will Never Heal'

On the train to London the next morning, which was unusually packed with Live 8 revellers, I had ample time to peruse the Manchester United-related news coverage in the papers. Although a tad cynical about our use of 'Pravda' MUTV, the reporting of the interview was largely straight, even faintly positive, with recognition that the preceding days' charm offensive had gone some way towards reassuring supporters of the Glazers' ownership. The *Guardian* wryly reported[12] thus: "In a piece of textbook if somewhat schmaltzy PR which saw him press every diplomatic button, Joel disarmed the doubters by presenting his family as change-resistant, caring capitalists who, far from regarding history as bunk, are enthralled by United's heritage." That weekend's *Observer* carried the headline[13] "Glazers make the right noises", while the august Patrick Barclay in the *Sunday Telegraph* opined[14]: "At a stroke, the Americans' takeover had been rendered less scary… it is time to wait and see, to give the Glazers a chance and, above all, call off those thugs".

On reflection, I think our three-day charm offensive – very much a product of the mutual goodwill and trust between Phil Townsend and me – served to steady a remarkably frenzied time. Key stakeholders were addressed – from the game's regulators through to the club's staff and supporters – leaving no one in doubt (if he or she were open minded enough to listen) that the Glazers were genuine in their desire to responsibly own and run the club. I also think the Glazers' unpretentious and low-key approach – a million miles away from the swaggering, cowboy-booted American cliché – impressed everyone they encountered. Moreover, the Glazers, I think, were a good fit for the culture of a football club that was straightforward in its dealings and, despite its high-profile glamour, a football club that coveted its privacy.

---

[12] *The Guardian*, 2 July 2005
[13] *The Observer*, 3 July 2005
[14] *The Sunday Telegraph*, 3 July 2005

Unsurprisingly, a contrary view prevailed among some sections of the media, who were resentful at not getting the access they felt entitled to, and were driven by disgruntled supporter groups who viscerally opposed the Glazers per se, particularly the debt used to manage their takeover. Perhaps there was no way back from the slogan "Love United, Hate Glazer", which had gained traction thanks to an illicit yet ubiquitous sticker campaign throughout Manchester and beyond. A *Telegraph* headline presciently summed up the chasm between United's owners and their core disgruntled fan: 'A wound that will never heal.'

After two months of non-stop work for the Glazers, July proved to be remarkably quiet. The takeover story had run its course, with many football writers by now either away on pre-season tours with Premier League clubs or snatching their annual holiday break. I recall feeling rather fatigued by then and, like many, would have to ride the emotional rollercoaster provided by the sunny euphoria of London winning the right to host the 2012 Olympics and the following dank, drizzly day when the city's ebullience was shaken to its core by the 7/7 Al-Qaeda bombs and the nerve-wracking aftermath.

Back in Smithfield's offices, my retained service to the Glazers had come to a formal end, coinciding with one of my other clients making a bold acquisition move and presenting another consuming PR challenge. Still, I was keen for the opportunity to continue representing the Glazer family. I had been excited by the career-defining last few months and by now felt very loyal to the family. So I wrote to Joel Glazer with some ideas regarding the forthcoming new season, convinced that the owners still needed a voice. Indeed, while there had been a welcome lull, requests for access to the family continued to pour in from every media organisation imaginable.

'This is My Childhood'

During the last week of July I received an email from the Manchester-based producers of ITV's *Tonight with Trevor McDonald* programme, listing 13 points likely to be included in a broadcast scheduled for the eve of the new football season. Most of these points were a rehash of anti-Glazer character assassinations published in tabloid newspapers during the takeover process.

The last point, though, was new. It cited Joel Glazer's recent MUTV interview in which he recalled his childhood thus: 'My family have always been very passionate about two sports, American football and British football. And it's because in the town I grew up, Rochester New York, we had the North American Soccer League. And in Rochester we had the worst team in the league. But week in and week out I was there to support my club...'

The producers had interviewed Charles Schiano who had held several senior administrative positions at the Rochester Lancers. He maintained that, contrary to Joel's comments, the Lancers were one of the strongest teams in the League, insisting the Glazers never attended or bothered to sponsor a game. The *Tonight* programme's emailed missive concluded: 'The Glazer family...are successful businessmen interested in making money not the traditions of Manchester United.' I forwarded the email urgently for Joel's attention, mindful of the personal nature of the attack.

Joel's telephone response marked the second and only other time in the six years of my dealings with him when he betrayed anything other than good humour (the first had concerned the *Daily Mirror's* headline 'Sir Bobby for the axe'). His frustration was palpable. 'This is my childhood. How dare they try steal my memories away from me...' protested Joel. 'I was a true fan of the Lancers despite their miserable record. I love the game.'

Joel told me that he had attended his first Lancers game in August 1977, when he was 10, and that he had continued to watch his team along with brothers Avie and Bryan as season ticket holders for three years until the team folded in 1980. Joel even said he had kept all the ticket stubs. He also pointedly remarked, 'Sure we weren't sponsors, not many 10 year-olds are.'

As for Schiano's claim that the Lancers were one of the strongest teams in the League: well, partly true. In the early seventies, when Joel was three, the team topped the Northern Division. But by the time Joel attended games regularly the Lancers were languishing at the bottom of their league.

When I put these facts to the programme, including several telephone conversations with Sir Trevor McDonald, one of the country's most venerable news broadcasters, I was given short shrift and told that unless Joel Glazer put the record straight with an interview the programme would not amend its allegations. I remember feeling strong-armed by the programme's producers over the most trivial of issues.

My advice to Joel was to not engage with the programme; any involvement would tacitly dignify its tacky journalism and provide the producers with the attention they truly craved. Joel agreed and I curtly replied to the *Tonight* programme that no interview would be forthcoming. We awaited transmission in mid-August.

When the illustrious *New Yorker* magazine also approached me to assist in its profile of the Glazers, I knew that although the takeover was done and dusted, there was definitely an opportunity for someone to do the Glazers' bidding, especially as the world's media continued to be vexed about two issues:

1. How will the debt impact on Manchester United?

2. If they didn't want to bask in the club's reflected glory, *why* did the Glazers buy the club?

Part Two
2005 / 06 Season

By early August I was formally retained by the Glazer family to represent their ownership of Manchester United. Naturally, I was thrilled at clinching such a high-profile client; not least for the kudos it provided me at my PR agency. By this time my managing director John Antcliffe had devolved the lead role on the account to me, which I had seized with alacrity, recognising the life-changing impact the past few months had had.

Champions League Qualifier

I could look forward to visiting Old Trafford again and attend the first competitive game of the new era, a pre-season match that United would rather not have to play; a Champions League qualifier against Debrecen of Hungary.

I had used the summer hiatus to invest time lunching and relationship-building with London-based business and sports journalists. As well as impressing upon reporters that the Glazers were not ogres – on the contrary they were an unusually down to earth, close-knit family – most of my time was used to mitigate the leveraged – or indebted – business model pointing to United's uniquely reliable cash flows to cover interest payments. I also stressed that the new regime would provide greater stability to Sir Alex Ferguson; more than he had received when the club was listed on the London Stock Exchange. It seemed bizarre that Manchester United PLC had been obliged to make public any issue that might have a bearing on the share price. This included having to respond to newspaper speculation and even disclosing when a key player had sustained an injury. By early August I already sounded like a broken record with a mantra comprising three simple key messages: 'business as usual', 'marathon not a sprint' and 'sorry, no further Glazer interviews planned.'

My visit to Manchester for the Debrecen game was the first since those heady 72 hours at the end of June. Six weeks on, with Manchester still basking in summer warmth, things at Old Trafford had seemingly settled down. Joel Glazer's MUTV interview, plus Sir Alex's signings of goalkeeper Edwin van der Sar and midfield dynamo Ji-Sung Park, helped to secure a degree of 'wait and see' acceptance among the majority of United supporters. To describe it as a honeymoon period for United's new owners would have been pushing it, though.

Stepping off the train at the bustling Piccadilly station I already had a routine, which I was to replicate many times over the coming years. An enjoyable 30 minutes' walk to my hotel on Peter Street; through the city centre past the vibrant but slightly menacing Piccadilly Gardens, down Market Street and the Arndale Centre and then left into Deansgate, a sympathetically regenerated area of Manchester's cultural quarter, resplendent with some of the city's finest examples of imposing red-bricked Victorian architecture. My hotel, the Radisson, had a glorious past of its own, with its previous incarnation as the Free Trade Hall in which Bob Dylan had infamously plugged his guitar into an electric amp to the cries of 'Judas'. But apart from the magnificent Italian palazzo facade at the front of the building, any historical significance inside had given way to a chic temple to corporate five star luxury.

That matchday afternoon I was struck by the lack of football shirts being worn by Mancunian United fans, in contrast to, say, Liverpool where half the population seemed to be clad in red or blue polyester jerseys. What I did see were hordes of red-shirted, high-spirited Debrecen supporters milling around the city centre. I would soon learn that a significant proportion of local United fans eschewed wearing the club's colours, preferring to differentiate themselves from the 'tourist' supporters in official Nike Inc. regalia.

Also wary of the Manchester United money machine was FC United, an alternative club that had been formed that summer by disgruntled United supporters who deemed the Glazer takeover to be the final nail in the commercialised coffin. Indeed, the Bury-based club was about to kick off its inaugural game of the season. I knew some Manchester United supporters resented FC United for turning their back on the bigger club, especially in the aftermath of the takeover when there was so much turmoil. But appreciating that a local FC United could co-exist with its older and bigger 'international' brother, it was difficult not to admire FC United's initiative and sense of purpose, inspired by the heartfelt desire of its founders to return to grassroots football. FC United also had a very good feel for public relations; aware that any reference to Manchester United and the Glazers would ensure media exposure, they succeeded in drumming up a favourable David v Goliath profile that exponentially dwarfed their start-up status.

The Press Pack

My return to Manchester also marked an opportunity to meet with regional football correspondents, who were tasked with following Manchester United for their respective national broadsheet and tabloid newspapers.

The football press pack struck me as a fairly homogeneous group of white, middle-aged men. Journalists worked long hours and racked up a significant number of travel miles together which no doubt helped to forge close social bonds. A few honourable exceptions notwithstanding, their dress sense tended to resemble that of someone about to embark on a long hike; heavy duty Manchester wind-chill resistant anoraks were *de rigueur*. While usually personable and good company on a one-to-one basis – most of these reporters were bright, well travelled and hard working – en masse I found them quite intimidating. At times their passion for football seemed soured by the relentless pressures of their dream job. Understandably, they resented the Glazers' lack of engagement and, at best, saw me as a necessary evil rather than reliable source of a juicy story. Also, I appreciated their dismay at having to consider football finance rather than focus on the artistry of the game they loved. So it was axiomatic why most would see me, a financial PR suit, as an unedifying development of the modern game; someone they didn't feel particularly well disposed to.

Given that Manchester United was the biggest football club in the land, the correspondents charged with reporting on it enjoyed an elevated status among their professional peer group. However, any reporter's vanity at getting to cover United would be promptly brought down to earth with the daily grind and deadlines issued from their news desks. Their editors appeared to have an insatiable appetite for stories on United, while the hacks had to contend with the frustration of dealing with an institution that valued its privacy more highly than its public relations. Unlike other football clubs, Manchester United generally sought to keep journalists away from its inner workings by being reluctant to engage with the media's agenda for relentless tittle-tattle. United could, of course, only sustain this aloofness by its bullet-proof track record of success; it would reinforce the positives of its sell-out stadium and its overflowing trophy cabinet as the true yardsticks to be judged by, rather than courting the ephemeral appeal of glowing newspaper headlines.

United's terse relationship with the press had long been shaped by Sir Alex Ferguson's frequent run-ins with the media throughout his Old Trafford reign. Famously, Sir Alex would not hesitate in having a journalist banned from his weekly press conference if he felt that the miscreant had unjustly criticised his team or had abused the club's conditional hospitality. His uncompromising stance was abhorred by the free press, but his wariness of the media was shared to some extent by the club's chief executive David Gill and its new owners, the Glazers.

There were remarkably few new entrants to the press pack during the six years under my watch, a testimony to how jealously-guarded a career in this area of journalism tended to be. I did observe how professionally incestuous it was, too; most reporters I had dealings with would have invariably worked for other rival newspapers at some point in their long careers, and it was not unusual to see a football writer switching seamlessly from a mass-market tabloid to a high-end broadsheet.

I soon discovered that the Manchester football correspondents generally hunted in discreet packs; reporters from the daily national newspaper titles like the *Daily Mail* and the *Daily Telegraph* would collude with one another, as would their colleagues from Sunday national titles like the *Sunday Times* or the *Sunday Mirror*. It appeared to me that any (usually non-newspaper) journalist who dared act alone would be treated with barely disguised contempt from his peers. While the reporters' cliques and bonds partially explained the unwritten pack system, football journalists were also acting out of professional self-preservation. Such were the incessant demands on them from their London-based sports desks that reporters would huddle in tight packs after each of Sir Alex Ferguson's press briefings, sharing what they had gleaned and agreeing on the main points they would *all* write about. This seemed a very efficient way to handle the constant stream of newsflow and reduced the threat of anyone getting an exclusive angle or indeed anyone missing the big scoop. This meant that, unless I stipulated otherwise, if I wanted to break a piece of news widely I could count on speaking to just one or two football reporters, whom I could rely upon to quickly disseminate it to their colleagues on rival newspapers.

My main messages to the football press were to assure them of the Glazers' wish for continuity, to accentuate their full support for Sir Alex Ferguson, and to stress the family's own sporting experience. In short, I aimed to emphasise the Glazers' ethos that the business of sport could equally be about managing the disappointment of losing as well as savouring the sweet taste of success.

The Directors' Box

As with my previous visits, I jumped in a black cab at the end of Deansgate for the ten-minute hop to Old Trafford. But on this particular matchday, my short trip to Old Trafford felt very different to my previous off season visits, with the route soon becoming clogged up with the dense combination of football and rush-hour traffic. With the arterial approach to the stadium closed off to cars on matchdays, I got into the routine of jumping out of the cab on the dual-carriaged Chester Way and walking down Sir Matt Busby Way to the stadium, past the thousands of supporters, indulging in their ritual of sloshing down plastic pint jars of beer from The Trafford pub and feasting on the greased carbohydrate delights from United legend Lou Macari's eponymous fish and chip shop. The intensely tribal atmosphere was always good-humoured and friendly, although I would always wonder whether my anonymous passage would have been so unfettered had some of Sir Matt Busby Way's loiterers known me to be the Glazers' spokesman and one-time Liverpool FC supporter to boot.

For my inaugural match I was seated in the directors' box a few rows behind Joel, Avie and Bryan Glazer. It was the first time they'd attended an Old Trafford match as its new owners, and each of them sported a brand new red silk club tie. The directors' box is one of the most coveted areas to sit inside the stadium, carrying immense snob value as well as the thrill of potentially being seated near to a visiting VIP or a well-known celebrity. It's also a large, impressive space, projecting the club's self importance with a stunning central view of the pitch. Each guest, usually dressed in his or her Sunday best, is cosseted in maroon faux leather upholstered arm-rested chairs, all with business class legroom. There are even luxury touches like ribbed carpeted aisles cordoned off from the adjoining seat block by an old fashioned red rope stand, attended to by a dapper club official.

While the directors' box is a special and privileged place from which to watch a football game, it can also feel rather repressive and formal, as demonstrations of high emotions are frowned upon. This avoidance of gloating stemmed from a tradition of respect for the away team delegation, seated separately across the aisle. I suspected it also reflected a time-honoured stiff upper lip desire among the VIPs to distinguish themselves from the marauding hordes in the adjacent stands.

Inside the stadium the atmosphere was largely convivial. The Glazers appeared relaxed, shaking hands with and signing autographs for curious spectators in front of them, some of whom took impromptu photographs with their pocket-size digital cameras and mobile phones. This was in stark contrast with the lingering venom and spite of the small but assiduously reported gathering of protesters outside the stadium. The *International Herald Tribune* wryly noted[15]:

---

[15] *International Herald Tribune*, 11 August 2005

'What the Glazer boys felt was a warm acceptance. Inside the stadium, they signed autographs and posed for snapshots with the fans. Outside, out of earshot and vision, a few hundred protestors… marched to the front entrance, some of them mouthing: 'I hope Glazer dies.' Oh, the passions of supporters.'

With summer holidays still in full flow, the Old Trafford attendance was, as expected, below the 67,000 capacity, at around 50,000. A legendary European night buzz may have been lacking, but the tone was lifted by the pocket of red liveried Debrecen supporters, all of whom were obviously thrilled at being at the Theatre of Dreams for this rare opportunity for their club to play Europe's footballing aristocrats. The crowd was also treated to a bravura performance from Wayne Rooney, who was embarking upon his second season at the club.

At the end of the game Phil Townsend gave me a quick behind-the-scenes tour of the stadium, including the players' areas, and introduced me for the first time to a suntanned Sir Alex Ferguson. Understandably he was pleased with the 3-0 final scoreline, appearing relaxed and chatty, something that was echoed in his post-match press conference. The Glazer brothers also spent twenty minutes or so with Sir Alex and the players in their dressing room; a post-match ritual they would fulfil each time they attended a game. Significantly, the Glazers met Sir Alex on his terms, in his domain: never the 'manager summoned by club owner' scenario that apparently took place at other less well-functioning clubs.

The Press Box

A few days later, on the eve of the new Premier League season, ITV broadcast its half-hour *The Man Who Bought United: A Tonight Special*. ITV's publicity machine went into overdrive with a press release widely circulated to journalists: 'Glazers' Football Passion Killer Speaks Out… One of Malcolm Glazer's son's claims that the Manchester United owner's family are 'passionate' football fans have been rubbished by a former chairman of the American club he said he supported as a young man.' True to form, the programme pursued its personal attack on Joel Glazer's credibility without broadcasting the facts I had provided them with. The programme's sensationalist agenda was an eye-opener and was not the last time the Glazers would receive a rough hearing on Britain's airwaves: given their refusal to engage with programme makers, the Glazers would become fair game for negative one-sided reportage.

One week on, with United having started the season with an away victory against Everton, I attended my first Premier League Old Trafford game, a lunchtime Saturday start against Aston Villa. Again, the Glazers were in attendance; Joel was accompanied by brother Bryan, who for the first time basked in the 67,000 capacity atmosphere, which felt welcoming and friendly. Aston Villa's supporters goaded the home fans with chants of 'USA, USA, USA...', an ironic refrain that every other away support would forever voice.

It was my first time in the press box, where I was assigned a couple of seats and from where I would watch most of my six years-worth of games. In addition to the thrill of a guaranteed seat at Old Trafford, I came to regard this perk as a very visible gesture to the surrounding press pack of my own commitment to the beautiful game. Access to the press area was gained via the South Stand tunnel, just opposite the directors' entrance, and echoed the VIP zone's modern white decor with flashes of red Perspex strips, albeit with a distinctly more workmanlike feel than its deluxe counterpart. Climbing a narrow staircase brought you into the press lounge, another windowless but airy white space, which was adjacent to the VIP lounge. Journalists were barred from access to this private area by a long corridor wall that was adorned with an impressive photographic collage of some of United's historic signings putting pen to paper, including George Best, Cristiano Ronaldo and Ruud van Nistelrooy.

The press lounge resembled a newsroom, albeit uncluttered; a working space centred on a large communal wooden desk wired up for journalists to plug in their laptops and modems. There was an additional desk along one of the walls, and an adjoining room comprising a small bar and airport lounge-like seating where a buffet meal was offered on match days. The food could most generously be described as being 'filling' and lacked the finesse of the VIP lounge's fare, although I would always relish the offer of the excellent Lancashire hot pot, particularly on a wintry Manchester night.

While the press lounge was a pleasant enough space on a quiet day, it seemed barely adequate to accommodate the throng of journalists on a big Premier League or Champions League game, when the room was often febrile with excitable reporters gossiping away and striving to meet their strict deadlines.

There were several flat screen televisions fixed to the wall, around which journalists would ritually cluster whenever Sir Alex Ferguson gave his interviews to Sky Sports or MUTV. With their dictaphones held high towards the TV speakers, they desperately tried to capture Sir Alex's every pithy utterance, which would likely lead their match reports. That's because, with the honourable exception of obligatory UEFA Champions League post-match press conferences, Sir Alex declined to give any interviews to the press pack after the game. This meant that the press conference room – a tiered, theatre-like space accessible from the lounge via a heavy soundproofed white door – was effectively redundant on a Premier League matchday, save for the (usually less newsworthy) post-match comments from the visiting team manager.

The press box, next to the directors' area, offered an equally prized view of the pitch and was buttressed against seated fans' areas, thus enhancing the intimate feel of the stadium. Unlike the VIPs' cosseted experience, however, the press box was unbelievably cramped with uncomfortable seats squeezed up against folding tables that would bite into your legs and chest, so unforgiving that they would often cause reporters' cups of coffee, mobile phones or even laptops to tumble onto the row of their unsuspecting colleagues seated below. I always wondered whether this discomfort reflected Manchester United's institutionalised wariness of the fourth estate. In reality, this sardine tin squeeze was due to space being at a premium in the stadium's most antiquated stand, while the supply of press seats was usually inadequate given the club's huge global media following.

Like the directors' box, there were unwritten codes of behaviour to reflect the prevailing workaday environment; idle chatter was avoided as reporters strove to concentrate and keep abreast of every moment of the game. Also, journalists always sought to appear impartial (especially those suspected to have an affinity for Manchester United), so no clapping or cheering for either team was tolerated. When I stood up during one particularly pulsating game to applaud a second United goal, I was duly scolded by the press pack: not in person, but more pointedly by having to read a stinging article criticising my behaviour in a following weekend's newspaper diary column. One journalist ribbed me that the article had placed me 'on the naughty step'.

Before the eventual installation of individual mini TV screens carrying live feeds and replays during the game, and with no large LED screen in the stadium, the press box was also an environment often gripped with frenzied rumour and speculation; a place where a journalist's take on a controversial occurrence during the game could spread quickly like Chinese whispers. But while the press box could sometimes feel daunting for an outsider like me, especially given how aggressively knowledgeable about football its occupants were, there was also occasional humorous banter and warmth among the cabal of reporters who, at a push, could go misty-eyed about their privileged journalistic positions.

Back in the USA

After the end of the Aston Villa game, a consecutive easy-ish victory for United, I snatched a few words with Joel Glazer in the directors' VIP lounge. He was waiting to be spirited away to the airport for his and his brother's flight back to the States, in time to watch their NFL team play in Tampa. He agreed that I should fly out to Florida to meet him.

Towards the end of August things seemed to have substantially calmed down with the Glazer brothers' two appearances at Old Trafford prompting friendly curiosity, in stark contrast with the seething contempt of a small gaggle of protesters outside, with the *Guardian* commenting[16]: 'The new men in power at Old Trafford

---

[16] *The Guardian*, 22 August 2005

could be seen high-fiving in the directors' box while, outside, the riot police were munching sandwiches and trying not to look too bored in the back of their armoured vans.'

However, as I waited in Virgin Atlantic's über-trendy Heathrow clubhouse for my Miami-bound flight, that morning's newspaper coverage pointed to the prevailing undercurrent of volatility. With United en route to Hungary for their second leg of the Champions League tie against Debrecen, the press reported that, while waiting at the luggage carousel, Sir Alex Ferguson and David Gill had been confronted by a supporter accusing them of 'selling out' to the Glazers. Newspapers claimed that Sir Alex told the fan that if he was so unhappy with the new regime at Old Trafford, he should 'go and watch Chelsea.'

This alleged incident was widely reported across that day's newspapers, and illustrated the media's insatiable interest in Manchester United and its owners. Indeed, it was this Glazer obsession that was to keep me in a job; something I would constantly remind myself, especially on the days when media interest – and hyperbole – became almost unbearable.

I arrived in the late afternoon at Miami airport, which was shrouded in a dark stormy gloom. I was due to meet Joel Glazer the following morning in Palm Beach – around 70 miles away – and I was chauffeured in a Lincoln limousine to a lavish, opulent hotel-cum-resort – The Breakers – that Joel had recommended to me. By the time I arrived at my destination the wind had stiffened significantly; high waves crashed onto the hotel's private beach, the sky over the Atlantic Ocean becoming a beguilingly beautiful orangey purple.

The next morning I awoke early, jet lagged and nervous ahead of my meeting, unsure whether to wear my tie or not (just like my advice to Joel ahead of the MUTV interview, I opted for formality). Gazing outside at the wind-battered palm trees, I started to fret at the deteriorating weather conditions, especially since the hotel concierge had passed a note under my door suggesting that all guests might want to switch to interior facing rooms. I spent my free morning recklessly attempting to walk towards the beach, but was buffeted by the strengthening gale and wisely reverted to the safe haven of the giant hotel lobby.

By late morning, and following a short taxi ride, I reached West Palm Beach. I headed to the office block where Joel and I were due to meet; a building which, like its neighbours, was becoming splattered by stormy rain and looked so nondescript I wasn't sure whether I had got the right address. Certainly no Tampa Bay or Manchester United nameplate was outside. Fortunately, at that moment, walking towards me on the immaculately clean pavement, was Joel, conspicuously without any bodyguard entourage. Dressed casually in a black Ralph Lauren polo shirt and beige chinos, with his demeanour breezily relaxed and friendly, he was at 180 degree-odds with the stereotype of a ruthless American business tycoon.

The Family Meeting

Joel accompanied me in the elevator up to his family's office suite, which was a modern wood-panelled affair, distinguished by a boardroom with a sweeping glass front offering a stunning view of Palm Beach's Intercoastal Waterway. Joel's sister Darcie and brother Avie joined us in the room while the voice of Bryan, dialled in from his Chicago home, emanated from the speakerphone on the boardroom table.

Compared with the casually-attired siblings, I felt overdressed sat there in my linen suit and tie. This was to be the first occasion that the Glazers would chat freely to me, outlining the logic of their purchase of Manchester United and their plans for the future. Two things soon became abundantly clear: the family were in it for the long-term and were committed to seeing the club regain its pre-eminence (many observers had argued that United's hegemony had been terminally dashed since Abramovich's purchase of Chelsea FC). The Glazers were also unequivocal in their trust in Sir Alex Ferguson and David Gill's leadership of the club.

At an early point the meeting was paused as the brothers deployed the many remote controls on the table to expertly tune the giant flat screen television, which dominated one of the walls to a US sports channel. This carried a live broadcast of the Champions League draw from UEFA's headquarters in Nyon; United were grouped with Villarreal, Benfica and Lille, a development the club secretary had cautiously welcomed in a subsequent interview.

It felt surreal – almost reminiscent of a scene in a John Irving novel – to be seated around a table with such a young and unassuming group of siblings…who just happened to own Manchester United. Although Joel maintained a brisk and businesslike pace, diligently following the agenda that I had drafted some days earlier, I was also struck by the informality of the meeting. The level of good humoured – but also at times vigorous – debate between the brothers and sister emphasised how well-versed each sibling was about Manchester United, and how freely they could air and kick around ideas. This was a family used to conducting business according to its terms.

Joel and Avie were sat opposite me with their backs to the window but I was occasionally distracted by the backdrop of a growing storm, the rain lashing against the building and the ant-like cars on the bridge battling through the gusts of wind.

Being acclimatised to Florida's hurricane season, the Glazers seemed nonplussed. However, when I expressed alarm about getting back to London – my flight was booked for the following day – they immediately suggested I book a plane out of Florida as soon as possible before the bad weather really set in. Rather than summon his PA as I would have expected any self-respecting tycoon to do, Joel reached for his cell phone and, speaking with his travel agent, booked me a plane, advising me that I should take a domestic flight out of Palm Beach to the north east coast. With our meeting abruptly curtailed by the escalating storm, Avie offered me a lift to the nearby Palm Beach airport in his made-in-Britain Range Rover, which sported a personalised Tampa Bay Buccaneers number plate.

I said my goodbyes, my mind buzzing with ideas following the meeting but increasingly concerned by the gathering storm. Indeed, I was feeling so disorientated that when Avie dropped me off at Palm Beach airport I realised I had forgotten my small travel case – with passport – at the hotel. By now soaked by the rain, I had to desperately hail a cab to The Breakers. Back in the hotel, I decided to dry off and take stock of the situation. I resolved to chance it and head back to

Miami Airport in order to get a flight home to London that day. My limousine easily exceeded the speed limit on the empty freeway, the opposite carriageway notably busier with evacuating Miami residents. Less than 24 hours after my arrival in Florida I was back in the air; my plane was one of the last to take off that stormy evening, in its ascent piercing through the swirling turbulence of sheet lighting and torrential rain. Within days of my return to London the storm I had managed to escape was to assume a much more startling significance that belied its innocuous name: Hurricane Katrina.

Clock Ticking for Ferguson?

As little substance came out of the Palm Beach meeting with the Glazers, no major communications initiative was agreed. However, the contact time – and the insights I would gain into how the Glazer family intended to conduct their business affairs – would prove invaluable, especially in the months ahead when I would discover at first-hand just how volatile the football industry could be.

Although the team had enjoyed a strong start to the 2005/06 season, by mid-September points were dropped against local rivals Manchester City and Liverpool. United went on to lose a home fixture against Blackburn Rovers which led to some supporters heckling their illustrious manager. The *Guardian* even speculated that Sir Alex's reign may be coming to an end[17]: 'This felt like the beginning of the end for Sir Alex Ferguson. That is some statement but what other inference is there to draw from a match that concluded with vitriolic abuse being directed at Manchester United's manager from the club's own supporters?'

With pressure heaping on Sir Alex, I began to take calls from journalists looking for any indication as to whether the Glazers' ownership might signal a change. To an extent it was 'box ticking' for reporters to put that call into me, and I duly refused to provide any

---

[17] *The Guardian*, Ferguson ducks a rising red tide of outrage, 26 September 2005

comment that could fuel speculation about the manager's future – or indeed any personnel at the club, a mantra I would stick to throughout the duration of my role. In any case, Joel's 'marathon not a sprint' ethos suggested that the new owners would be phlegmatic about the team's relatively poor run of results.

However, despite two wins and a draw during October, the team's subsequent 4-1 away defeat to Middlesbrough would trigger a chain of events that returned Manchester United to the same high-octane crisis coverage last experienced six months earlier. The new Glazer regime soon became a lightning conductor for the club's travails.

The loss, predictably, prompted further speculation in the press. The *Daily Telegraph* headline read[18] 'Clock Ticking for Ferguson', but it was the remarks made to MUTV by the then-injured club captain Roy Keane – he allegedly lambasted his teammates' performance against 'Boro before the footage was pulled – that provided the perception of a club in turmoil. This would, of course, be heightened by the inherent melodrama of the 24/7 rolling news agenda.

The media pressure was to intensify a few days later when Manchester United travelled to France for their away Champions League tie in Lille. That morning, the *Daily Mail's* Matt Lawton even questioned the wisdom of expanding the stadium[19]: 'The Glazers... must now wonder if 8,000 new seats that will help pay off their debt will ever be occupied. Construction in the stands is being accompanied by self-destruction on the field. As Old Trafford rises, the empire begins to fall.'

Later that day Manchester United lost 1-0 to Lille, which unleashed a further wave of harsh criticism for Sir Alex and his players. The *Times*[20] pointed to a 'deepening sense of crisis'. There was also a degree of schadenfreude among some reporters that the Glazers had unknowingly bought a club in decline, with the *Guardian* pronouncing[21]: 'There is no minor tinkering that can rejuvenate

---

[18] *The Daily Telegraph*, 31 October 2005
[19] *Daily Mail*, Fergie Fighting Talk, 2 November 2005
[20] *The Times*, 2 November 2005
[21] *The Guardian*, Red alert as United slump again, 3 November 2005

United and major upheaval lies ahead. It will cast doubt on the future of Sir Alex Ferguson and also show whether the Glazer family have the means to nourish a club bought at such expense.'

The scene was set for United's next game, a home fixture against Chelsea, the unbeaten leaders of the Premier League. During the intervening days I had been inundated with calls from journalists, their prevailing attitude could have been summarised thus: 'Surely the Glazers – who, as Americans, clearly have no idea about football – must be convulsed in panic with the team losing and all that debt to service?' In truth, speaking to Joel Glazer frequently over this period I knew just how calm he and his family were. Now would not be a time to flinch, and I sought to convey this in my countless briefings, seeking to replicate Joel's measured tones and unfailing optimism.

Still, with the country that weekend marking Guy Fawkes Day with the traditional bonfires and fireworks (and despite my best efforts to relay the owners' 'business as usual' message) the press coverage was incendiary ahead of the Chelsea game. The *Times* headline speculated:[22] 'Glazers can be counted on to demur at high price of failure,' and the editor of *United Rant*, a popular fanzine, wrote in the *Guardian*[23]: "The strength of feeling against Ferguson has become so forceful recently that the hated Glazers may even win over some fans by removing him".

Mindful that the Glazers would not be making the trip to Manchester – their NFL team were due to play in Tampa that day against the Carolina Panthers – I contemplated the prospect of being harangued by a packed press lounge should United go down to Chelsea. That said, I was really looking forward to this most anticipated of glamour ties, having attended three games up to that point at Old Trafford, which had all been comfortable wins against middling teams in front of what had struck me as a subdued home crowd.

United's duel against Chelsea became one of the most memorable matches I ever attended, reflecting the intense rivalry between the

---

[22] *The Times*, 4 November 2011
[23] *The Guardian*, 4 November 2011

country's two leading clubs. The tension was ramped up by the London club's manager, José Mourinho, who had transfixed the nation with his cocksureness. It was a match that United simply *had to* win. As the two sides emerged from the players' tunnel, the atmosphere inside Old Trafford was gladiatorial, the intensity persisting right through to the final whistle. The only goal, a looping header from United's Darren Fletcher, prompted a deafening roar of unbridled joy from the 60,000-or-so home supporters inside the stadium. I shared their emotions, too, engulfed with a huge sense of relief after what had been a very stressful week.

The metaphorical knives that reporters had sharpened in the event of a United loss were put back in the drawers. However, true to form, the press could not resist a dig at the Glazers' conspicuous absence. The *Times'* columnist Matt Dickinson pronounced[24]: 'The Glazer heart beats with such passion for Manchester United that, on the day that the empire was in greatest peril, not one member of the family bothered to cross the Atlantic. No doubt they watched the match on television, but that was no substitute at all for witnessing the stirring of a mighty beast within Old Trafford.'

Vodafone Hangs Up

On Friday 18th November, the same day that Manchester United announced the departure of its emblematic club captain Roy Keane, Joel Glazer called me. He informed me that Vodafone was intending to use its break clause to terminate its shirt sponsorship deal to focus, it would later transpire, on a partnership with UEFA's Champions League competition.

Joel was his usual calm and positive self as he insisted that this marked an opportunity for the club to seek a new sponsor at a more lucrative rate. My reaction to the news was a mixture of apprehension

---

[24] *The Times*, Champions fire blanks as undefeated sequence ends, 7 November 2005

and excitement; while I anticipated that this would fuel the perception of post-takeover upheaval, I also relished the prospect of dealing with a classic crisis communications situation. My advice to Joel was indeed time-honoured; to be proactive with the announcement and to seek to control the messages as much as possible. Given the sensitivity of the news, it was inevitable that it would leak. With this in mind, Joel agreed that we should sign off any activity as soon as possible, coinciding with his brothers' next visit to Old Trafford, namely the Champions League tie against Villareal the following Wednesday. It was a match which had a must-win feel to it, with United trailing third in the group of four.

In fact the game against Villareal proved to be a disappointing goalless draw, prompting mutinous chants of 'Keano' to reverberate around Old Trafford. The tension inside the room of Sir Alex's post-match press conference was palpable; the manager provided curt, sarcastic responses to the questions volleyed at him, with one enquiry from the *Times'* correspondent being totally dismissed. Manchester United would need an away win at Benfica if they were to progress to the knockout phase of the Champions League, a feat the club had routinely achieved in nine previous seasons.

After the game, my meeting with Joel, held inside the directors' private dining room in the VIP lounge, was typically ad hoc, and we stood huddled in discussion with his brothers Avie, Bryan and commercial director Andy Anson. All provided me with their comments on the press release which Phil Townsend and I had drafted, already reflecting the advice of Vodafone. Despite the lacklustre result, the mood that night was bullish; having already sounded out potential sponsors United's senior executives seemed confident at the prospect of securing an improved shirt deal. If anything, I stood my ground by advising caution, arguing that we needed to tone down any statement by the club in the press release, lest it make us hostages to fortune.

Mindful of the team's indifferent result and the aftermath of Roy Keane's departure, Phil Townsend and I shared the view that the news would likely prompt a torrent of negative coverage. Nevertheless we agreed to release the announcement the following day, realising that any delay in doing so would risk a leak from elsewhere. The Glazers, who had made a hasty exit for the flight back to the States, left me in charge of finalising the press release, the key messages and the Q&A documents in time for sign-off as soon as they landed in Florida.

So I returned to my hotel room, working through the early hours to finish off the statement. The next morning, Phil and I met with Andy Anson in his spacious Old Trafford office to ready ourselves for a demanding day. After further discussion in a conference call, a sleep-deprived Bryan Glazer approved the press release, giving us the go-ahead to coordinate the news dissemination with Vodafone.

Just before we went live, Phil and I had to contend with one further concern: the ailing health of Manchester United legend George Best. The previous weekend the *News of the World* had printed a front page photo of Best in his hospital bed[25], with a personal 'Don't Die like Me' message for his fans. This fuelled press speculation that George Best's death was imminent, and Phil and I were extremely anxious that the Vodafone announcement, were it to coincide with news of Best's death, would be perceived as a cynical attempt by us to 'bury bad news'. In fact, we knew our only option was to put out the Vodafone statement regardless, knowing that we had no choice but to weather any likely storm.

Once we issued the press announcement, Andy Anson gave a remarkably robust series of media interviews in which he stressed the club's optimistic prospects. For a few hours that day, communications-wise, we were on the front foot. Later that afternoon, while travelling on the London-bound train, I confess to being one of those irritating passengers with a mobile phone glued to his ear. I spent much of the journey responding with adrenalin-fuelled passion to the multitude of journalist calls, explaining to them that Vodafone's decision represented an opportunity rather than threat to the fortunes of Manchester United and the Glazers.

The following morning, the tenor of the Vodafone newspaper coverage was expectedly but annoyingly negative. The development was seen as a further blow to the club's esteem, which had already been

---

[25] *News of the World*, 20 November 2005

rocked by Roy Keane's exit. There was even wild speculation that Nike, United's kit supplier, would review its partnership with the club.

I was now accustomed to the level of press interest in Manchester United's business affairs, especially relating to the club's post-takeover financial position. While the *Financial Times* astutely speculated that the Glazers could be looking to Asia or the USA for a potential sponsor[26], most commentators concluded that United might even struggle to trump Chelsea's then record 2005 deal with South Korean electronics firm Samsung, reported to be worth £50 million over five years. Moreover, with the household name of Vodafone – burnished in no small part by its sponsorship of United – on the way out, there was a presumption that Manchester United would need the prestige of a high-profile sponsor like Apple or Sony. This defied logic, as it was more likely to be a lesser-known brand that would prize having its name emblazoned on that famous red shirt, assuring wide exposure to millions of global supporters.

A few days after the Vodafone announcement, while I was having lunch with sports journalist Mihir Bose, I received the sad news that George Best had died. It evoked my own memories of the Old Trafford legend, as I had worked with him in 1993 during a stint as an assistant producer for a Sky Sports outside broadcast. Despite the pressures of live television, the George Best I recalled was sparkly-eyed, calm and courteous. Having also met Bobby Moore many times through his son Dean – a prep school class mate – I felt myself to be serendipitously intertwined with the elite echelons of our national game.

European Exit

Aware of the Glazers' input into the shirt process, I was hopeful that a strong deal would provide a lift to their reputation. However, in the meantime, I was resigned to the doom-mongers and naysayers warning of difficult financial times ahead. I didn't legislate for a sudden

---

[26] *Financial Times*, 24 November 2005

escalation in the perceived 'crisis' at Old Trafford, though, courtesy of a crisp winter's evening in Lisbon.

The run-up to Manchester United's must-win game against Benfica was dominated by press speculation regarding the financial impact of the team's failure to progress to the knockout stage of the Champions League. This ranged from a loss of £2.5 to £15 million, depending on which newspaper you read, the general consensus being that troubled times lay ahead for the club's seemingly beleaguered new owners. On the morning of the game the *Times* thundered[27] that 'exiting Europe would be disastrous for the bottom line.'

Acutely aware that United *could* lose, especially as the game involved a potentially tricky away trip to Lisbon's famously intimidating Estádio da Luz (Stadium of Light), I took the precaution of putting in a long call to Joel Glazer, advising him that the morning's press could be an omen for a likely barrage of further hysterical coverage. Joel's response, as usual, was measured and collected: 'Yes, the team could lose, that's the nature of sport and if that happens it's not the end of the world, is it? Business as usual, Tes!' Joel went on to brush off the prospect of any negative bearing on the club's finances, and his family's support for Sir Alex remained unequivocal.

Not having a Sky Sports subscription I ended up watching the game in an empty run-down bar perched on the outskirts of Crouch End. After Paul Scholes' early goal I felt optimistic about the final outcome, probably like most viewing United supporters. However, the ensuing – and edgy – 80 minutes exposed United's fragility against an ebullient Benfica. The Lisbon team's equaliser, meant that Manchester United were consigned to playing in the UEFA cup. But United's ignominy was completed when Benfica's 34th-minute winner dumped the Reds out of European competition altogether. My gloom was compounded by a group of noisy Portuguese fans, who had piled into the bar during the latter stages of the game to celebrate their compatriots' victory.

During the short walk home I rehearsed my PR angle in my head in the aftermath of this seismic disappointment. I considered calling

---

[27] *The Times*, 7 December 2005

Joel again to seek a fresh response but thought better of it; I knew his pre-match comments remained 100 per cent salient.

Back at home I sat at the kitchen table, the radio tuned to angry United fans phoning in their frustration, and scribbled some notes in readiness for the next day's media enquiries. One poor result had no bearing on the family's long-term ownership; the show must go on. Acutely aware that an owner's public backing of a manager could be decoded as a kiss of death, Joel and I had agreed that I would not provide any comment relating to the manager. Perversely, but predictably, this was inferred by some journalists as 'a deafening silence' and 'a refusal to publicly back Sir Alex.'

Not Pygmies

As expected, the following morning's press coverage, with the recent exits of Roy Keane and Vodafone still ringing in journalists' ears, did not make for easy reading. Many football writers jumped to the conclusion that the Benfica defeat could mark the end of Sir Alex's tenure.

Just as I walked into the office, the BBC telephoned me asking for a comment. I echoed what Joel Glazer had told me the previous afternoon, explaining that his family were naturally disappointed but that I was convinced that their resolve was unabated. These comments, straight from the book of anodyne common sense, were duly reported. This 'statement from the Glazer family' was even transcribed for a graphic on the BBC's News 24 channel, which I could see clearly on the office's large, wall-mounted LED TV screen. This development unleashed calls from every news outlet, all of whom wanted more of the same.

I was surprised by how some journalists presumed the Glazers to be so hopelessly out of their depth that they would be panicked and crushed by the past month's travails. Alternatively, some journalists seemed to imagine the Glazers to be ruthless ogres, seething with rage, bent on meting out swingeing changes to the club they had bought only six months previously. A sort of naïve cynicism on the media's part, if that isn't an oxymoron.

That afternoon I was deluged with calls from newspaper reporters, on the usually quiet Thursday for football stories. All relished the opportunity of extending the news cycle of United's defeat by a further 24 hours; my office colleagues around me certainly didn't relish my broken record repetition.

While I had planned to stick to my simple messages, I was becoming exasperated by the level of suspicion towards the Glazers, causing me to resort to an unfortunate analogy. I asserted that the family were not 'pygmies' who were ignorant of the inherent risks of sport, and also cited their experience of mixed on-pitch fortunes with their NFL team. My loose use of the word pygmy meant I would endure a largely sleepless night, anxious that a newspaper might seize upon it, perhaps featuring a cruel caricature of a half-naked, pot-bellied Malcolm Glazer with a bone pierced through his nose replacing the obligatory leprechaun outfit?

The amount of column inches on Friday morning (as well as the weekend) more than matched the level of coverage at the height of the takeover in May. Football and business journalists, commentators and columnists, some barely concealing their schadenfreude, all questioned how the servicing of the debt could survive the disappointment of an early Champions League exit. A small positive: no pygmy caricature. What a relief.

Most newspapers looked forward to the end of Sir Alex's reign, speculating on his successor. Even the *Financial Times*, renowned for its measured and dispassionate reportage, opined[28]: 'Malcolm Glazer must wonder what he has got himself into. The cracks in Manchester United evident before his takeover are gaping fissures now.'

I was particularly riled by a story on the Bloomberg newswire[29] quoting a business school professor that United's early exit 'could be a disaster in the short, medium and long terms… It could impact on the perception of United as a truly global team and ultimately cost 50 to

---

[28] Champions League exit means financial penalty for Manchester United, *Financial Times*, 9 December 2005

[29] Champions League Exit May Cost Manchester United $173 Million, Bloomberg, 8 December 2005

100 million pounds.' Demonstrating the hysteria that often pervaded the media, the influential Bloomberg headlined its story 'Champions League Exit May Cost Manchester United $173 Million,' its hyperbole reminding me that when it came to Manchester United and the Glazers it was open season, regardless of the reputation of the news outlet. The story also highlighted how quickly some academics, marketing and sports finance 'experts' would jump on the Manchester United bandwagon, generously providing the media with frequently ill-informed opinions in pursuit of the heady oxygen of self-publicity.

Meet Ed

Just as Christmas decorations were being put up, a disappointing draw against Everton would mean that United had all but conceded the title to a rampant Chelsea. A few days' later, on the eve of the club's encounter against Wigan Athletic, Sir Alex Ferguson walked out of his pre-match press conference after a reported 74 seconds, giving the bemused gathering of journalists further opportunity to sharpen their vitriol. But away from the headlines, which had peddled doom and gloom for over a month, there was – paradoxically – a remarkable sense of calm inside the club and among the owners, unified by a siege mentality and tacit commitment to ride out the media storm. United's Phil Townsend and I kept in frequent contact during this period, our sense of perspective and humour intact, aware that only football results, not PR initiatives, would shift the media's pessimistic agenda. Indeed, Phil and I would go on to compare any future crises with this period, resting assured that, as with the forces of nature, being at the eye of a media storm could often be the most tranquil place to be.

The atmosphere inside Old Trafford on the crisp mid-December night of the Wigan game was unusually raw, reflecting the shredded nerves of many a Manchester United supporter. There was press speculation that Bryan Glazer had cancelled his attendance for fear of fans' protest, but the truth was far more straightforward; a stateside snowstorm meant that he was unable to make the flight in time. Fortunately, United's emphatic 4-0 home win would serve as a cathartic moment, providing, with hindsight, a bookend to the previous two months' frenzied press coverage.

Earlier that week Joel Glazer had informed me that the family had recruited an Englishman, Ed Woodward, to fill a new 'chief of staff' role, and that he wanted me to hook up with him as soon as was convenient. Although I had not met Ed before, I was familiar with his JP Morgan email address, which had appeared on the press cutting distribution list that we routinely sent during the takeover. I put a call into Ed to introduce myself, and we arranged a brief meeting inside the VIP lounge following the Wigan game.

Fortunately, Ed and I hit it off immediately, his friendly and unpretentious manner belying the tough *Equalizer* image I had subconsciously shaped in my mind after his famous television namesake. Over the next five years Ed and I enjoyed as good a working relationship as I have ever forged. Together with my regular dealings with Joel Glazer and Phil Townsend I appreciated, and would never take for granted, just how fortunate I was to be working at the heart of such a fascinating and volatile story with such pleasant and genuine colleagues.

Meeting Malcolm Glazer

Manchester United had enjoyed a decent run of results over the 2005 Christmas period, although Chelsea's equally strong form meant that United would be stuck in the runners-up position right through to the final whistle of the season. With Nemanja Vidic signed over Christmas, and Patrice Evra poised to join the squad, 2006 began with the Glazers pledging their support to Sir Alex Ferguson to strengthen the squad. This made United among the biggest spenders of the January transfer window; a deed acknowledged widely by the press, even endorsed by the *News of the World* which commented[30]: 'Manchester United could not have a better man in charge if they are to stand a hope of catching

---

[30] Glazer key to beating the Blues, *News of the World*, 8 January 2006

Chelsea. And I'm not talking about Sir Alex Ferguson. Malcolm Glazer is the key figure at Manchester United now… The fans might not want to hear it but the Glazer takeover could be the best bit of luck the club has had all year.' However, some journalists privately warned me that the signings of players relatively unknown in the UK suggested a certain penny-pinching by the owners. This cynicism was indeed corroborated by irate United fans at that time who contacted radio phone-ins and posted hostile messages on Internet message boards.

At the end of the first week in January I flew to Tampa in Florida to watch the Glazers' NFL team play their biggest game since the Super Bowl triumph three years previously. A victory in the play-off against the Washington Redskins would mean that the Tampa Bay Buccaneers would be just two games away from another stab at American sport's richest prize.

The atmosphere around the Raymond James Stadium that Saturday evening was charged with hope. As expected, the pre-match entertainment proved to be an event in its own right, and I was not disappointed by the carnival of conviviality from impeccably good natured fans and their families. Many were decked out Tampa Bay red and pewter regalia as they expertly tended their barbecue cook-outs in the vast surrounding car parks, and toasted the game with a steady flow of ice-cold beer kept in giant portable chillers.

This was my first time inside the Buccaneers' stadium since my visit in May 2005. I took advantage of my 'access all areas' pass by standing on the edge of the field as dusk fell, watching the seats fill as the Florida warmth was slowly replaced by the biting cold January air.

The pitch was congested with huge television rigs and vast amounts of training apparatus for the players to warm-up on, attended by hundreds of personnel who all seemed to have a vital role to play, unlike the many VIP hangers-on like me. The colour, noise and energy in the run-up to the game was in complete contrast to the simple sanctity of English football where only 22 players, a small crew of coaching staff, match officials and fork-wielding groundsmen are bestowed the privilege to roam the pitch.

All the Glazer brothers were gathered on the field. Joel, Bryan and Edward, the Buccaneers' co-chairmen, huddled in animated discussions which I managed to eavesdrop. Their conversation centred on concerns that every one of the 65,000-plus seats would be properly equipped with the souvenir Tampa Bay flag they had had specially commissioned for the event; such was their attention to detail. I also spent time with Kevin Glazer, the second eldest sibling (after Avie) whom I had briefly met at Old Trafford. He patiently, but vainly, tried to explain to me the delphic intricacies of American football, the rules of which always produced a mental block.

Not long before the start of the game, Malcolm Glazer emerged onto the pitch, the first time I had seen him in person. Joel called me over and introduced me to his father. Looking dapper in an expensive navy blue blazer and a beige cashmere pullover, Malcolm's wispy ginger hair was finely groomed and, holding my gaze with his piercing blue eyes, he offered the silkiest, softest handshake I had ever experienced. The silky aspect was also, bizarrely, chronicled by the BBC journalist Jonathan Legard[31] who had briefly met Glazer Senior a couple of months later. Malcolm jokingly quipped to me, 'Ah, you're the man I need to be nice to.' Disarmed by his flattering charm, we small-talked a little longer about the spectacle surrounding us. He then moved onto meet and greet some VIPs waiting patiently to glad hand. It was the one and only time I would get to meet Malcolm Glazer.

The pre-match razzmatazz that many a Stretford Ender had feared would be imposed on Old Trafford by the Glazers' ownership, was, of course, a full-blown, star-spangled affair which marked the rare occasion of a Bucs' home play-off. Goose-pimpled cheerleaders and immaculately uniformed military personnel cheered on the teams as they ran onto the field amid a national anthem crescendo of intense and fervent flag-waving. This colourful display of patriotism, I suspected, carried even more intensity post-9/11. I watched the first quarter from the sidelines, struggling to make sense of the game but also mesmerised by my proximity to the jungle of heaving on-field activity. I then decided to retire to the warmth of the press lounge. In line with other NFL stadia, it was housed in the highest echelons of

---

[31] In search of the Glazers, Jonathan Legard, BBC Online, 11 April 2006

the stand, allowing a bird's eye view of the field and enabling me to better analyse the appeal of gridiron, particularly the sheer speed of movement. The sport reminded me more of cricket rather than football or rugby as, to my untrained eye, most of the action seemed to be performed in a staccato, stop-start manner. On-field play was interspersed every few minutes with television advertising breaks, providing ample opportunity for spectators to explore, à la Homer Simpson, the stadium's multitude of fast food concessions.

The Raymond James Stadium's press facilities were superlative, their impressive scale and activity dwarfing what Old Trafford had to offer on a match day. This reflected the very labour-intensive effort required to report on a sport renowned for its obsessive attention to live, quasi-scientific statistical analysis. Behind the main press gantry, a large lounge stretched the length of the stadium and had been transformed into a food hall of epic proportions. Extravagant quantities of junk food (and some healthy stuff too) provided constant nurture to the hundreds of working journalists. I wondered whether Manchester United's press pack would be more mollified if they were catered for so opulently.

Despite an enthralling game in which the fans' fervour – and noise – was at times the match of anything I had experienced at an English football game, the Buccaneers lost 17-10 to the Redskins. It was a bitterly disappointing way to end the season.

The next morning, I hooked up with Bob Leffler, a PR professional who had been a close associate of to the Glazers and, in 2004, had made some tentative remarks to the UK press when the family were initially looking to buy Manchester United. Bob was immaculately dressed in black, ensuring that his giant gold and diamond Super Bowl winners' ring – which had been bestowed to him by the Glazers to mark his service – sparkled with maximum conspicuousness. While he regaled me with his stories of working close up with the family I managed to glean just how privileged an upbringing Joel and his siblings seemed to have enjoyed. Many of Bob's insights of the Glazers mirrored my own experiences and, although I'd served them for just one year, I felt even more resolved to work for this remarkably successful but unusually unassuming family.

However, despite their riches and past successes, the Glazers would have to contend that weekend with the dual disappointments of not only seeing their NFL franchise lose, but also learning that, back in the UK, their recently-acquired Premier League club had been humbled in a goalless draw away to lowly Conference side Burton Albion in the third round of the FA Cup.

Better than a PLC

In mid-January, and ahead of the weekend's Manchester derby, Sir Alex Ferguson remarked on his experience of the Glazers' ownership for the first time during his routine press conference. 'Without question, I have found the owners excellent… They have supported me 100 per cent. They have never caused me one bit of a problem and they have given me the money I wanted. What do I do? Tell lies? They have been great. It is much better than a PLC, I can tell you that. We don't have to go through all the procedures of a PLC board meeting and football club board meetings. We don't have to inform the Stock Exchange. The whole thing is far more straightforward now and it is much quicker. You can get an answer yes or no without going through the whole procedure."

Sir Alex's comments provoked a flurry of press coverage, which equally reported the hostile response from the Manchester United Supporters' Trust (MUST), formerly known as Shareholders United. With a strong whiff of condescension, it denounced Sir Alex's comments as those 'of a shrewd man on a one-year contract. It would be an extremely foolish and short-lived employee who does anything other than praise his employer in public.' Echoing MUST's line, the fanzine, *United We Stand*, more colourfully decried: 'Ferguson's toadying comments… are sickening, inflammatory but, above all, sad.'

Throughout my association with Manchester United Sir Alex would repeat his mantra of approval of the Glazer family many times over, which as night follows day, would be duly reported with much fanfare before being attacked by the likes of MUST and other supporter groups with their, depressingly tedious, dollop of vitriol. Perhaps their response marked United supporters' strong tradition of (healthy) cheeky iconoclasm, never afraid to have a dig at the club's great and good? Just as likely, the battle lines, already drawn for two years prior to the Glazer family's eventual ownership, were now taking firm root with Ferguson, widely revered by United supporters, seen by some as a feeble proxy for the American owners.

Sir Alex's comments were important as they reflected his obvious pleasure in being involved with a club that was no longer accountable to the likes of City of London pension fund investors as well as vigorous Stock Exchange rules governing a pre-takeover PLC. Now, Sir Alex enjoyed considerable autonomy under the Glazers' experienced sports ownership, inasmuch that he and his chief executive David Gill would be able to sign off a new addition to the squad with an instant telephone call to Joel Glazer. The recent signings of Vidic and Evra were also significant as, prior to the Glazers' purchase of United, the previous PLC board had warned that, in light of Wayne Rooney's £25.6 million transfer from Everton, no more money would be available to spend for two seasons. Given the arrival of one Roman Abramovich to Stamford Bridge it seemed absurd that a top football club competing for the highest honours would dare think this, let alone have to outline it in a legally binding public statement.

On the day Sir Alex had given his press conference the *Times'* Ashling O'Connor, one of the most thorough journalists I would come across, called me to say she had got wind of Ed Woodward's appointment and intended to report that this marked the prospect for a refinancing of the debt used to buy Manchester United. While accurate, I sought to steer Ashling's expectations and to quash media speculation by explaining that that such refinancing was possible rather than imminent. Her story, which was filed in the following day's newspaper,[32] prompted a spate of articles pointing to a possible change in the debt arrangement, which, along with the ongoing story of the next shirt sponsor, would continue to excite the sport-business community, and would continue to keep me busy.

---

[32] Glazers bank on help from new City man, Ashling O'Connor, *The Times*, 13 January 2006

A Baptism of Sorts

Manchester United's home fixture against Liverpool was my first opportunity to sample live at Old Trafford one of the bitterest rivalries in world football. This was complicated by my conflicted support for Liverpool whom I had followed with some passion for around two decades before working for the Glazers, but had since consciously sought to put into 'trust' following my involvement in the takeover. With United having succumbed to a 3-1 defeat in the Manchester derby the previous weekend, Sir Alex's team were once again on the back foot and had a point to prove. Upping the ante, it was the first time Liverpool's vocal away supporters had visited Old Trafford since the team's astonishing victory in Istanbul in May 2005, which they commemorated by proudly waving cardboard placards bearing the simplest of messages: '5'. This referred to the number of European Cup trophies Liverpool had won, dwarfing United's tally of two. Liverpool's fans would continue to taunt their Manchester rivals throughout a tense and goalless 90 minutes, with a constant refrain of 'USA, USA' chants and the occasional unfurling of a large banner which mischievously read 'Agent Glazer: Mission Accomplished.' However, it was the 60,000-odd United fans who would have the last laugh, with a decisive last-minute goal headed in by defender Rio Ferdinand prompting delirium among United's supporters. Controversially, club captain Gary Neville proceeded to rush towards Liverpool's supporters, provocatively tugging his shirt's club crest and ensuring mayhem throughout the stadium.

For me, this match marked a baptism of sorts. During the entire game I felt content at the prospect of a goalless draw, thus maintaining my United Nations-like support for both teams. But my eruption of pleasure during injury time, when Manchester United snatched its victory, effectively marked the end of my love affair with Liverpool. I knew this stance would curry me neither credibility nor favour among either group of fans, but it reflected a genuine desire of mine to support the team that I was now putting most of my waking hours into.

The game against Liverpool coincided with the club's decision to put out its financial results for the 11 months to the end of June 2005, effectively the final season prior to the Glazers' ownership. Before the takeover these results would have been vigorously marketed by the club's financial public relations advisors and would have been closely scrutinised by fan and City analyst alike, their impact on the club's share price widely reported. But now as a privately held company, the results were already more than six months old and, to our satisfaction, received a modicum of media interest. The drop in Premier League television revenues had already been trailed; this resulted in a fall in operating profits to £46 million (these profits being the key metric in football, representing the balance of cash coming into the club minus all operating costs) and met a muted response in the following day's newspapers. This was aided, no doubt, by the improved mood music generated by the defeat of Liverpool.

Still, the press continued to be fascinated with the club's ongoing finances, especially centred upon the debt obligations to service. By mid-February the shirt sponsorship process was in full swing as Bryan Glazer (who took a leading interest in the marketing of Manchester United) and commercial director Andy Anson clocked up thousands of air miles flying to meetings with potential suitors. An array of overseas companies such as Middle Eastern airlines Etihad (Arabic for 'United') and Qatar Airways, as well as Mansion – a Gibraltar-based online gambling company – were all reported to be close to clinching a record sponsorship deal.

Deloitte published its annual Football Money League, effectively a snapshot of revenues at the biggest clubs and a great means for the accountancy firm to drum up some publicity. For the first time in nine seasons Manchester United had lost top spot to Real Madrid; while there was recognition that this could be a blip (given that United could look forward to an uplift from the new shirt sponsor deal and greater ticket receipts from an increased Old Trafford capacity) the Deloitte report would rankle with me. A significant portion of United's commercial revenues, some £25 million a year from its apparel deal with Nike, would not count by Deloitte's specious reckoning. That day I sought to put on a brave face, bolstered by how bullish the owners and Ed Woodward were privately regarding future revenue streams. But over successive years I would feel frustrated by the manner in which Deloitte's questionably collated report would fuel the media's negative post-takeover narrative.

First Cup Final

Having been well beaten by Liverpool at Anfield in the fifth round of the FA Cup, Manchester United's only opportunity of securing some silverware that season (and potentially the first under the new ownership) rested with the Carling Cup final against Wigan Athletic at the Millennium Stadium. Admittedly, for those United fans weaned on League and European success under Sir Alex Ferguson it was hardly the stuff of dreams. I made my way to Cardiff on a packed train from London Paddington, seemingly corroborating the jibe that most United fans originate from within the M25's boundary. There was a convivial atmosphere in Cardiff as United and Wigan fans mingled easily, taking advantage of the stadium's prime location at the heart of Wales' first city. This goodwill would permeate the covered stadium which, despite the organisers' best efforts at injecting American-style razzmatazz to the proceedings, lacked the gladiatorial tension had United been playing a more prestigious rival. Joel, Avie and Bryan Glazer were in attendance, and walked around the pitch before kick-off, just as they liked to do ahead of an NFL game. They cannot have failed to notice a large banner ironically reading 'Malcolm Glazer: forever in your debt,' which, for long spells during the match, would glide serenely over the United fans' heads.

While the game began competitively, the underdogs from Wigan found themselves overwhelmed by a rampant five-minute, three-goal spree that contributed to a 4-0 lead for United. With the last 30 minutes of the game effectively a victory parade for United, I found myself having a stressful altercation with a newspaper journalist seated alongside me who I knew to be a United supporter, and who was someone I had had frequent dealings with. Despite his team being on the brink of a cup win, his mood was dark. He claimed that he could not condescend to be happy at a Carling Cup triumph, maintaining that the Glazers' ownership would prevent United from competing for the more illustrious titles. I disagreed, breezily arguing that the club was surely on a more secure footing under the Glazers than when it was a PLC, but my comments, which he perceived as glib, only served to feed his contempt. Several months' later I texted him about an article under his byline that had contained a wholly wrong allegation. His SMS response was direct and menacing: 'Don't ever text me again. Everyone at Old Trafford knows you're a joke.' This animosity, I would later rationalise, reflected the raw anger felt by many fans and reporters towards the Glazers. Raw anger that, in this case, was channelled through me, their loyal messenger.

After the game, and feeling quite shocked after the cross words with the journalist, I made the long descent inside the stadium's bowels and waited for the Glazers to come down to the dressing room to congratulate the players and coaching staff. The bittersweet mood of the day was compounded by my witnessing the undisguised disappointment of the club's then leading scorer, Ruud van Nistelrooy. As he had not got off the substitutes' bench that afternoon, he contemptuously ripped his token winners' medal from around his neck before making an early exit from the dressing room, sweeping angrily past me as he did so. Moments later I joined the Glazer brothers inside the large, starkly-lit dressing room to behold the victorious players in genuinely high spirits, the hard floor already dangerously slippery from the spillage of champagne. I enjoyed watching a particularly exuberant Wayne Rooney savour the triumph as he celebrated his two goals and his first winner's medal as a United player. The moments, digitally captured by the club's father and son duo of photographers, would presumably find their way into each team member's personal photo album, but would probably be superseded by the greater triumphs to come.

While it certainly did not feel like a particularly momentous victory, a win was a win; a first trophy under the Glazer regime. I think the *International Herald Tribune* succinctly summarised the mood[33]:

---

[33] United wins first trophy for Glazers, *International Herald Tribune*, 27 February 2006

'There surely can be no fooling hard-headed businessmen like the Glazers. The League Cup is fourth in priority, behind the Champions League, the English Premier League and the FA Cup.'

Middle-Class Billionaires

One of the more frustrating aspects of my role was that so few of my contacts had met the Glazers in person. Of those business associates and regulators who had dealt with them, most if not all corroborated my description of them: that is, as sensible and measured businessmen and sports fans, rather than cynical, ruthless carpetbaggers. Of course, every journalist would have loved to have met or interviewed them – their allure was enhanced by their aloofness – but, like Chelsea supremo Roman Abramovich, the Glazers had elected to take a vow of silence.

I appreciated that this stance was probably more controversial for the owners of Manchester United than Chelsea, taking into consideration the Red Devils' unique position in British cultural life which, arguably, transcended football. So it was understandable that the Glazers' silence would be viewed with such frustration, even contempt.

One of my favourite phrases to describe the Glazers, used in off-the-record press briefings, was 'middle-class billionaires.' Yes, they were rich, with wealth beyond most people's dreams. Yes, they happened to own not just one, but two top-flight football teams. But the Glazer brothers I came to know were surprisingly modest and unassuming people. Married to equally grounded women, they would have not looked out of place at a chartered accountants' convention.

But, while most journalists appreciated that they were not clichéd, cowboy boot-clad Americans, not being able to meet any of the Glazers in person led to an overriding suspicion of their motives. This would foster an enduring cynicism towards their ownership of Manchester United and led to a perennial fodder of unattributed reports, particularly in the tabloid press, pointing to the Glazers' alleged parsimony and bloody-minded business practices.

Towards the end of March, Jonathan Legard, BBC Radio 5 Live's football correspondent, called me from the States. I enjoyed a good relationship with Jonathan, whose sensible and authoritative commentary on the Glazers' takeover – with his trademark crisp delivery – proved highly influential. He had attended the NFL owners' meeting in Orlando in order to research a feature on the Glazer family and, at some point, was also hoping to doorstep them. 'I get it, I get it!' exclaimed Jonathan down the phone line, excitedly explaining that he had managed to meet Joel Glazer and had grabbed an off-the-record chat with him. This provided the BBC journalist with the missing link by which to appreciate the Glazers' personal sincerity as regards their ownership of United. I was happy to share Jonathan's enthusiasm, but it also made me further appreciate the 'Mission Impossible' task I had in courting the journalists who would never gain any access to this most private of families.

AIG

By April, with the production cycle deadline of United's kit supplier Nike looming, speculation was mounting that Manchester United had found a new sponsor to replace Vodafone. The *News of the World* predicted[34] that United were days away from signing a £60 million deal with Mansion, the online poker exchange. However, two days later, newspapers reported the termination of talks between Mansion and United, bolstered by angry comments from the former's chief negotiator who accused the club of 'double dealing.' Only the *Daily Mail's* Charlie Sale correctly mooted that a deal with US Insurance giants American International Group (AIG) was likely, despite a lower fee. It seemed that the club and the Glazers, for ethical reasons, had opted to avoid the controversy of having a betting company on United's replica shirts, traditionally so coveted by young children.

The press conference to confirm AIG's sponsorship on Wednesday 6 April was presided over by Sir Alex Ferguson, David Gill and the

---

[34] £60m United Poker Deal, *News of the World*, 2 April 2006

insurance giant's supremo Martin Sullivan, an Englishman and a passionate football fan (albeit of Tottenham Hotspur). Bryan Glazer sat in the front row of the audience, away from the media's glare and thus avoiding any contact with the nearby journalists. Team members paraded the shirts with the AIG logo mocked up on their chests, one of the several kits that United had produced sporting different sponsor names so as to scupper any potential leaks.

The deal provided quiet satisfaction to United's owners. Reportedly valued at a British record of £56.5 million over four years, it was worth considerably more when a financial services tie-up was factored in (Manchester United credit card anybody?). It also marked their first obvious hands-on involvement in the club's day-to-day operations, and would escalate their efforts to grow United's commercial muscle worldwide. The Glazers' exacting attention to detail would also come to the fore, with their insistence that the shirt deal meant just that. AIG would have had to pay extra to have their brand logo emblazoned on the East Stand's seating area, unlike Vodafone which had that benefit thrown in when it had negotiated its £36 million, four-year shirt deal.

I was relieved at the outcome; not least because I had spent the previous six months seeking to lower expectations of a lucrative deal so as to maximise the final impact. It also represented the first nugget of good news for the owners after a turbulent few months. Chatting to Joel Glazer, it was clear that AIG felt like the right – and safe – choice for the family; an American blue-chip behemoth with a global footprint that matched United's, particularly so in Asia where both partners were seeking to capitalise on their household profiles. What could go wrong?

'A Great Franchise'

That week ended with the BBC's press machine going into overdrive while publicising Jonathan Legard's radio programme, titled 'In search of the Glazers'. Slated for the following week, its accompanying press release noted: 'The report includes the first British interview with Malcolm Glazer, albeit a short one, in which Glazer refers to Manchester

United as a 'franchise' twice and refuses to answer United fans' concerns about the future. Glazer says: 'We are enjoying it [owning United] greatly, it is a wonderful franchise, we just love it. I just want to say hello to the fans. It is a great franchise, it will do just great.'

Admittedly, the term 'franchise' was unfortunate to prickly English ears and would be pounced upon and derided by the Glazer sceptics, who cited it as an example of the owners' ignorance regarding the traditions and sensitivities of English football. Commonly associated with American sports teams, the word 'franchise' – in BBC English – suggested transience and commercialism. These two elements can indeed characterise American football, wherein it is possible for an owner to close down a team and move it lock, stock and barrel to another part of the country; a sacrilegious anathema to English football fans. That said, the word 'franchise' in the context used by Mr Glazer Sr. seemed innocuous enough to me, no more contentious than a Brit referring to the home of the Boston Red Sox as a stadium rather than a ballpark.

The BBC went on to replay its sound bite with Malcolm Glazer across its news bulletins – perhaps too frequently for my comfort – but, to be fair to Jonathan, it did represent a journalistic coup and was a tribute to his tenacity as an interrogator. The in-depth documentary – which featured an extensive interview with David Gill – was balanced and thoughtful, reflecting the grievances and suspicions of those angry at the debt but also featuring insight from people who had encountered the Glazers and could vouch for the family's commitment to sporting success. Perhaps I could look forward to a thaw in media relations with the Glazer family? Maybe the press were finally recognising the virtue of their hands-off ownership? A few days later Martin Samuel, one of the most eminent of sports columnists, penned an article in the *Times* acknowledging the benefits of Sir Alex being only a short telephone call away from a signing. The headline posed the question:[35] 'Is it time for United fans to concede they owe a small debt of gratitude to the Glazers?'

---

[35] Is it time for United fans to concede they owe a small debt of gratitude to the Glazers? Martin Samuel, *The Times*, 12 April 2006

Ticket Prices

As the days started to grow longer, United's board – just like other clubs in the UK – began to internally debate the merits of a season ticket price rise. Ticket receipts that year had been strong and a waiting list augured well for a full uptake of the 8,000 new seats in the corner quadrants of the enlarged Old Trafford. Factor in the UK economy – which continued to bask in a period of uninterrupted growth, providing for virtuously low unemployment – and add to this the loyalty of Manchester United supporters, and any potential rise would likely have had a negligible effect on demand, thus enabling greater revenues to be recouped.

A decision was made to push for an average 12 per cent rise in ticket prices. Amazingly, the press reaction was moderate, perhaps as club spokesman Phil Townsend and I succeeded in communicating that standard seats remained reasonably priced (especially compared with other clubs) and that it was the executive box holders – the so-called 'prawn sandwich brigade' – who would bear the brunt of the rise. The muted media response might have been due to the fact that United were enjoying a resurgent league campaign, with that weekend's important win against Arsenal marking a nine-game unbeaten run. That said, the Independent Manchester United Supporters' Association (IMUSA) received substantial coverage as they warned that the price rise would produce large swathes of empty seats. This sentiment would chime with the more pessimistic of the press commentators, who were convinced – even hopeful – that the Premier League 'bubble' would burst.

Any increase in ticket prices would represent a sure-fire public relations hurdle, as supporter groups would vigorously argue that, without the debt service to fork out, the club could comfortably pay its players' wages and have plenty to spare for the transfer market without having to inflate admission fees.

Ticket prices did indeed rise under the Glazers. The cheapest general attendance ticket price for the 2005/06 season was £21; by the 2010/11 season it had increased to £27 per game, representing an annual five per cent rise over five years. Equally, the most expensive seat at United had climbed from £37 to £49, which equated to a six per cent rise each year. But what about the five years that had preceded the Glazers' takeover? In 2000 the lowest-priced ticket was £17, which the then PLC board gradually increased to £21, or an annual four per cent rise over five years. Meanwhile the most expensive ticket rose from £26 to £37, a seven per cent rise for every year between 2000 and 2005. So, with inflation factored in, United ticket price rises since the Glazers' takeover were consistent year-on-year when compared with the actions of the PLC board (and indeed most other football clubs in the country), thus invalidating the argument that ticket prices rose to service the debt.

The Debt

Notwithstanding the fact that Old Trafford was full to capacity, suggesting that tickets were appropriately priced, the debt imposed by the Glazers' takeover was deeply controversial. On one hand, the debt proved to be manageable and was comfortably serviced by the club's growing cash flows, which also covered investment in a squad that would go on to dominate its rivals and win silverware. On the other hand, there was resentment that *any* of the club's revenue – generated in considerable part by paying fans' hard-earned money – should be devoted to servicing the interest on a debt that didn't exist before the takeover, when the club had already been incredibly successful under Sir Alex Ferguson as a public listed company. Add the fact that the new American owners did not actively engage with the fan base to allay their financial concerns, and it wasn't difficult to understand how debt would dominate and define all debate regarding the Glazers' ownership.

My attitude to debt was equivocal. Personally, I grew up to be relatively risk averse; weaned on free university education, I had avoided carrying any borrowings into adult life (apart from a mortgage) and was conscientious about paying my monthly credit card bill in full. And just like anyone with a mortgage on a home, I coveted the day when I would no longer have to fork out a portion of my income to meet interest payments. Equally, as long as I could comfortably afford the mortgage service with my earnings, I didn't spend any time fretting about the debt and didn't think that having a mortgage gave me any less right to my home versus those neighbours who owned their houses outright. Ditto the Glazers' Manchester United, where as long as interest payments were manageable they were, in my view, perfectly entitled to use debt to buy the club – something that was publicly listed, and therefore for sale – just like thousands of other companies on the Stock Exchange.

I would also get frustrated with the ambiguous meaning of debt in the English language: it can mean an arranged manageable loan or it can refer to spending beyond one's means. It was frightening how most sports journalists and supporters would so easily confuse the two concepts to make the wild assumption that *all* debt was bad.

Indeed, on a corporate level I would point out to reporters that debt was a legitimate way to finance a business and was appropriate to use against an appreciating asset like a solid business or property, the interest service costs being offset by its rising value. While studying for an MBA, one of the mantras drilled into me by my finance professors was 'debt is cheaper than equity.' To put it simply, taking money from any person or institution always involved some strings being attached. The restrictions from a lending bank tended to be less onerous and intrusive than the demands of a shareholder, who would perhaps interfere in the running of the company and would seek an on-going dividend as reward.

In 2005, the Glazers did rely on a sizeable amount of debt to complete their purchase. In a world subsequently shaped by the global credit crunch, such a takeover would be rendered inconceivable, it being at a multiple of some 20 times the free cash (i.e once all the wages and bills are paid) that the club was able to generate. Yet, unlike other highly leveraged buyouts that went on to encounter significant trouble, the Glazers were prudent and oversaw a more than doubling in operating profits. This was thanks in part to a sharp lift in media and expanded stadium revenues (which they were not directly responsible for but had the sense to factor in) but also to the strong rise in highly profitable commercial revenue, which they were to personally drive.

So, while for many the hundreds of millions of pounds that did leave the club to service the debt (and serve to boost the lending bankers' bonuses) may indeed have been eye watering, the buffer of cash to service the interest payments and the investment in a successful squad was to grow substantially under the Glazers' ownership: some £54 million of discretionary cash generated by 2010 compared with £28 million in 2005.

Therefore I accepted the Glazers' rationale of buying Manchester United using debt, especially as it involved a one-third deposit of their own money – totalling £270 million in cash – in order to proceed. But with the lesson of Leeds United still ringing in supporters' and journalists' ears, it was always going to be an impossible sale to the very many who were vexed by debt. Not least as Roman Abramovich had managed to buy Chelsea, returning them to the top of the Premier League through a self-financed, no-holds barred spending spree on players.

A Cautionary Tale

English football is an inherently risky business: for every Abramovich there are scores of clubs enduring financial woe, with Leeds United's demise being an infamously cautionary tale[36]. From the glory of being Premier League stalwarts and 2001 Champions League semi-finalists, by 2007 the Yorkshire club had suffered the ignominy of relegation to football's third tier. While the team had once boasted a who's who of British talent, the club would soon become synonymous with profligacy and financial mismanagement. Its high wage bill was mortgaged via notoriously complex sale and leasebacks and securitisation schemes on the pretext of future Premier League and Champions League success. When that gamble failed to materialise, one of England's great football clubs spiralled into rapid financial meltdown.

---

[36] Money to burn, Brian Cathcart, *The Observer*, 7 March 2004

Why wouldn't this happen to Manchester United, mused concerned supporters, especially as the Glazers' acquisition debt substantially dwarfed any of the borrowings accumulated by a desperate Leeds United board. In any case, an acceptance of the Glazers' approach to owning Manchester United would be anathema: it was more than a business, extolled angry detractors, much more, and the Glazers were leeches. Quietly suggest to them that United was also a global brand, and their visceral hatred of the commercial exploitation of their beloved football club would provoke even more intense anger.

Of course Manchester United, like any other established football club, was a significant community asset; some might even say a quasi-religion, pulling in thousands of fanatical supporters, or worshippers, to Old Trafford week in, week out, and many millions more via television. But it was always clear to me that any great institution like United could only remain successful if it were run according to business lines, with the discipline meted out by Ferguson towards his players matched by the financial rigour of a profit-centred culture looking to grow its revenues.

While United's phoenix-like re-emergence from the doldrums of the seventies and eighties owed much to Sir Alex Ferguson's leadership, it was underpinned by a club board that recognised the need to modernise along commercial orthodoxies by expanding revenue streams to allow for sustained investment in the squad. Hence the redevelopment of the Old Trafford stadium and the pioneering efforts to market the club worldwide. Contrast this with England's other true global football brand, Liverpool FC, which made a virtue of its old-fashioned club set-up and failed to invest in its off-the-field business activities. Brian Reade in his book *Epic Swindle*[37] analogised: 'Throughout the 1990s, Old Trafford was Harrods, while Anfield was a corner shop. As this century progressed, United's brand, fired by repeated Premier League wins and Champions League successes, grew even stronger. While Liverpool's flat-lined.'

---

[37] *Epic Swindle*, Brian Reade, Quercus 2011

The truth was that Manchester United was unusually insulated from much of the risk that blighted most of its counterparts, thanks to a bullet-proof track record of footballing success: never finishing outside the top three in the Premier League; a consistent capacity audience at the country's largest club stadium; and – due to its illustrious history and pedigree – possessing a brand coveted by hordes of sponsors wanting to tap into United's millions of worldwide supporters.

The subsequent efforts to refinance the acquisition debt served to prove the Glazers right, although they were soon preoccupied with more pressing personal matters.

On Monday 24 April Joel called me to say that his father had been discharged from hospital after suffering a stroke the previous week. I advised that we should put out a statement to control the message and avoid any misleading speculation. We traded emails and Joel signed off a short quote stating 'My father's spirits are high and doctors expect his condition to improve with rehabilitation.' We also agreed that it was important to communicate that his father's illness would have no impact on the running of Manchester United; 'business as usual.' Before I sent round the statement, I teed up the BBC and Press Association so that there would be blanket coverage of the news, with Joel's quote given due prominence. The next day's newspaper coverage was restrained and respected the Glazers' request for privacy, and the key 'business as usual' message that I had sought to emphasise during the previous evening's briefing was widely reported. Ominously, however, the *Times* reported[38]: 'While the Glazer family has enjoyed a thaw in its relations with United's supporters in recent months, a rise in ticket prices earlier this month notwithstanding, there were some predictably cruel and tasteless taunts and gibes surfacing on Internet chat rooms last night.'

Some three weeks later, around the unheralded first anniversary of the takeover, I put out another statement confirming that Malcolm Glazer had suffered a second stroke. Again, there was barely any

---

[38] Glazer in high spirits on the long road to recovery, James Ducker, *The Times*, 25 April 2006

coverage in the papers, the 'business as usual' message being firmly understood. Minding my own business, I would never ask Joel about his father again, deferring to his and his family's intense desire for privacy.

Refinancing the Debt

By the spring of 2006 it had become an open secret among banking circles that the Glazer family would seek to refinance the £540 million or so borrowings they had raised to purchase Manchester United. Approximately half of the debt comprised bank loans syndicated by JP Morgan and the remaining half comprising Payment-in-Kind (PIK) notes, which would charge a rolling credit card interest rate upon redemption. Just one year into the Glazers' ownership the club had secured its first silverware for two years, a creditable second place in the Premier League, and an automatic berth into the Champions League group stage. Admittedly there were few plaudits of the Glazers, but at least off-the-pitch United could also look forward to a strong uplift in TV rights from 2007, thanks to the entrance of Setanta which sought to break BSkyB's monopoly over live broadcasts. Revenues would also enjoy a strong boost from an expanded Old Trafford, with AIG's shirt sponsorship deal the icing on the cake and an indication that United's brand value was potentially far higher than most pundits had thought.

The Glazer family's recently-appointed chief of staff, Ed Woodward, led the process from his small serviced office suite, which he shared with Kay, his PA, a former JPMorgan colleague. Their offices were housed in a stunning white-stuccoed block just off Belgrave Square Gardens in London's upmarket diplomatic quarter, which also hosted a cluster of extremely discreet hedge fund boutiques. The office block was plush, with expensively tiled mosaic floors and exquisitely polished rosewood banisters. Ed's working area, however, had an endearingly slapdash, informal air; his desk was actually located in the office foyer alongside a small, worn Chesterfield sofa and a coffee table piled high with documents, while Kay had one of the two adjoining rooms to herself. The main focal point of Ed's ad hoc office was the whiteboard which he would always use in subsequent meetings to enthusiastically take me through the club's occasionally Byzantine finances. He delivered these briefings with as much aplomb and didactic fervour as a star university finance lecturer, sketching out the many permutations that a refinancing could involve.

The refinancing proved to be a long drawn out affair, with Ed presiding over draft after draft of spreadsheet and PowerPoint presentations involving numerous pitches in banks' meeting rooms, as well as conference calls with advisors, lawyers and potential investors. Of course, Ed's JPMorgan credentials proved invaluable in his dealings with his former employer, which continued to lead the syndication of the debt.

With the credit market in full swing, and with all the swagger of dealing with an obsequious bank manager after a big pay rise, Ed Woodward was able to project a considerably more bullish outlook about the club's finances compared to just 12 months previously. At the heart of the process lay a desire by the Glazers to reduce the annual interest bill which, in terms of cash, amounted to a hitherto affordable £30 million a year but with the PIK's notional interest rate clocking up a staggering £60 million on top. Now that the transactional risk of the takeover was history, replaced with the certainty of increased revenue projections from United, Ed sought to scale back the PIK borrowings and negotiate better terms for the outstanding debt.

For any company experiencing the aftermath of a takeover, the refinancing would have been a routine exercise of good housekeeping. The fact that it involved Manchester United ignited heightened press interest and speculation, fuelled by the inevitable leaks from third parties contacted during the process as well as prospective investors who had received presentation packs.

In the meantime, Manchester United's board was expanded to incorporate the remaining Glazer siblings not officially involved as non-executives: Kevin, Edward and Darcie. The move was interpreted as a sign that Malcolm Glazer, convalescing after his two strokes, was handing over the reins of power to his children. More prosaically, this was something that had been discussed during my meeting with the Glazers in Palm

Beach the previous August; it marked their efforts to keep another arm of their business empire across the family, all of whom, remarkably, had a hand in commercial affairs (no renegade Glazer sibling had dropped out to pursue a bohemian existence). I was somewhat surprised that this news barely raised an eyebrow; perhaps it reflected the growing acceptance of the Americans' ownership among media circles.

The Leak

By early July speculation was mounting that a refinancing deal was imminent. The *Sunday Telegraph* announced[39] that the Royal Bank of Scotland was planning to securitise future match day revenues for a £500 million loan. Just the mention of the word 'securitisation' would prompt feverish online comparisons with the tortured experience of Leeds United; old rumours of post-takeover ramifications were even regurgitated, such as the selling of the naming rights to Old Trafford.

The actual package, signed off in mid-July while the team were limbering up on a pre-season tour of South Africa, was a relatively simple (or 'plain vanilla' to use City jargon) refinancing of the £265 million acquisition debt achieving less expensive interest rates. However the debt level raised against Manchester United's assets increased significantly to £525 million, absorbing the redemption of half of the original £270 million PIK plus the expensive interest charge it had rolled up. The outstanding Glazers' £135 million exposure to the PIK lenders was also renegotiated to more favourable (although still double-digit interest) terms. The refinancing prompted the paradox that, while the total debt had climbed significantly, interest costs were reduced; a sign of the buoyant credit market. Significantly, the Glazers' original cash investment of £272 million remained intact, reinforcing the family's commitment to the club. This was an important key message that I would stress in briefings, along with the deal's neutral impact on Sir Alex's transfer budget.

---

[39] Man Utd seeks £500m loan, *The Sunday Telegraph*, 9 July 2006

While some of the details had already found their way into the *Daily Telegraph*[40] (presumably fed by the many disappointed investors who had failed to get a slice of the oversubscribed debt) I was keen that the news should be reported in as controlled a manner as possible, given the complexity of the deal and the potential controversy it could stir. I suggested that the *Financial Times* was the best business forum to expound United's fiscal position, the newspaper's esteemed journalists being well-versed in the specialist jargon of the debt market. On a glorious early summer's day, I furtively went to the newspaper's headquarters, its brown glass walls shimmering with the reflection of the River Thames. I was armed with a sheaf of papers outlining the refinancing, including the obligatory key messages and Q&A documents that I would routinely draw-up for big announcements, and would often redraft many times before they were carefully studied and signed off by Joel Glazer. The briefing took place in the staff canteen, its smell and surroundings acutely familiar to me from the time when I was a reporter for Financial Times Television during the mid-1990s. I delivered it in hushed tones, my relief at disseminating the news being tempered by the need for discretion to ensure that the leak was unattributable.

A leak via an exclusive briefing is the PR operator's time-honoured way to control news flow by taking advantage of a media outlet's intense desire to break a story ahead of its rivals. Choosing a single outlet can usually maximise a story's impact – an exclusive is usually proudly splashed by the editor – and granting exclusivity can also curry more favourable coverage in the chosen platform. A win-win situation. On the downside, a leak to one outlet can also alienate rival reporters and newspapers, understandably peeved at missing out on a significant story.

The following day the *Financial Times* carried the story prominently in its Companies and Market section, even featuring an action shot of midfielder Paul Scholes as a teaser on its front page[41]. More pleasingly,

---

[40] Manchester Utd refinancing £500m debt to pay off PIKs, *The Daily Telegraph*, 14 July 2006

[41] Man Utd reduces interest bill, *Financial Times*, 18 July 2006

the FT would stretch the story to the following day with the headline 'Man Utd refinancing hits sophisticated level,'[42] commenting that the new package 'demonstrates a new level of sophistication by football clubs in methods used to generate cash. The Glazer family has made full use of Man United's power to generate revenues via gate receipts, TV broadcasting rights, sponsorship and merchandising in striking its new debt package.'

The press backlash was more subdued than I had anticipated, reflecting the quiet summer lull and the fact that, in 2006, sports correspondents were still wary of writing about finance, deferring to their business desks. Only the ever-astute David Bond of the *Daily Telegraph* called me to protest at the *Financial Times'* privileged access, his report the next day ominously noting[43]: 'the package... has increased the money borrowed against the club's assets and will mean no extra money for players... That could raise concerns among fans who remain suspicious of the Glazers' long-term intentions for United.'

Another Quiet American

As the *Financial Times* had wisely observed in the aftermath of the refinancing, there was a growing recognition of the riches that the Premier League could offer, especially to overseas investors. The Glazers' takeover of Manchester United a couple of years after Roman Abramovich's purchase of Chelsea marked a new era when only the seriously wealthy tycoon – usually non-British – could afford to buy into the quickly inflating assets of English football. The notion of a prosperous local English businessman and fan owning a team for the vanity of entertaining friends and associates in the directors' box already seemed an anachronism, certainly confined to the lower football divisions. The latest suitor was Randy Lerner, like the Glazers an owner of an NFL franchise, who by mid-August was locked in negotiations

---

[42] Man Utd refinancing hits sophisticated level, *Financial Times*, 19 July 2006
[43] United defend £660m refinancing deal, *The Daily Telegraph*, 19 Jul 2006

with the same team from Rothschild that had advised the Glazers and on this occasion were representing Aston Villa chairman Doug Ellis.

However, unlike the Glazer family, from the outset Randy Lerner attracted admiration from the British press. Unquestionably well-heeled and planning to buy Villa outright with cash rather than debt (although the forensic *Guardian* investigative reporter David Conn would claim in 2010 that Lerner's money had been lent to Villa, routed via a shell company Reform Acquisitions, charged at an interest two per cent above inter-bank lending rates[44]), his formative year at Cambridge University in his early twenties gilded his anglophile, football-loving credentials. His PR was pretty good too: humble and generously philanthropic, Lerner also provided access to journalists, albeit limited. Moreover, after the death throes of Doug Ellis's ownership, Villa fans hailed the American's riches just as the majority of Chelsea fans had lauded Ken Bates' exit and Abramovich's arrival. This reinforced one of the core resentments that many United supports would feel towards the Glazers: unlike Villa and Chelsea, their club was already accustomed to winning ways, so why should they welcome aloof Americans, especially those who had dared to dump loads of debt onto their beloved club?

As well as speculation that the Premier League's two American owners might seek to impose an NFL style salary cap, Lerner's takeover would prompt unavoidable scrutiny between his and the Glazer family's regimes. However, I would insist to journalists that it was like comparing apples with pears. Villa had been bought for a fraction (one twelfth to be precise) of what Manchester United had cost – or for approximately £210 million less than the cash the Glazers had put into their purchase of United – reflecting the considerable difference in scale between the two clubs and the dissimilar expectations of their respective fan bases.

Before the year was out, Icelandic businessman Eggert Magnússon had fronted a consortium to buy West Ham United, backed by

---

[44] Aston Villa live the American dream with Randy Lerner, *The Guardian*, 27 January 2010

financier Björgólfur Guðmundsson. His spokesman was quoted as saying[45]: 'Long term this is also a business opportunity. English football has become a very high-worth entertainment, like Hollywood films. There is a great deal of television money and you can see commercial opportunity flowing from that.' This sentiment had struck me, like most observers, as a touch too brazen from the owner of a Premier League team languishing at the foot of the table, but it was something that echoed my own private thoughts on the motivation for overseas investors into England's national game. This was something I would discuss off-the-record with the press but would avoid airing publicly, mindful of the taboo surrounding the discussion of football as a 'business'.

This taboo always struck me as perverse but intelligible; a paradox of British life, where there was a grudging appreciation that football involved huge amounts of cash, but to address this in an a matter-of-fact way – as the Americans did – could somehow tarnish the game's quasi-religious spell. Indeed the code governing how off-the-field football is reported is highly nuanced and is rooted in a sentimental Corinthian idyll where sport and business are uncomfortable bedfellows. Borrowing money, of course, was frowned upon but being seen to 'splash the cash' with abandon was a virtue. This conflict felt particularly pronounced in Manchester. Traditionally a politically left-wing bastion, some local observers had told me that the city prided itself on a radical edge rooted in its industrial trade union past, a counterweight to the financially-engineered capitalist boom of London.

So, for football press and fans alike the main virtues of those involved in *administrating* football were, firstly, an unequivocal love for the club and, secondly, a love for the game. In that order. These could hide a multitude of board directors' sins, from profligate spending to benign neglect. By contrast, my one year's experience had shown me that football was best administered by people who loved and understood the game, but who were not necessarily so emotionally

---

[45] The real power behind West Ham, *The Guardian*, 29 November 2006

attached to the club. Indeed, did anyone dare to cast aspersions on Sir Alex Ferguson for never being a lifelong Manchester United fan? At Old Trafford, perhaps as many as one-third of employees were not professed Red Devil supporters. That said, almost all the staff I encountered would root for the team regardless, such was the impact of the team's performance on sentiment and morale. In fact, in the rare event that Manchester United did suffer defeat, I found it easier to face the next working day having made a concerted effort to avoid that crushing feeling of disappointment.

Part Three
2006 / 07 Season

The arrival of the new football season in August 2006, the second in my role as the Glazers' spokesman, felt just like the start of a fresh school year; the optimism and excitement of the new adventures ahead wiping the slate clean of the previous season's turmoil and disappointments. Depressingly though, the new season would also mark the football media's continuing expression of cynicism towards Manchester United's now established owners. In spite of the £18 million outlay for Michael Carrick from Tottenham Hotspur, much continued to be written about the Glazers' perceived paucity of summer signings, especially when Ruud van Nistelrooy's £11 million departure was factored in. There were also stories of a poor take-up of season ticket sales at the redeveloped stadium. In truth, sales patterns mirrored previous seasons' and a 'sold out' sign could eventually be raised once the new campaign was under way; the record number of 64,000 season tickets contributed towards a league-beating £3 million in income recouped for each home match.

But, on the pitch, the last few months of 2006 would unfold serenely and would be remembered for the right reason: the *football*. A residency at the top of the Premier League (bar a few weeks in September) would eventually lead to the regaining of the coveted title and would mark a new spell of Sir Alex Ferguson's hegemony, replacing the interloping figures of Arsenal's Arsène Wenger and Chelsea's José Mourinho. The team also managed to top their Champions League qualifying group, which included two wins against Benfica, their unlikely nemesis in that dark evening of autumn 2005.

Ringing in Changes

With the team winning on the pitch, the mood music off it felt significantly more benign than 12 months' previously, giving weight to the truth that, in sport, it's the results that count (a mantra frequently espoused to me by Joel Glazer). In fact, during the first few months of the season my telephone barely rang, allowing me to focus on my work for other corporate clients, save for one diverting exception. In mid-October, Nick Humby and Andy Anson resigned from the board and left their respective roles as finance director and commercial director. Internally, both departures had been on the cards for some time; Humby had successfully project-managed the building of the recent extension of Old Trafford but his finance role had effectively become obsolete at the moment the club had ceased its Stock Exchange listing and had become private. Meanwhile, Andy Anson, having helped steer United to the record AIG kit deal, had been poached to become chief executive of the professional men's tennis organisation ATP Europe. The news reminded me of the Oscar Wilde quote: 'To lose one parent, Mr Worthing, may be regarded as a misfortune; to lose both looks like carelessness.' Indeed, there were some inevitable stirrings among the press, who questioned whether Humby and Anson had jumped or had been pushed. There was even speculation over chief executive David Gill's future, with the *Independent* describing him as 'the last pre-Glazer man left standing.'[46]

The Glazers were indeed incrementally ringing in the changes to United's operations, but in close consultation with Gill who, since the start of 2006, had maintained a regular transatlantic telephone dialogue (as well as face-to face-meetings) with Joel Glazer and Ed Woodward. Gradually, the commercial aspects of the club would become devolved to Ed and the Glazers while the Manchester-based football and operational matters would remain under Gill's supervision. This de facto split in responsibilities was to become the Glazers' USP, which would provide a level of stability unmatched by

---

[46] Gill is the last pre-Glazer man standing, *The Independent*, 18 October 2006

other Premier League clubs. This was underpinned by a powerful triumvirate of trust: Joel Glazer would liaise with David Gill, who in turn would work closely with the untouchable Sir Alex Ferguson, who felt assured that his football management would not be interfered with by the owners.

Financial Times

The *Financial Times* had appointed a new leisure correspondent, Roger Blitz, whose first assignment on United was to report on Humby and Anson's departure (he described David Gill as 'left looking isolated as chief executive.'[47]) A good working relationship with the FT was vital in my view given its fully-deserved reputation for journalistic excellence and its global reach among the business community. Having worked for its television arm for several years I also held a sentimental attachment to the title, so I was particularly keen that Roger Blitz was given as good an insight into the business end of the club as possible. Towards the end of November I invited Blitz up to Manchester to provide him with an immersion course in all things United. We kicked off by hooking up with Phil Townsend, who gave us a behind-the-scenes tour of United's training ground. Known by all as 'Carrington' after the Manchester suburb in which it was located, the complex was immediately adjacent to Manchester City's counterpart. Since Carrington housed the manager, the players, the coaching staff and medical team, security was understandably tight; a handful of fans would maintain a constant vigil outside the security gate in the hope of catching a glimpse of their United idols as they swept down the narrow lane in their luxury cars.

Carrington looked and felt like an out-of-town business park, replete with spacious and modern glass-fronted buildings that housed sophisticated training and treatment facilities (including swimming pools and a giant patchwork of outdoor and indoor pitches) as well as

---

[47] Man United to lose two of its top directors, *Financial Times*, 18 October 2006

the usual array of offices, meeting rooms and catering units. As our visit took place on a match day, the complex was eerily deserted as the players and coaching staff were resting up in a Manchester hotel.

Later at Old Trafford Phil and I introduced Roger Blitz and his Manchester-based colleague James Wilson to David Gill. We met in his chief executive office, which shared the same dated-looking green leather furniture and old-fashioned carpets as the nearby boardroom. That said, the room was distinguished by its highly covetable collection of miniature replica trophies and souvenir photographs which, in the early evening wintry darkness, helped to provide a cosy welcoming feel to proceedings. The meeting was predicated on the FT journalists agreeing to not report or cite anything from it; a so-called off-the-record relationship-building affair designed to forge trust rather than generating any news. The meeting – which lasted well beyond the allotted time slot – went well, with David Gill elaborating animatedly on his role at United and the multifaceted business issues he was confronted with.

I then hosted Roger and James over a pre-match meal of steak and profiteroles in one of the stadium's more traditional South Stand suites, which were hermetically sealed behind toughened glass. In the early eighties, this barrier might have provided corporate guests with a rarefied refuge from the scourge of hooliganism; now, however, it seemed to smother the infectious (and largely benign) Old Trafford atmosphere. United's clash against Everton resulted in an easy 3-0 victory, the score line actually flattering the Merseysiders. At the start of the game, the three of us traded a particularly surreal conversation. The United players routinely ran out onto the pitch to the opening bars of the Stone Roses' anthem *This Is The One* (the band's frontman, Ian Brown, was a passionate United fan). As its trademark guitar riff blared from the sound system I pointed out to the journalists that '*This Is The One* is the song the team always come out to.' 'What's the song?' James enquired. '*This Is The One*,' I replied. 'Yes, but what's the song called?' he fired back. '*This Is The One*,' I exclaimed. And so the exchange continued until we realised the cyclical charade of our inane dialogue and were reduced to giggles.

As 2006 drew to a close, the team continued with its string of impressive results (notwithstanding a surprise defeat to West Ham at Upton Park). The press duly shifted its focus towards the prospect of another foreign takeover of a Premier League club, namely Liverpool FC, perhaps Manchester United's fiercest rivals. There had been a longstanding expectation that Dubai Investment Capital (DIC) were a likely buyer and had even agreed with Liverpool's board to study the club's books. However, it was an American, George Gillett (who owned Canada's biggest ice-hockey team, the Montreal Canadiens) who also emerged as a serious suitor for the club.

I suspect both the DIC and Gillett would have studied the *Times'* Christmas Eve edition with interest. Two-and-a-half pages of coverage[48] outlined the presentation that Ed Woodward had paraded in front of prospective investors during the previous summer's refinancing. The *Times* had developed a knack of getting hold of these documents from its City source; we had always assumed that they would see the light of the day at some stage, following on from the pre-takeover business plan presentation that gave the paper its June 2005 splash. My response to its highly regarded football correspondent, Oliver Kay, who called me for a comment, was similarly phlegmatic.

Just as with the business plan publication in 2005, I felt relief that the document's contents had been revealed, not least because it contained nothing that I wasn't already privately communicating to journalists interested in learning more about the Glazers' ownership. The *Times* article concentrated on the £25 million net transfer budget, with the additional admission that an extra £25 million could be made available for a marquee player. There were also statements supporting the owners' conviction there was scope to boost United's commercial potential. The paper also reported that ticket prices were 'undervalued' and were projected to rise further. Oliver Kay commented: 'In many areas [the Glazers] speculate boldly. Predictions of playing performance are relatively cautious – a third-placed finish in the Barclays Premiership and progress to the last 16 of the Champions

---

[48] Glazers setting aside £25m to pay for next Old Trafford 'superstar', *The Times*, 22 December 2006

League each year – but their projected commercial and broadcasting revenues rely heavily on the latest football boom being sustained.'

That football boom was top of everyone's mind at the start of 2007, with David Bond of the *Daily Telegraph* heralding the Premier League's negotiation of more than £2 billion in media rights deals. This included £625 million for overseas television and media rights covering 208 territories (double the previous amount) as well as £400 million for Internet and mobile phone rights on top of the astonishing £1.7 billion domestic TV rights deal. Bond predicted:[49] 'The winner of next season's Premiership will collect at least £50 million as a huge cash windfall from a new global television deal spills over into the pockets of England's top 20 football clubs.'

The explosion in the value of media rights reflected the efficacy of Rupert Murdoch's Sky TV strategy to charge viewers for the privilege of watching live sports. Although the audiences would never match those pulled in by the traditional free-to-air channels like BBC and ITV, Sky customers were predominantly male and were in their consumerist prime, and were therefore highly coveted by firms selling cars, beer, online gambling and even disposable razors. Advertisers recognised the growing value of live football whereby an audience was 'captive,' rather than alternative programming in which digital and online technology would enable viewers to watch on demand and to skip through the advertising.

Against this backdrop of expanding media revenues, the team started the New Year firmly perched at the top of the Premier League with a six-point lead over Chelsea. At that time, the only controversy surrounding United was a sensationalist tabloid report regarding an alleged spy plane seen flying over the Carrington training ground. So it felt like a good time to publish Manchester United's accounts, which would reflect the first 12-month period with the Glazers in charge. While the accounts were fairly straightforward, showing the beginnings of a rise in sponsorship income helping to produce a trebling in pre-tax profit, I advised that we should use the results to

---

[49] Premiership shares £900m TV windfall, *The Daily Telegraph*, 18 January 2007

build some momentum behind the club's strong commercial story. Ideally, I wanted to secure an authoritative piece in one of the UK broadsheets off the back of a rare interview opportunity with David Gill. As with the 2006 refinancing story, it felt better to feed a single paper with an exclusive in order to maximise impact; it was also a more efficient use of David Gill's precious time.

Initially I considered going to one of the four established broadsheets – the *Times*, the *Daily Telegraph*, the *Guardian* or the *Independent*. However, by favouring one of these papers I would automatically be creating enemies from the marginalised three, such is the rivalry between the four titles (seemingly as intense as the catfights that went on between their tabloid brethren). In the end, however, I opted for the *Financial Times*. The newspaper attracted a global business audience that didn't tend to muscle in on the other broadsheets' readerships, and I also hoped to capitalise upon the knowledge of Roger Blitz, whose fresh understanding of the club had been gleaned from his recent trip to Old Trafford and his meeting with David Gill. Aiding my decision was the fact that David was often reluctant to speak with the other national titles, given their fixations on delicate player contracts rather than corporate issues. So Roger was given a lengthy telephone interview with the club's chief executive, which was as far-reaching as their previous face-to-face conversation.

The resulting coverage,[50] trailed by a front page 'Winning Formula' strapline accompanied by a photo of Wayne Rooney celebrating a goal, reported the improved accounts as well as the club's growing roster of international sponsors: Air Asia, Tourism Malaysia, Kumho Tires, Budweiser and Audi. David Gill used the interview to place on record his optimism about the club's finances and his satisfaction with the club's owners: 'They don't interfere, they are interested, and particularly in areas they can add value. The relationship now is as it's going to be. They know us and we know them. It's working extremely well. They have been true to their word.'

While I was pleased with the *Financial Times* piece (and even other

---

[50] Club getting its kicks after going private, *Financial Times*, 26 January 2007

news outlets' subsequent coverage of the financial results) I felt we were probably living on borrowed time ahead of the mandatory publication of the accounts of Manchester United's holding companies, Red Football Ltd and Red Football Joint Ventures Ltd, which would be announced sometime in the spring. These documents would outline where the debt and PIK were held respectively and would, I suspected, be more forensically and suspiciously examined. But back in early 2007, the controversy surrounding the acquisition debt had seemed to settle down, thanks in no small part to the team's strong on-field performances, often the acid test as to whether a club is sinking or swimming. However, that calm was to be rocked as Liverpool's new ownership became evident.

'Glazers Lose the PR Battle'

In early February it was confirmed that the Premier League was to welcome a new set of American owners in the form of George Gillett Jr. Mooted for several months as a possible buyer, he had been brought to the table by the same Rothschild team that had advised the Glazers, as well as Aston Villa's selling owner. Gillett had teamed up with private equity entrepreneur Tom Hicks to purchase Liverpool FC for what seemed a bargain price of £220 million (plus a commitment of a further £215 million for a new stadium). That was after Dubai Investment Capital (DIC) had angrily pulled out of its proposed takeover, accusing the Liverpool board of behaving in an underhand manner. DIC's bid had been gravely compromised at the back end of 2006 following the leaking of a document to the *Daily Telegraph's* Mihir Bose[51]. It outlined DIC's plans to borrow £300 million to finance the takeover, and claimed that the Dubai private equity fund planned to flip the club after seven years. 'We don't want another Glazer,' exclaimed Liverpool fans across online forums.

---

[51] Buyers plan to sell Liverpool in seven years, *The Daily Telegraph*, 27 December 2006

So after countless years of uncertainty, Liverpool's exasperated fans could breath a huge sigh of relief, optimistic that the Americans would revive the club's fortunes. I telephoned my Liverpool fanatic friend – the same person in whom I'd confided just after the United takeover to reveal my work for the Glazers. In stark contrast to May 2005 – when his despondency at his club's ownership was palpable – he now sounded jubilant, optimistic that the promise of a sparkling new stadium on Stanley Park and new signings would usher in another golden era for Liverpool. Mindful that he now adjudged me to be a partisan working for the sworn enemy, I suspect my response that Liverpool missed an opportunity of a lifetime to be backed by an Arab sovereign wealth fund too proud to fail, and instead opted for a 'partnership' between two American businessmen with mixed reputations, just seemed to wash over him. Certainly that was the sentiment among colleagues at United, who could look forward to not having to compete with a rich Arab emirate.

Also, having endured Liverpool's unhappy flirtation with two co-managers (Roy Evans and Gérard Houllier) I wondered aloud why things should be any different as far as its new owners were concerned. From my experience of advising successful corporate clients – and in every MBA case study I'd pored over – most business decisions needed to be made swiftly and decisively and were best handled by a single responsible entity.

But, back in early 2007, one thing was for sure: Gillett Jr and Hicks had a considerable flair for public relations that would weigh heavily upon the reputation of my charges. The new owners' press conference was a master class in seductive charm and not a little cheek. 'This is truly the largest sport in the world, the most important sport in the world, and this is the most important club in the most important sport in the world,' declared George Gillett to a starry-eyed press pack, well and truly succeeding in putting the hype into hyperbole. Indeed, the media had appeared to leave its usually world-weary bullshit sensors at the door, replacing them with a grovelling gratitude towards a football owner who – unlike the Glazers and Abramovich – had the decency to address them en masse. Gillett was widely reported to announce: 'We have purchased the club with no debt on the club.'

Ouch. But hold on, I wondered, the Offer Document on the computer screen in front of me detailed considerable borrowings from the Royal Bank of Scotland – some £298 million – and in the form of just a one-year loan; this was effectively an overdraft, which would need to be refinanced sooner rather than later. That was inferior to the long-term lending that JPMorgan had made available to the Glazers.

I soon received a call from a confused and baffled United chief of staff, Ed Woodward. 'Are we following the same Hicks and Gillett press conference as everyone else?' Ed enquired. 'Didn't Gillett just thank RBS? Didn't Gillett say there's no debt?' he asked rhetorically. Our frustration shared, I suggested I could go on the offensive and bring this matter to a head, but then surmised that 'Glazer spokesman says Liverpool owners have debt too,' might not serve our own interests very well. Ed agreed. In fact we were both able to see the funny side of the new owners' ill-conceived chutzpah, and hoped that time would tell.

To the outside world, however, Gillett appeared to have taken his communications style straight out of the rulebook that dictated 'if you say something enough times, it becomes true'. So, with their Internet-researched platitudes regarding Liverpool's glorious traditions, and with their bullet proof promises about the future, the UK press took their oleaginous words as read: Hicks and Gillett good; Glazers bad.

The media's unequivocal support for Liverpool's new owners was not a surprise. After years of restricted access to Abramovich and the Glazers, sportswriters were suddenly welcomed into the open arms of Hicks and Gillett; some favoured correspondents were even given access to their personal mobile phone numbers.

That weekend's Liverpool-centric coverage gave the PR momentum to Hicks and Gillett, arguably to the detriment of the Glazers. Even Jonathan Northcroft, one of the most sensible journalists on the football beat, gushed in his authoritative *Sunday Times* piece:[52] 'They may be in English football for the same hard dollars as the Glazers but 'The Yanks of the Mersey' seem softer beasts. "The Glazers showed us

---

[52] Fistful of dollars to take on world. Liverpool's new owners are acting local but thinking global with their purchase, *The Sunday Times*, 11 February 2007

what not to do," said Hicks. Having thrashed their compatriots in the field of public relations he and Gillett, who paid £470m for Liverpool, see the Glazers as who to beat on a football pitch. Both tycoons projected sincerity when suggesting the target was to make Liverpool once more England's preeminent team.'

All this appeared to be water off a duck's back for Joel Glazer, who had better insight than most into Hicks' and Gillett's Stateside business track records, and seemed to me entirely nonplussed at the prospect of competition from his compatriots. However, I found it hard to not take their stinging criticism of the Glazers personally, especially as Hicks and Gillett were effectively attacking the owners' public relations, for which I was so closely responsible. Still, the Liverpool owners' successful PR offensive also made me wonder whether we had got ours so wrong.

In a *Daily Telegraph* comment piece titled 'Glazers lose the PR battle,'[53] David Bond argued that 'Hicks and Gillett have handled their takeover of a famous football institution far more astutely than the Glazers. Hicks and Gillett have turned up at Anfield, shown their faces, enthused about the Kop and the club's history… and come across as businessmen who care. Hicks and Gillett are at Liverpool for the money, but they are also there for the trips and trophies. They seem keen on a shared adventure with Kopites. The contrast with the Glazers could not be more marked… the Glazers seem disinterested. It's a business deal for them. Show me the money, not the step-overs. At least Hicks and Gillett are enjoying their commercial venture.'

Bond's view was echoed by the ever insightful Martin Samuel who, having witnessed Hicks and Gillett rapturously cheering on their team's victory against Barcelona FC, wrote in the *News of the World*:[54] 'In certain ways, by keeping a low profile and stumping up the money for transfers, the Glazers are the perfect football club owners. But there is a difference between shunning publicity and refusing to engage with the supporters. It would have been so easy to win friends in this of all

---

[53] Glazers lose the PR battle, *The Daily Telegraph*, 10 March 2010
[54] Glazers Miss Out, *News of the World*, 11 March 2007

seasons... the Glazers may yet look like interlopers at their own victory.'

Armchair Supporters?

Admittedly, the Glazers *did* seem disinterested in Manchester United: the lack of media interviews was at best interpreted as indifference, or at worse as not even caring for the club (apart from making lots of money). But that could not have been further from the truth. Within the family, the club's co-chairmen Joel and Avie were particularly passionate supporters who genuinely loved football and cared for all things United – especially its traditions – and who fully appreciated the nuances and subtleties of the game.

But the Glazers' reticence would also infuriate those supporters who wanted their club's owners to be more demonstrative and passionate. Even the taciturn Roman Abramovich would often be seen excitedly watching Chelsea at Stamford Bridge or visiting his players at their Cobham training facility. To most Chelsea fans, the Russian's singlehanded bankrolling of consecutive title wins entitled the removal of any suspicion that he didn't care about his club.

Admittedly, the Glazers' reluctance to give wide-ranging press conferences and interviews was a PR fail as far as reporters were concerned, whose livelihood depended on access to the subjects they sought information about. Other than the Queen, it was difficult to think of many heads of major British institutions – of which Manchester United was one – who did not court approval from the media. Even the Queen regularly gave speeches, performed walkabouts, attended functions and met her subjects in full view of the media glare. Ironically, only the owners of the Telegraph newspaper group, the Barclay Brothers, seemed to ape the Glazers' reluctance to engage in British public life. The very fact that they lived in a castle on a remote Channel Island sometimes made it easier for me to justify the Glazers' aloofness, particularly to occasionally despairing *Daily Telegraph* journalists.

To me, that justification was simple and sincere. The Glazers were a private family who bought Manchester United to make it more successful on an off-the-pitch, *not* to embellish their profile. This reticence and natural modesty was something I admired, particularly since that, in the past, I had become somewhat jaded when dealing with huge egos who had courted the media. Plus, with a conviction that would harden during my six years with the club, it is difficult to imagine what upside there actually was in owning Manchester United and looking to engage with the press.

It was understandable why the Glazers wanted to avoid spending a significant amount of time dealing with demanding journalists; this was especially impractical when they were based five time zones' away. It had also seemed clear to me, after just a few months of working for the club, that the British football press were ill-disposed towards measured and thoughtful reportage of Manchester United's main power brokers, despite their coverage of the club often dwarfing its rivals. This reflected the perceived wisdom that the British press had a dubious quest to harshly chip away at successful institutions and people; what Australians refer to as 'tall poppy syndrome'. Why *wouldn't* the press want to cynically tear further strips off the Glazers, challenge their knowledge of football, bang on about the debt ad nauseam and look for friction and discord between the owners, manager and chief executive, even when there was none?

On April 10th Manchester United were to host AS Roma in the second leg of the Champions League quarter-finals. They had lost 2-1 in Rome but had gained an all-important away goal, which had the potential to be decisive should the goal aggregate be all-square. That day, the *Times* published a wry piece by Oliver Kay[55] who questioned the Glazers' passion for the club, centred around Joel Glazer's assertion in his sole post-takeover interview for MUTV that he intended to visit Old Trafford 'very often.' With the press box adjacent to the directors' area at Old Trafford, it was common for reporters to take note of which club VIPs had taken their seats. The row containing seats designated

---

[55] Old Trafford family outings off agenda for absent Glazers, *The Times*, 10 April 2007

to the Glazer family were often conspicuously empty. Hitherto it might not have been a big deal, but with Hicks, Gillett and Aston Villa's Randy Lerner frequently seen spectating from their directors' boxes – often with their family in tow – I felt some pressure about the Glazers' no-shows. Oliver called me to say that he had hardly noticed any Glazers that season, speculating as to whether the family members' interest in United had indeed waned.

Throughout my time working for the Glazers I would decline to confirm whether they would or wouldn't be at a game, keen to diffuse the significance either way. But with the NFL season in the States coinciding with the first half of the Premier League season in the UK, I would guide journalists away from expecting the Americans to be in attendance. Also, I thought, the Glazers had a lot of young children between them and it was understandable they would rather watch a Premier League game live on television rather than making a 24-hour round trip. Oliver Kay concluded: 'In short, the Glazers have become happy to be armchair supporters and, given that they continue to be viewed with either suspicion or hostility by the overwhelming majority of United fans, in one sense that is understandable. On one of their only visits this season, for the opening Barclays Premiership match away to Fulham, they leant out of the directors' box to sign autographs for some before kick-off, but later, at their city centre hotel, were forced from their bedrooms when an attempted break-in by a 30-strong mob led to an evacuation. Much of the overt hostility has dissipated — perhaps in many cases because the doomsday scenarios laid out when the takeover was completed in the summer of 2005 have not unfolded – but ill-feeling remains.'

Although Avie Glazer was at Old Trafford, I grabbed the opportunity to watch the hotly-anticipated Roma game from a seat in the South Stand rather than in the press box. While not a die-hard United fan, I would always feel very nervous before a game, especially prior to high-stake matches such as this. In the blink of an eye, my sentiments would veer from fantasies of triumphal optimism to nightmares of crushed pessimism. There was a real tension in the city that afternoon. Just one week earlier the eternal city's Stadio Olimpico had witnessed crowd trouble, so the thousands of Roma fans who'd made the trip to Manchester, and who were gathering in Piccadilly Gardens, were chaperoned by a heavy police presence. That tension was significantly heightened outside Old Trafford during the lead up to the game, as Greater Manchester Police sought to segregate the masses of United fans from the baying maroon-and-gold-shirted Roma supporters.

I suspect Joel Glazer in particular would have rued not attending the game, which saw a total 7-1 demolition of AS Roma, with each and every United player – apart from the largely redundant Edwin van der Sar in goal – putting in a bravura performance. Even lone striker Alan Smith shone brightly. At first Old Trafford had almost cowered in deference to the deafening taunts from thousands of 'Ultra' Roma fans housed high up in the East Stand. However, this soon gave way to celebratory ecstasy as the Reds served up their football feast. By nature a restrained spectator, even I managed to let rip and ended up deliriously hugging neighbouring supporters as each goal was hammered in.

Red Debt

Of course, the overriding concern among those supporters disgruntled at the Glazers was less the owners' low profile, but rather the level of debt now carried by *their* club. In April the deadline was looming for Manchester United's holding companies, Red Football Ltd and Red Football Joint Venture Ltd (where the debt and PIK were held respectively) to file their accounts with Companies House. As the accounts related to the twelve months to the end of the club's financial year – 30th June 2006 – the numbers were already significantly out of date as they referred to the period before the refinancing had taken place in the summer of that year. Moreover, most of the debt figures had already been widely flagged up in the press by events such as the takeover and the refinancing and release of the United accounts. That said, the Reds' accounts revealed a sharp headline £137 million accounting loss, reflecting £85 million in total debt interest, of which £27 million had come out of United's cash flow. The loss could also be attributed to the heavy deductions of non-cash items like the depreciation of assets (mostly the value of players) and, significantly, the amortisation of goodwill, some £39 million. In layman's terms, the Glazers paid approximately £800 million for United, some £500 million more than the *book* value of the club. This notional figure – 'goodwill' -would have to be discounted as though it were an asset over 15 years, and would constitute a significant negative on the accounts' balance sheet for many years to come despite having absolutely no bearing on the real health of the club's finances.

We decided to release the accounts while the newspaper ink was still wet from the crushing of AS Roma and just ahead of an FA Cup semi-final, where United were expected to triumph against Watford, who were rooted at the foot of the Premier League. This optimum timing would also be augmented by the news that the club's star winger Cristiano Ronaldo – who had enjoyed scintillating form that season – had signed a new five-year contract worth a reputed £30 million. This would end the nonsensical speculation that the Glazers had been dragging their feet over the sizeable deal.

Although the team's fine efforts on the pitch had served to deflect much of the noise off it, debt was still a potential flashpoint and I was keen to quash as much interest in the Red accounts as possible. Like the 2006 refinancing and United's accounts, where I had sought a positive high profile in the papers, I advised that we should again offer an exclusive which would aim to achieve, paradoxically, as muted coverage as possible. This time we would be liaising with polar opposite news outlets, namely the *Financial Times* and the *Sun* (the latter's City editor, Ian King, was one of the best financial reporters on Fleet Street).

I hoped that by providing a story to journalists on a Friday – traditionally a quiet day for news – the subsequent publication on the Saturday morning would herald little interest. Many business-minded people would be tied up with weekend pastimes and would be more likely to focus on the back pages rather than the home pages. By contrast, however, a splash in one of the Sunday business broadsheets would have been a tried and tested way to guarantee good coverage and pick-ups from other outlets to drive the following week's business news agenda.

While the *Financial Times* couldn't resist splashing with 'Man Utd goes £137m into the red,'[56] the actual reportage was sensible and included my then mantra that 'the accounting losses had absolutely no bearing on the strong underlying financial performance of Manchester United, which is presently enjoying record revenues.' Every word was the honest truth.

I was also relieved there was little follow up to the two papers' stories, a tribute to the team's storming season, which superseded all off-the-field issues. It also reflected a bygone era in which news tended to stay confined to the newspaper pages as originally intended, unless an eagle-eyed journalist had picked it up. The subsequent advance of the Internet and the prevalence of smartphones would mean that news is disseminated like wildfire via applications such as Twitter.

A Full-time Role

That weekend, with talk of United winning another historic treble, with the Premier League title within tantalising reach and the team still in the Champions League and FA Cup competitions, Sir Alex Ferguson provided a further ringing endorsement of life under the Glazer regime. He told the *Scotsman* newspaper:[57] 'The Glazers have been fine since they took over. They haven't interfered with anything we do. I've had a couple of meetings with them, although David Gill, our chief executive, obviously deals with them more regularly. Any time I've been with them, they've simply said to let them know if there's anything I need.'

While I bore the role of Glazer spokesman, it was clear that only Sir Alex's pronouncements on the American owners would carry true weight among the media and the supporters.

By spring, Manchester United had announced that its executive board would be replenished with the appointment of a new commercial

---

[56] Man Utd goes £137m into the red, *Financial Times*, 14 April 2007
[57] Ferguson's Power of Persuasion Secures Ronaldo, *The Scotsman*, 14 April 2007

director, Lee Daley, who had a strong advertising background, as well as the creation of a new chief operating officer function filled by Michael Bolingbroke. This would enable David Gill to take on more responsibilities at the FA. Michael was an Englishman who had served a lengthy stint abroad as a senior executive in the entertainment industry, including the Cirque du Soleil: this was significant in as much as it reflected the Glazers' open mindedness to go beyond sport for ideas on how to grow Manchester United's interests off-the-pitch.

I too was beginning to explore how I could work for the Glazers on a full-time basis to become more immersed in their ownership of Manchester United. That said, during the previous two years it felt that much of my work life and private life had been consumed with all things United. I also felt convinced that I could do more to bolster Manchester United's corporate profile were I to have a full-time focus. This was in part prompted by the positive coverage Barcelona FC had gained in the *Sunday Times* Business section when they had agreed a sponsorship deal with computer firm Acer; if I was reading this in my English newspaper, surely we could put more effort into promoting United's commercial deals to an overseas audience?

So I began to covet working exclusively for the Glazers, ideally retaining my spokesman role to represent their ownership, but incorporating a wider remit to work more closely with Ed Woodward's expanding office in London. However, I felt my ambitions would be dashed at the first hurdle as I was resigned to leaving my agency without the Glazer account, given the industry standard covenant restricting a parting director from exiting with a client. It felt like a Catch 22: I couldn't leave the agency and lose the Glazer account, but I felt significantly hampered by staying at the agency and trying to meet United's increasing communication needs.

Then came a lucky break.

By the end of March there was strong speculation that yet another American was eyeing up a stake in a Premier League club. Stan Kroenke already had a marketing tie-up with Arsenal and newspapers excitedly reported that he was looking to buy ITV's 9.9 per cent stake in the club. His subsequent purchase of those shares, and his efforts to purchase more, prompted a fall-out among the Arsenal board leading to the sudden resignation of David Dein, a long-serving director and a close confidante of manager Arsène Wenger. A few days later the club's chairman, Peter Hill-Wood, accused Dein of being in league with Kroenke and issued one of the most memorable outbursts to come from the mouth of a football administrator:[58] 'Call me old-fashioned but we don't need Kroenke's money and we don't want his sort. Our objective is to keep Arsenal English, albeit with a lot of foreign players. I don't know for certain if Kroenke will mount a hostile takeover for our club but we shall resist it with all our might. We are all being seduced that the Americans will ride into town with pots of cash for new players. It simply isn't the case. They only see an opportunity to make money. They know absolutely nothing about our football and we don't want these types involved.'

Hill-Wood didn't need to say it but everyone presumed that Malcolm Glazer would have been one of those 'types' that the Old Etonian so despised. But, by a strange twist of fate, Hill-Wood and his well-respected managing director Keith Edelman would seek counsel on how to ward off a potential hostile takeover bid from the best advisory team in the football business: NM Rothschild. This would mark their fourth commission involving the Premier League's most high-profile football teams, having served the Glazers' bid to buy United, having advised Doug Ellis on selling Aston Villa and having held George Gillett's hands during his long-baked purchase of Liverpool FC.

My agency, Smithfield, bolstered by its reputation for good work for Rothschild and the Glazer family, were invited to pitch for the opportunity to represent the Arsenal board. It was clear to me that should we win the brief, it would be odd for a boutique agency the size of Smithfield to be representing the boards of two top clubs, especially when there could be a conflict of interest. That said, the agency had operational screens to ensure client privacy between the Glazer and Arsenal accounts. It was also conceivable that the Arsenal board would

---

[58] 'We Don't Need Kroenke's Money' blasts Hill-Wood, *The Guardian*, 20 April 2007

be keen to pour scorn on the type of acquisition debt used by the Glazers; in addition, the board's hostile stance towards the non-English Stan Kroenke might not sit well with my clients, who held the Missouri businessman in high regard. In any case, knowing Joel Glazer, I was sure he would not be happy for Smithfield to represent a rival.

When I learned that Smithfield had succeeded in securing the partnership with Arsenal, I knew that the prospect of extravagant fees meant that my agency would be prepared to lose the Glazer family as clients. I was hopeful that this could facilitate my smooth exit from the agency with Joel, Bryan et al in tow. However, I would have to endure an agonising wait in order to establish whether I would be able to transfer directly to the Glazers, as part of me was still nervous that they might choose to forgo Smithfield and my services altogether.

In the meantime, I had the happy distraction of another big European night at Old Trafford to savour as Manchester United hosted AC Milan in the Champions League semi-final. This game would prove to be the most enjoyable match of my career, tugging every emotional string during a heart-stopping battle between Europe's football aristocrats. The game had everything: world class marquee players like Cristiano Ronaldo and Milan's Kaká at the height of their pomp; a surfeit of dramatic twists and breathtaking goals and an intense, fervent atmosphere. The Old Trafford faithful roared with so much passion that they almost wished in Wayne Rooney's last-minute winner. On this occasion, four of the five Glazer brothers – Joel, Avie, Bryan and Edward – were in attendance, a confident Avie reassuring me at half-time, just after Milan had gone 2-1 up, by saying: 'No worries Tes, United will win.' United's 3-2 triumph ensured a festive post-match mood in the packed directors' VIP lounge, and later in the bar at Manchester's Radisson Hotel. The victory, however, proved to be pyrrhic. Milan's two away goals gave them the psychological edge for the return leg, in which an inexplicably lacklustre United would be dumped out 3-0.

Ticket Price Rise (Again)

The following morning's newspaper coverage of yet another glorious night at the Theatre of Dreams contained two stings in the tail. Firstly, there was news of a further rise in season ticket prices, with both me and Phil Townsend being accused of burying bad news by trying to sneak the announcement amid the euphoria of the game. Secondly, there were reports that a car thought to belong to the Glazers had been attacked by an angry mob outside the Lowry, Manchester's five-star hotel. (The Glazer brothers had by then flown out of the UK and into the USA).

As anticipated, the average ticket price rise of 14 per cent prompted an angry response from fans' groups, already incensed by the 12.5 per cent rise the previous year. It also riled many in the wake of the record revenues from the money-spinning television deals and the lucrative AIG shirt sponsorship, both of which had been trumpeted heavily by me and the club during the preceding few months. Two years into the role, I would look forward to this stage in the season as much as a doctor telling a patient they had a terminal illness. Trying to defend a price hike would never be easy, especially when the vilified Glazers were seen as driving it. Phil Townsend and I would stubbornly point to the continued value for money that the normal seats provided – especially when compared with United's rivals – as well as a sizeable season ticket waiting list.

United's cheapest matchday ticket after the price rise was £25, against £34 at Liverpool, £35 at Chelsea and £46 at Arsenal. Moreover, Old Trafford's most expensive standard ticket was just £44, with children only having to pay £10 regardless of where they sat in the stadium. These facts, however, would get drowned out by the concerted protests from supporter groups enraged by the Manchester United board's decision to introduce an Automatic Cup Scheme (ACS). The ACS would oblige *all* season ticket holders, rather than the established practice of just new ones, to buy tickets for the early rounds of home cup games, even the usually less sought after midweek Carling Cup ties. Arsenal had brought in a similar system following the club's move to the Emirates stadium, but London supporters would broadly empathise with their board's desire to maximise stadium earnings to service the £260 million debt the club had taken on to build the Gunners' gleaming new home. But in Manchester, the overriding perception among angry supporters was that the debt represented an unjustifiable curse wreaked unto the club by the Glazers. The ACS struck many as a further cynical ploy by a distant ownership, and duly unleashed the prospect of summer protests not seen since the takeover.

'Chinese Takeaway'

In early May, however, the focus quickly returned to the football pitch where, after United achieved a narrow win against Manchester City (and following Chelsea's failure to beat Arsenal) Sir Alex Ferguson won his ninth Premier League title, which went some way to assuage the bitter disappointment of losing to Milan in the San Siro a few days earlier. David Gill, a diehard 'southern' United fan exulted in the triumph and heaped lavish praise on the Glazers:[59] 'Joel rang me last night to express his congratulations to everyone at the club. All the doomsayers who said we would be in trouble have been proved wrong… They have brought a stability to the club, and stability is the key element of any football club.'

Nick Harris, one of the most perceptive sports journalists around, commented in the *Independent*: 'As long as the massive debts remain, there will be doubts over how they will be repaid… So the Glazers' £790m takeover of May 2005 was a gamble, and remains so. Yet it would be churlish not to recognise the positives. Their gamble is paying off so far, more through design than luck. They took a business that they saw with potential for expansion with proven and aggressive US marketing, and are growing it… The Glazers will also benefit from the new three-year £2.7bn Premiership TV deal, which kicks in next season. If they envisaged that when they took over, they are seers.'

---

[59] Glazers praised for bringing 'stability' to Old Trafford, *The Independent*, 8 May 2007

On the eve of the last league game of the season, a home match against West Ham after which Manchester United would be officially crowned Premier League champions, I took a call from the *News of the World* reporter, David Harrison. He sheepishly told me that he had heard that the Glazers had turned down a bid to buy Manchester United for £850 million from a Chinese consortium. Too right they would have turned it down, I thought, especially given how measly the price tag appeared. But it was never my business to speculate and I immediately put a call into Joel Glazer who was also amused at the seemingly derisory figure attached to the club, but who also agreed that we put out an unequivocal message confirming that no approach had been received, and that the club was not for sale. We also saw this as an opportunity to talk up the club's credentials to the newspaper's multi-million readership, so I dictated to Harrison a statement that I had drafted on a scrap of paper during my conversation with Joel. 'Manchester United is the world's biggest club and, of course, it is coveted but anyone who thinks that it is up for sale is mad. The Glazers are in it for the long haul and are determined to ensure success both on and off-the-pitch.' (Joel had steered me from making a stronger and more sarcastic statement.)

Come Sunday morning, the potent combination of Manchester United and the clichéd pun of 'Chinese takeaway' must have proved irresistible to the *News of the World's* sub-editor and it was duly splashed as an exclusive on the paper's back page[60]. It meant that my rare drive up to Manchester for the game on a beautiful May morning (weekend engineering works on the train line would have made the Pendolino journey unbearably slow) was constantly interrupted by a barrage of calls to my hands-free phone from reporters testing the credibility of the story. While there wasn't any, to the mild-mannered David Harrison's credit he did report for the very first time *speculation* that Manchester United might be up for sale, ushering in an inexhaustible procession of similarly wild stories.

---

[60] United No To Chinese Takeaway, *News of the World*, 13 May 2007

Although I was happy that my statement featured in the article, I did feel the story to be pretty feeble for the Sunday tabloid to lead with. However, I had already learned by then that any United-related story would trump the sports agenda, especially when it was tied in with the heightened interest of that day's West Ham game. More annoyingly, though, I resented how the report would serve as an obvious self-publicity vehicle for the advisors cited in it. This was certainly neither the first nor the last occasion that people and organisations would succeed in jumping on the Manchester United bandwagon, claiming a spurious connection for the purpose of blatant self-aggrandisement.

A Damp Squib

By the time I had arrived at Old Trafford, the warm promise of summer had given way to a dank cool afternoon with rain in the air. The Glazer brothers had taken their seats early in the directors' box, watching the stadium gradually fill to its near-76,000 capacity while a trickle of curious United supporters asked for their autographs.

The game itself was a dour and frustrating affair, played out in front of a distinctly subdued crowd huddled under the Manchester drizzle. While the match was billed as United's first title coronation in three years, West Ham United had their own agenda; to avoid relegation, they desperately needed an unlikely win, and were reliant on rival teams' results to go their way. Perhaps the home players wanted to avoid injury ahead of the following weekend's trip to Wembley for the new stadium's inaugural FA Cup final, but when Carlos Tévez scored just before half-time for the Hammers, the London team appeared fated to pull off the same unlikely result against United that they had achieved at Upton Park before Christmas.

By the final whistle, football had dealt the crowd a rare win-win scenario for both teams, with West Ham surviving the drop and United, fully indifferent to the 1-0 loss, looking forward to grasping hold of the Champions' trophy again. The delirious euphoria of the Hammers fans in the corner of the South and East Stands did not, however, seem to have infected the rest of Old Trafford, and I was struck by how so many United supporters seemed almost nonchalant, appearing to take the title win in their stride while their team jubilantly paraded the Premier League trophy around the rain sodden pitch.

Back inside the directors' lounge, a clearly shocked West Ham entourage downed freely dispensed alcoholic drinks to settle their nerve. The group was led by its easily-recognisable 'egghead' chairman Eggert Magnússon, who received plaudits from just about everyone – myself included – which he duly reciprocated with a warm bear hug. Unusually, Joel Glazer, who was significantly more restrained than his West Ham counterpart, did not have to make a mad dash to the airport and seemed happy to hang around in the lounge, so I introduced him to the TV presenter Eamonn Holmes who was a trustee of the MU Foundation, United's charitable wing. For the most part, however, Joel, Ed Woodward and I stood together talking shop, although I dared not raise the subject that was really preying on my mind: whether my services would be retained now that my agency had become conflicted with Arsenal.

By early evening we were among the last to leave the lounge. I noted how Joel made sure he scooped up the freebie – now souvenir – '9' glossy flash cards marking Sir Alex's title triumph – which had been distributed to every home supporter to hold up at the start of the game. He also carefully stored away his match programmes to take back home with him, behaving just like any United devotee would. Ed, his PA, Kay, and I headed back into Manchester to have a full-blown celebratory dinner at San Carlo, a bustling Italian restaurant. This eaterie was a bastion for the city's bigwigs, its entrance area adorned with signed photographs of its many celebrity football diners. Situated just off Deansgate, it was reassuringly far away from the nearest Chinese takeaway.

The FA Cup Final

The following weekend, United were up against Chelsea in the FA Cup Final. It was to be staged in the brand new Wembley Stadium, whose grand opening after a succession of embarrassing delays had become a national talking point. By May 2007 it was finally ready to welcome some 90,000 fans in front of the FA's President, Prince William. The previous week I had liaised with Paddy Harverson who, before working as the press secretary to Prince Charles and his sons, had been the communications director at Manchester United. Paddy advised me on the protocol that the Glazers needed to follow when they met the Prince, which I duly forwarded to the family.

Wembley was an easy half-hour Tube ride from my north London home. Unlike its decrepit and dangerously overcrowded predecessor, arriving at the spanking new Wembley Park underground station felt surprisingly civilised, made special by the vista from the top of its steps, from where – along with the thousands of fellow passengers streaming out of the station – I would stop in awe to gawp at the sight of the stunning stadium, with its beautiful, shimmering 1000-feet arch spanning the North stand. The long walk towards the new Wembley resembled the feel of the pilgrim-like approach to the old twin towers, the huge crowd of red and blue-clad supporters in carnival mood as they excitedly approached this shiny new construction. The stadium had taken some four years to build and, judging by its scale of ambition, its deluxe hospitality areas and its sprawling gigantic atriums (filled with the usual overpriced fast food outlets) I could understand where every penny of its eventual £800 million price tag had been spent. Even the multitude of toilets with turbo-powered hand dryers – a relative novelty in 2007 – were impressive.

The press lounge was particularly striking and looked out onto the lush green (albeit controversially patchy) Wembley turf. One area housed banks of carrel desks for journalists to file their stories, adjacent to which was a spacious dining area and which served surprisingly tasty hot food and a large selection of drinks to the hungry hordes of journalists. But it was the outdoor press box, located in a central position above the eye-wateringly expensive members' enclosure, that impressed the most. Around 400 comfortable seats were split across two blocks, all with generously appointed desk spaces. Each chair came with an ingenious mechanism which allowed reporters to change their positions which, as well as keeping my geeky sensibilities entertained, also provided a welcome distraction from what turned out to be as insipid a match as the previous weekend's at Old Trafford. When Chelsea's Didier Drogba scored in the dying seconds of extra time I felt crushed with disappointment. Within seconds I had evacuated the stadium, deciding against applauding Chelsea's grudgingly deserved victory and instead making a mad dash to the Tube station to beat the rush.

Within an hour of leaving what had been a largely pleasant Wembley experience – save for the result – I found myself back in the comfort of my living room. I was later to learn that the Glazers and their co-VIPs had endured an altogether more frustrating day at Wembley. Their limousines had been stuck in huge traffic queues, there had been confusion over accreditations and, by all accounts, the catering had been haphazard. While it had hosted its first momentous and prestigious fixture, it seemed that Wembley still had some gaping deficiencies to overcome.

The Celebration

That evening, Manchester United hosted a formal bash at the Royal Lancaster Hotel opposite Hyde Park. The party was primarily intended to mark United's title win, and hopefully an FA Cup victory (sadly not to be on this occasion), and the guest list was strictly limited to the club's administrative hierarchy, the players, the coaching staff, their spouses and some close family members. In effect that meant no sponsors, no agent hangers-on, and no buyable invites. The celebrations were strictly off limits to the press, too. While I was immensely excited to be attending, I still had not received word of whether my services were to be retained, and I remember pondering, 'well, if this is the last thing I do in connection with Manchester United and the Glazers it's not a bad way to bow out...'

The paparazzi gathered outside the entrance gave a strong clue to the status of many of the guests assembled inside the hotel's Nine Kings Suite, which had been extravagantly draped with shimmering black satin and dressed with freshly-cut flowers. The dim lighting added both glamour and intimacy to the proceedings. I attended as one of

Joel's guests and sat next to his father-in-law around one of the room's many exquisitely decorated circular dining tables. We were served a three-course banquet comprising a Prosciutto ham and seasonal melon appetiser, followed by a rack of English lamb entrée. As we nibbled on our petits fours and sipped our coffee, the party's official host, chief executive David Gill, stood up and gave a rousing speech, serving to lift us from the gloom pervading the room in the wake of the Wembley defeat (and the traffic jams). David reminded everyone in the room – most of whom had been intimately involved in the day to day running of Manchester United – of the need to celebrate the team's very special title success.

After the dinner an exuberant live band helped to add some zest to the party while guests freely mingled from table to table, with many, especially the players, gravitating to the large and lavishly stocked free bar. I made sure I looked up Phil Townsend, with whom I had already shared a reasonably intense two-year working relationship. We chatted about the club's successes of the previous twelve months, ruefully contrasting them with the tribulations that we had experienced in the first twelve months.

The party marked the first occasion that I had encountered the club's players in one space, most of whom appeared to be celebrating the hard work of the previous eleven months while at the same time drowning their sorrows after the FA Cup disappointment. All were slightly incongruously attired in elegant dark lounge suits rather than the Nike sports apparel I had become accustomed to seeing them wearing. During my time at the club I would never cease feeling a tad self-conscious around them: firstly, I could not help being naturally star-struck by some of these hugely famous household names. Secondly, I felt considerably older among the players; I was twice the age of many of them and was aware that, when I came close to their youthful faces, I had little or nothing to chat about except patronising small talk regarding cars and the like. There were a few occasions when I would strike up a conversation with an overseas player, often in a hotel lift, only to realise that he had barely understood a word I had said.

Moreover, since Manchester United's players were cemented by a strong bond, there seemed to be an invisible force field surrounding them, making it feel unusually awkward for anyone to stroll up and talk to one of them, the honourable exceptions being the more mature players like Ryan Giggs and Edwin van der Sar who seemed to share some of my middle-aged weariness. At the party I also fondly remember seeing Henrik Larsson, the Swedish striker who had joined United for a short spell earlier that year, being warmly courted by his ex-colleagues, their respect and admiration for him plain for all to see.

But the real star that night was a beaming Sir Alex Ferguson, who appeared relaxed and seemed to have put that afternoon's disappointment behind him. United's nine-time-winning Premier League manager held court for much of the evening, standing alongside the gleaming trophy as a procession of party guests queued up for a cherished photo opportunity.

While the end-of-term do had been billed as a formal affair, I was struck by how welcoming and friendly the mood was, perhaps reflecting the natural Mancunian warmth of the majority of the attendees, but also the paternal kindness – symbolised by Ferguson and Gill – that was woven into Manchester United's DNA. I left the party in the early hours of Sunday morning, lifted by having come so close to the heart of this very special club, and craving even more the opportunity of staying there.

No Job Description

The following week Ed Woodward broke the very welcome news to me that my services had indeed been retained, meaning that I could leave my agency and work for the Glazers full-time. When, a few hours later, the call came from Joel Glazer to welcome me on board I felt more relief than joy. The long-term stress of not knowing about my future had taken its toll on my nerves. The job came with no description, title nor office (and even for a time no business card). This reflected our shared view that news of my role should be handled as discreetly as possible and should certainly not be construed as a club appointment, whereby I could – albeit mistakenly – be seen as a threat to the club's communications director Phil

Townsend. In an industry like football, where gossiping tongues could wag as mischievously as those in politics, it was important to guard against any misunderstanding from the outset.

Indeed, my unwritten remit was very much a continuation of my previous role in order to compliment Phil's duties; my position would involve acting as the Glazers' communications advisor and spokesman, plus taking on the responsibility for the club's financial and commercial public relations. Phil would maintain his wide reaching purview of the club, which included the players, Sir Alex Ferguson and David Gill. Both operating within our comfort zones, Phil and I would continue to enjoy a harmonious working relationship, our mutual trust ensuring that our communications would be as joined-up as possible.

My appointment coincided with the eve of the Champions League final in Athens between Liverpool FC and United's semi-final conquerors, AC Milan. It was the third consecutive final to feature an English club and was a rerun of 2005's meeting in Istanbul when Liverpool had snatched an improbable victory. That morning the *Guardian* carried an extraordinary interview with Tom Hicks, Liverpool's co-owner, wherein he compared the purchase of the club to another business he used to own, the breakfast cereal Weetabix. 'When I was in the leverage buy-out business we bought Weetabix, and we leveraged it up to make our return. You could say that anyone who was eating Weetabix was paying for our purchase of Weetabix. It was just business. It is the same for Liverpool.'[61] Hicks went on to describe the Glazers' takeover as a 'blueprint of what not to do' although he acknowledged: 'They were the first. There were fans who honestly believed that, if an American owner came in and borrowed some of the purchase price, it could be the end of the club's success. I think things changed when people saw that the Glazers didn't necessarily turn out to be the end of Manchester football.'

The Liverpool owners' latest brickbat to be hurled at the Glazers did not irk me, especially in the context of his considerably more brazen comments about my once beloved club. True, Weetabix may have been

---

[61] Liverpool profit will service new owners' loan, *The Guardian*, 22 May 2007

a national treasure just like Liverpool, its distinctive yellow packaging and blue logo ubiquitous in the nation's food cupboards, but surely Hicks should have realised that to affirm that Liverpool Football Club, like Weetabix, was 'just business' would rile even the most hard-headed, least sentimental of Liverpool fans? Also, Hicks' frequent use of the word 'leverage' (aka debt) appeared gratuitous given that, just three months previously, his co-owner had claimed that no debt had been used to buy Liverpool. I immediately felt sorry for Hicks' London-based PR man. He enjoyed an excellent reputation in the business and there was no way he would have advised his loose cannon of a client to speak in such a feckless manner.

On the morning of the final, Hicks and Gillett gave another bravura performance in a joint television interview with Sky Sports News extolling their love of Liverpool FC, its traditions and fans (although no mention of a wheat-based breakfast cereal). When asked about their transfer budget for the club's manager, Rafa Benítez, Gillett – with a complete absence of irony – sought to demonstrate 'loads' by stuffing the breast pocket of his jacket with a wad of dollar and euro notes. Presumably Gillett wasn't a student of the comedian Harry Enfield, whose notorious 1980s creation 'Loadsamoney' was also known to brandish handfuls of cash.

Now on-board, and feeling even closer to the Glazers, I felt sure that they would not be so crass with regard to their ownership of Manchester United. If anything, their continued vow of silence seemed to be winning some plaudits, who appreciated their reluctance to grandstand and preferred their more dignified silence; Charles Sale the most dogged of sports diarists, noted in the *Daily Mail*[62]: 'Manchester United may have lost the Cup final to Chelsea but next season is likely to be another one of stability behind the scenes at Old Trafford, in contrast to the daily turbulence on and off-the-pitch at Stamford Bridge. The five Glazer brothers, Joel, Avi, Bryan, Kevin, and Edward, only sister Darcy [sic], who has just had a baby, was missing from the clan, were all at Wembley supporting their club but making

---

[62] Glazers will be seen and not heard, *Daily Mail*, 22 May 2007

no fuss. The same strategy is planned for next season, with the Glazers remaining in the background.'

Sat glued to the television, my bitter disappointment at United not getting to the final still lingering, I watched with initial indifference to the result from Athens' Olympic Stadium. However as Liverpool began to outshine their Italian rivals, I found myself cheering the Anfield side on once again, driven on by my visceral fervour (no doubt lacking among most United fans that evening). My sadness at seeing the team lose was compounded by my having to witness George Gillett, his affiliation with Liverpool just a few months old, leading the crushed team towards the podium to collect the losers' medals. Now, that was definitely something I couldn't see Joel Glazer doing, I thought.

Still Not for Sale?

One story that was almost stifled by the Champions League media circus was the unexpected arrival of another prospective Premier League club owner who appeared to fit the new archetype of football's elite: mega-rich, little-known and with no previous connection to the sport. However, unusually, Mike Ashley – who had launched a £133 million takeover bid for Newcastle United by buying out the club's largest shareholder, Sir John Hall – was English. This served as a useful benchmark against overseas owners, especially the Glazer family who, as Americans, were consistently pilloried for not understanding the beautiful game. Ashley, in fact, was arguably more enigmatic than my new bosses; until he had floated his sports retail business earlier that year and banked £929 million in cash, he had not provided any interviews and there seemingly existed only one obscure photograph of him. Still, most Newcastle supporters – among the most passionate and loyal in the land – broadly welcomed Ashley's arrival, not least because the outgoing chairman, Freddy Shepherd, had not exactly endeared himself to fans following a *News of the World* sting which reported him as describing female supporters as 'dogs' and calling the club's beloved star striker Alan Shearer the 'Mary Poppins of football.'

And all this while allegedly visiting a brothel. However, Ashley's non-sports pedigree was not that auspicious, either: the *Financial Times* commented that[63] 'Mr Ashley's interest is all the more unusual because he is patently not 'a football man'... one associate said of his knowledge of football: "He's not at all interested."'

An eventful week for Premier League clubs ended with me having to manage yet another media issue. The *Daily Mirror* had decided to splash on its back page: 'For Sale. Exclusive: Glazers will listen to offers for United.' The article went on to claim[64]: 'The Glazer family are ready to consider bids for Manchester United – potentially throwing the club into off-field turmoil once more... One well-placed City source said: "What we're all hearing is United hasn't turned out to be what the Glazers thought it was. When they paid so much, they were convinced a lot of money was to be made. Buying United wasn't about owning a football club, but a business decision and from an investment point of view it's been little short of disastrous."

That's news to me, I thought, after a year that had seen a first Premier League title in three years, record TV and shirt deals, a successful refinancing, and Old Trafford's attendances becoming the highest in Europe; hardly economic meltdown. Calls from other journalists poured in that Friday morning; it was too early for me to touch base with Joel Glazer in Florida but, in any case, I knew the *Mirror* story to be complete nonsense, particularly since it had feebly cited chief executive David Gill as being in a 'really bad mood' before the Wembley FA Cup Final as evidence of a boardroom rift. Tellingly, the article's author hadn't had the inclination to put a call into either myself or Phil Townsend to provide us with a prior notification before publication, knowing that we would have rubbished it from the outset. It was another friendly journalist who revealed the identity of the 'City source'; apparently, the unusually publicity-shy banker had tried to feed this story into a number of outlets for some weeks. It made sense that a City type – who had probably heard talk in the market that

---

[63] Buying up Magpies may prove a steal, *Financial Times*, 24 May 2007
[64] For Sale. Exclusive: Glazers will listen to offers for United, *Daily Mirror*, 25 May 2007

United was exploring a further refinancing package – would have had an agenda to ruffle some feathers; by doing so he could point potential suitors to articles painting instability and crisis at England's top club to try and expedite a possible deal. Welcome to the murky world of football finance.

The Supporters' Trust

With the football season now well and truly over, the *Mirror's* story had a curious traction among football writers scrambling for some content to fill the back pages. It became open season for further attacks on the Glazers' ownership, stoked up by the Manchester United Supporters' Trust (MUST), which had seized upon the unpopularity among some fans of the season ticket price hikes, in particular the introduction of the Automatic Cup Scheme. Whether MUST actually believed reports of United's imminent economic malaise or not, its hierarchy took the tactical decision to jump on the bandwagon calling for the Glazers to sell the club. It would be a precursor to more concerted action a few years down the line.

The respected journalist Jim White would regularly pen diatribes against the Glazers in his *Daily Telegraph* column which, disappointingly, always failed to disclose that he had an axe to grind, being one of MUST's founder members. In June he rounded on the season ticket hike[65]: 'Far from being proven wrong by what has been happening recently, what the anti-Glazer movement said all along is coming to pass: it is the fans who are buying the club for a set of owners they were never consulted about in the first place. The only choice they have in the issue is to walk away and no longer support their team… Don't be fooled by glitzy promises of new investment. The only investment the new style of foreign owner makes is in the initial purchase. For everything else, there's the fans.'

---

[65] United fans' wallets cup-tied club funding scheme, *The Daily Telegraph*, 9 June 2007

MUST, which in 2007 claimed to have some 9,000 paying members and a 20,000-plus mailing list, was able to exploit the open goal of the Glazers' silence and expertly drum up coverage within a media sympathetic to the David versus Goliath narrative. The Supporters' Trust could also rely on a well of goodwill and credibility among its strong network of influential journalists. This dated back to its inception in 1998 (as 'Shareholders United Against Murdoch', later abbreviated to 'Shareholders United') when it was formed to represent fans fiercely opposed to a potential takeover of the club by media tycoon Rupert Murdoch; a cause that was naturally supported by the sections of the press who weren't owned by the Australian. In April 1999, the surprise decision by the UK government to block Murdoch's bid earned MUST significant plaudits, although it is moot how much influence its lobbying carried in the final government decision.

I had felt that Shareholders United had missed a trick during the run-up to the Glazer takeover in 2005. Given its reputation for good work representing supporters' interests I wondered why they had not tried to eke out a constructive dialogue with the Glazers as their takeover was taking shape. Perhaps they could have garnered a voice at the club on fans' matters, especially since Shareholders United had so opposed the Manchester United PLC board seeking to do a deal with Murdoch, the same board that was set square against the Glazers. Instead, perhaps emboldened by the collapse of Murdoch's takeover, Shareholders United had focused their efforts on an avowed ambition to own the club itself and would meet their Waterloo by taking such an unequivocally aggressive stance towards the American suitors, from where it would be impossible to come back once the Glazer family had assumed control in 2005.

Two years on, and with most supporters adopting a wait-and-see approach to their new owners while watching their team returning to winning ways, the bright bods at the reincarnated MUST might have wondered whether they would ever find their voice again. But the Automatic Cup Scheme was a cause, which stirred MUST's political antennae, and its spokesmen duly announced that it was taking legal advice over its validity. This measure would ensure continuing interest in the fate of the unpopular scheme.

Shockwaves

Joel Glazer was one of life's natural listeners and, as the media knew all too well, was not prone to verbal outbursts. Joel's laconic style was borne out by mantras he would often repeat to me, and which he used in his sole MUTV interview – like the aphorism 'marathon not a sprint' – to describe his family's long-term approach to owning United. Another favoured expression maintained that his family must be judged by its 'deeds not words', a riposte to the era of the sound bite in which George Gillett and Tom Hicks could rightfully claim to have wiped the floor with the Glazers in terms of public relations.

One such deed, at the start of the summer transfer window, was Sir Alex Ferguson's swoop for two wingers – the Portuguese Nani and the Brazilian Anderson – for a reputed £35 million. With the impending midfield addition of Bayern Munich's Owen Hargreaves, the *Guardian* wrote[66] that the move 'represents the most lavish spending of the Glazer era at Old Trafford to date. United's initial outlay to buy the pair from Portugal is more likely to be around £15m. The trio of signings will send shockwaves through the Premiership. While Chelsea could match such financial clout if they desired, it remains to be seen whether Liverpool and Arsenal can match such spending power. Indeed, not since Wayne Rooney's arrival in the autumn of 2004 for an initial £20m have United spent this much to refresh their playing squad.'

I was not usually privy to transfer activity, except for getting a heads-up prior to any announcements by which time the news had usually been extensively leaked to the media, often by the player himself, his family, his agent or the selling club. Manchester United, understandably, was very sensitive about leaks and operated on a strict need-to-know basis, which normally meant that transfer matters were confined to a coterie of trusted club officials: Sir Alex (and his Carrington-based coaching and medical staff); Old Trafford-based chief executive David Gill, who would broker the deal with the selling

---

[66] United to splash £35m on Nani and Anderson, *The Guardian*, 31 May 2007

club; and finally Joel Glazer in the States, who would provide Gill with the sign-off.

In the PLC days, United was obliged under Stock Exchange rules to publicly release the fees it had paid to secure (and had obtained to release) a player, reflecting the material bearing that these outgoings had on the club's bottom line. But ever since United had become private under the Glazers, it enjoyed the prerogative of not having to disclose transfer finances. This did not, however, prevent the media from reporting figures, usually based on guidance from the players' agents who would always be keen to talk up their clients' values thus increasing their cut from future earnings and transfers.

I would also adhere to this non-disclosure of transfer fees, either because I wasn't in the loop or, increasingly, because I had developed a capacity to listen to sensitive information in one ear, only to let it flow straight out of the other. Indeed, contrary to popular perception, it was often an advantage *not* to be told sensitive club information such as transfer fees and sponsorship values. Not only would it mean being spared from the firing line in the event that the information illicitly found its way to the press, it would also save me from having to lie and plead ignorance among reporters hungry for information. This, trust me, was a virtue in public relations where the only abiding rule is to never lie to journalists.

The 2007 summer transfer window, in which Sir Alex had added the loan of Argentinian Carlos Tévez to his three other signings, was largely seen by the press and the fans as evidence of the Glazers' support to Ferguson. The owners clearly wanted their manager to kick-on from the success of the Premier League title. It seemed the sports media were also impressed by the unusual speed with which the transfers had been expedited, which had left United's rivals trailing in their wake.

A phrase I particularly hated was 'splash the cash,' and I made a point of never boasting about sums that might have been spent. Instead, I would stress that player acquisitions demonstrated what I had been saying all the time: that the Glazers would always support Sir Alex Ferguson and David Gill in the transfer market. 'Just imagine if they hadn't?' I would speculate to journalists in my frequent off-the-record briefings. 'Believe me, you'd be the first to know about it.' Reporters agreed that, during the club's PLC days, Sir Alex Ferguson had made crystal clear his frustrations with the board's tight grip on the purse strings, but had stopped short of making any public criticisms.

However, as the summer went on I would get accustomed to the cynicism among some quarters of the press, touted I presumed by briefings from MUST. This dictated that the spending sanctioned by the Glazers, a reported £50 million to £70 million depending on which newspaper you read, was all 'smoke and mirrors' and subject to the 'crippling' debt repayments. Or, as the *Daily Telegraph* put it: [67] '(Ferguson's) spree is more a result of good housekeeping rather than the sudden generosity of the Glazer family' given the likely receipts from the sales of Gabriel Heinze and Kieran Richardson and the presumed money left over from the previous summer.

Indeed, as far as a football club is concerned, an actual cash outlay for a player is rarely made in one headline-grabbing instalment. Rather, the deal may be structured over the period of the player's contract, meaning that a lump sum may be credited to the selling club upon his signing with the promise of further annual payments, which may also be tied to the amount of player appearances and the team's performance in cup competitions. One of the first insights I gleaned regarding football's idiosyncratic finances came from a conversation with the then finance director Nick Humby during the Glazers' first visit to Old Trafford. As we gazed at the jam-packed trophy cabinet in the club's museum, Nick explained to me that winning a trophy can, ironically, be cash negative for a club where extra media and prize revenues are outweighed by substantial bonus payments to playing and coaching staff. Factor in the issue of timing, as well as which accounting period the cash paid out on a transfer is made, and also when monies due from selling players hits United's account, together with the effect of foreign exchange fluctuations over a contract's lifetime and a club like United does not think about player expenditure in a concrete lump sum. It considers it a constantly monitored,

---

[67] New faces show United's intent, *The Daily Telegraph*, 1 June 2007

moveable feast centred on a collection of valuable assets subject to the human vagaries of physical and emotional well-being.

'The Disgust of United Fans'

An insight into the effectiveness of the Supporters' Trust's anti-Glazer campaign surfaced in early June when Brian Viner, a columnist with the *Independent*, opined[68]: 'All those Manchester United fans who waged such a frenzied and deplorable campaign of hate when the Glazer family took over their club. Those same Glazers, consistently lauded by Sir Alex Ferguson, have now presided quietly over a triumphant league championship campaign, and since it ended have already stumped up more than £50m in pursuit of further glory, with the signings of Owen Hargreaves, the Portuguese prodigy Nani and the Brazilian midfielder Anderson. And from the "Glazers out!" bile-merchants? A resounding silence, which I suppose is the nearest thing the Americans can expect to an apology.'

At last, a sensible commentary piece from a respected sports writer, I thought. However, by the following weekend Viner had performed a dramatic *volte face*[69], writing: 'I have read every email sent from outraged United fans, or at least the relatively temperate ones, and I have also consulted journalistic colleagues who know more than I do about the situation at Old Trafford. As a consequence, I realise that what I wrote was ill-considered, naive, and as spectacularly wide of the mark as a penalty kick hitting a corner flag. The Glazers, and chief executive David Gill, and even to a certain extent Sir Alex Ferguson, are plainly entitled to the disgust of United fans... I have had my eyes opened, to the determination not only of the Glazers but of all the Americans flooding into Premiership football to make money, not least Messrs Hicks and Gillett at the other end of the East Lancs Road. They are not interested in the trickledown effect, in the grassroots of

[68] Saturday column, *The Independent*, 2 June 2007
[69] I was as ridiculously wide of the mark last week as a penalty hitting the corner flag, *The Independent*, 9 June 2007

the game being watered, because they are not interested in the game. I apologise for elevating them on this page last week. I should have known better, and now I do.'

While Viner's blistering comments may have been prescient as far as the Liverpool owners were concerned, they did not ring true of the Glazers. His abrupt change of mind seemed to have been prompted by a missive from Nick Towle, the chairman of MUST, who was cited at length in the column: 'The money for these transfers does not come from the Glazers. It comes from the club's own funds. The Glazers have not put a penny of their own money into the team and never will.'

Did Manchester United's previous 'owners' when it was listed on the Stock Exchange like John Magnier, JP McManus, Harry Dobson, Legal & General and countless other pension funds and tens of thousands of small shareholders each receive erudite letters from Nick Towle castigating *them* for not dipping their hands in their pockets to fund transfers, instead of taking millions in dividends, I wondered?

My sarcastic thoughts aside, I always felt to pick apart MUST's arguments would be as futile as arguing with an angry drunk, as was addressing certain journalists whose sympathies were so viscerally entrenched against the Glazers who, to them, symbolised the worst excesses of the commercial exploitation of football. Indeed, in all my time with the club I never contacted or engaged with any of the Supporters' Trust's representatives, nor did they ever approach me. The fact that United enjoyed huge success under the Glazers on and off-the-pitch would count for nothing, so incontestable was their resentment of the Americans' use of debt and rise in ticket prices.

MUST, understandably, wanted to own and run United their way, and there seemed no sense in dealing with an organisation hell bent on bringing an end to the Glazers' ownership. Moreover, I did not trust them and was never keen to debate the merits (or otherwise) of debt; I thought that was best left to the people who would have to decide whether to put their money where their mouths were and invest in the club. My job was to communicate that debt did not undermine the club's pursuit of football success. If MUST did not appreciate this within months of Sir Alex winning his first title in three years, there was no way I could have even fractionally succeeded in persuading them.

The Demonisation of Debt

By mid-May, and with the season over, the financial press had returned their attention to Manchester United's off-the-field affairs, picking up newswire reports that the Glazer family were considering a further refinancing of the debt to take advantage of the strong credit market and to reduce the outstanding £138 million PIK loan, which had been accruing interest at around 14.25 per cent per year. These reports helped explain the spurious rumours that the Glazers were looking to sell the club. When contacted by reporters, I would respond with the tried and trusted formula to not lie and deny any refinancing discussions had taken place. I was equally eager to maintain secrecy over potentially sensitive negotiations, and would curtly comment: 'We continue to assess all options.'

Indeed, even before the ink had dried on the last refinancing in the summer of 2006, Ed Woodward – joined by his London office new recruit Jamie Reigle, who shared his line manager's sharp mind, good nature and devotion to sport – had begun investigating further options for the Glazers to continue to make the debt more manageable off the back of growing cash flows generated by the club; just as any corporation would do. For much of the previous season, Ed could be frequently seen hosting an array of bankers at his designated dining table in the VIP lounge. Here, he would entertain the conservatively-suited visitors with United's finest dining and directors' box seats, all the time impressing upon them the club's unique ability to drive success off as well as on the pitch. After a few post-match drinks in Manchester's best cocktail lounges and bars, these bankers – some striking me as absurdly young – would often have to take the earliest train back to London the next morning in time for a full day's work in the capital; presumably to report back on the club's projected strong increase in EBITDA margin rather than rave about Rooney's scintillating strike at goal.

There was speculation that Ed was in talks with RBS and Deutsche Bank looking to securitise the club's debt into a bond using ticket sales as the collateral, an idea that would conjure up the unfortunate spectre of Leeds United.

Spring 2007, however, represented the high water mark for the booming credit market, symbolised by what would later be regarded as a grotesque tussle between Barclays and RBS for the Dutch bank ABN Amro. 'Cove-lite' was the buzzword, when bankers were throwing themselves at corporations with tantalising offers to lend at knock-down rates and competing with each other by offering fewer strings – or covenants – attached to the loans.

In this environment – under the project name 'Hercules' – the Glazers and Ed Woodward were considering a simple amendment to the existing capital structure which, as with the refinancing of the previous year, was aimed at reducing the annual overall interest charge. In early June the *Daily Telegraph* reported that the Glazers were[70] 'studying a series of refinancing options presented by advisers at Deutsche Bank, Royal Bank of Scotland and JPMorgan, the US investment bank which engineered the £790m takeover. The advisers are expected to meet the Glazers in the next few weeks to discuss their preferred route towards refinancing the club's £660m debt. Sources close to the talks say they expect a deal to be secured before the start of the football season in August.'

However, within a few weeks of that article, 'cove-lite' was beginning to be usurped by an altogether more powerful and polarised expression: the credit crunch. While at this stage confined to the pages of the financial press, this phrase was steadily taking hold of the imaginations of financial markets players, who may have been looking forward to the lull of the summer holidays for a respite from the seemingly relentlessly enriching boom. But reports soon began to surface of nervous banks that had gambled away obscene amounts of money in US sub-prime mortgage lending. As fear began to displace greed, day by day the credit markets tightened. Nothing yet like the dramatic levels we were to witness in the subsequent months which prompted a run on the British bank Northern Rock and a year later the demise of investment bank Lehman Brothers but enough to make the Glazers, Ed Woodward and their advisors, JPMorgan, pause for

[70] Glazers poised to refinance Man Utd, *The Daily Telegraph*, 9 June 2007

thought. My advice was clear: we should maintain our radio silence and avoid if at all possible the spectre of *failing* to refinance.

In the second week of July, with all the documents finalised and the formal invitation letter to investor ready to go, and with my family holiday at the behest of minute-by-minute developments on my BlackBerry, the Glazers decided to not pursue a refinancing, lest the prospective market volatility which was threatening to push interest rates higher caused any of the potential lined up investors to pull out at the last moment.

The letters were never posted. The refinancing had been pulled.

Even without the benefit of hindsight it struck me as a prudent piece of judgement. Had United pursued the deal, it would have been as closely watched as a bellwether in an increasingly choppy market which, were the project not successful, would have prompted a high-profile backlash. With hindsight, the 2007 decision not to refinance proved to be a positive too; the club was in an increasingly strong financial position with a stable capital structure put in place only in the previous summer. As the credit markets deteriorated into 2008 and interbank interest rates (LIBOR) soared, the prospect of an amended 'cove-lite' capital structure with a higher debt number might not have sat comfortably with the ensuing market turmoil.

The next couple of weeks would involve a nervous waiting game as I readied myself to react to the inevitable news of the Glazers' decision. Unsurprisingly it fell to the same *Telegraph* business reporter, Far East-based Mark Kleinman, who had speculated about the possible move in early June. This time Kleinman told me that he had got wind from 'a reliable source' that United's planned refinancing was being significantly scaled back because of adverse market conditions and took advantage of the team's Far East Asian pre-season tour to doorstep David Gill[71]: 'The decision to temporarily withdraw the Glazers' latest refinancing plan was confirmed last night by David Gill, Manchester United's chief executive, who was in Macau for the latest leg of the club's pre-season tour of Asia. Gill said the benign state of the debt markets until recent

---

[71] Man Utd loan deal stays on the bench, *The Sunday Telegraph*, 22 June 2007

weeks had presented an opportunity to examine financing options. "The last refinancing in August 2006 put in place a long-term structure and we have been looking at both refinancing the existing debt as well as a securitisation of [matchday] revenues. It's correct that the debt markets have become choppier recently, so we are not going through with either of those options right now.'"

A watching brief was maintained during the summer in case the credit markets improved but, with the UK mortgage provider Northern Rock succumbing to a funding crisis in mid-September, the window to refinance was well and truly shut. While I could take comfort that United had wisely sought not to attempt a refinancing and avoided the opprobrium of failure, this episode – amid the gathering credit crunch storm cloud – provided for a paradigm shift in how the Glazers' ownership of Manchester United would be perceived. For the first two years while the Americans' use of debt had been disapproved by many in the press and among some fans, there was a broad acceptance that it was a viable means of finance. But the credit crunch in 2007 and its intensification in ensuing years, which would also unleash financial insecurity into many people's everyday lives, germinated the false idea that the Glazers were struggling to manage the debt and therefore their ownership of United. It also led to the demonization of debt and the 'financial engineering' that businesspeople like the Glazers had been so adept at practising. This heightened resentment among some supporters that United revenues were going in interest charges, which would ultimately top up the bonus pots of bankers now so discredited and increasingly vilified by the wider public at large.

Internally, Joel Glazer and Ed Woodward were calm personified. It was business as usual. One opportunity missed simply meant another needed to be pursued. But although the existing capital structure, negotiated in the summer of 2006, allowed for interest payments to be comfortably covered by the club's existing cash flows, the prospect of a continuing rise in LIBOR rates, which governed the amount of interest charged to United, would encourage the Glazers to take an even more active involvement in growing the club's commercial revenues to form a cash buffer.

Strangely, while the credit crunch would mean the bubble may have burst for large sections of the UK economy, investment in English football continued to thrive, suggesting that the rich really did get richer in times of crisis. As the new season was drawing closer, the Premier League confirmed that it had sanctioned the arrival of a new overseas owner in its midst, the controversial figure of Thaksin Shinawatra, the former Prime Minister of Thailand, who paid £82 million for Manchester City. While there were significant misgivings over his human rights record while in office in Thailand, 'Frank' Shinawatra (a sobriquet fondly provided to him by fans on account of the similarity of his surname with that of the legendary American crooner) was warmly welcomed by the blue half of Manchester who, like their counterparts in Liverpool and Newcastle, had become exasperated with their previous owners and desperately sought investment in their clubs to help them compete with the likes of Manchester United, Chelsea and Arsenal. The Glazers' continued silence was again to be brought into sharp focus as Shinawatra's public relations were exemplary, with generous amounts of time provided to the media and widely-reported grand gestures to City's supporters, including a street party in central Manchester that laid on live Thai music and free samples of his home country's food. Shinawatra even drafted in Sven-Göran Eriksson as Manchester City's new manager. The Swede had once been talked up as Sir Alex Ferguson's natural successor, after the Scot had prematurely announced his retirement in 2002.

Part Four
2007 / 08 Season

A Hesitant Start

While I was excited about the start of the new season – the third since the Glazers' takeover and my first in my full-time role for the family – the signs were not altogether auspicious. Although the arrival of new players Nani, Anderson, Hargreaves and Tévez had assuaged fears that the debt would preclude investment in Sir Alex Ferguson's squad, sceptics nevertheless insisted that the net expenditure had been deceptively modest. Not only that, the press were predicting empty seats at Old Trafford off the back of the double-digit rise in season ticket prices and the controversial introduction of the Automatic Cup Scheme. My understanding, though, was that season ticket sales had gone well that summer, certainly in line with previous years, although advertisements on the club's website publicising availability did not help reverse negative perceptions. However, the prospect of some unsold season tickets did not necessarily augur the doom and gloom that some at the Supporters' Trust had predicted: more tickets could now be made available on a match-by-match basis, providing some hope to the casual punter who was accustomed to seeing a 'sold out' sign at the stadium.

Despite a surprisingly intense Wembley rematch between Manchester United and Chelsea in Community Shield – won by United in a penalty shoot-out – the Premier League champions made a spluttering start to the season. Two draws and a painful away defeat to Shinawatra's Manchester City condemned United to a lowly 17th place in the table.

That hesitant start was mirrored by my early foray into my full-time role. Somehow I managed to commit the heart-stopping error of erroneously copying a journalist into a series of emails I'd sent out to the Glazers. While the content of the emails was not sensitive, the owners' private email addresses were laid bare which, in the wrong hands, could have been catastrophic. Fortunately – very fortunately – the journalist at the receiving end of my missives was one of the most decent in the business, who immediately assured me that the emails had been deleted, and that it was the end of the matter. Still, I thought it wise to take full responsibility for my error and offered Joel Glazer my resignation for the breach. Thankfully, he declined.

But one United colleague who did leave the club at that time was Lee Daley, who had only joined the club at the end of the spring from advertising agency Saatchi & Saatchi but had left in August by mutual consent. The London *Evening Standard* quipped:[72] 'Four months in and he's gone… Whatever the reason, it's an embarrassment for headhunters Odgers, who spent six months finding him—two months more than he lasted.'

The new season's indifferent start seemed to precipitate more United-related 'exclusives' in the *News of the World*. Most of these stories had a negative tenor – based on tenuous connections with reality – but given the paper's multi-million circulation, they would have a far-reaching impact. But, having lunched that summer with the newspaper's editor Colin Myler at London's celebrity haunt, The Ivy Restaurant, I felt I had enough insight into the paper's amoral agenda to not take his paper too seriously, or its sensationalist revelations to heart.

Of course, some four years later the *News of the World* – for a long time reputed to be the best-selling English-speaking newspaper in the world – would be abruptly shut down following the phone hacking scandal, in which journalists had allegedly accessed voicemail messages by illegal means. By the time of my lunch with Myler I was already on my guard. An associate at another high-profile organisation had already called to alert me that the newspaper was aware of our planned – albeit innocuous – meeting over coffee. The only conceivable way the *News of the World* could have gleaned this, he reckoned, was if his voicemail

---

[72] City Spy, *London Evening Standard*, 22 August 2007

had been hacked. Fortunately, I felt assured that my mobile phone security was foolproof, if any of the countless voicemail messages I would leave with Joel Glazer were anything to go by. I would always stick to 'Joel…Tes here, please call back,' and Joel would never veer from 'Tes, Joel here, call me back.' Absolutely zero news value to any illicit private investigator.

In early September the *News of the World* phoned me to say that Manchester United had been subject to two £1 billion takeover bids from rival groups in Dubai and China. I repeated my unequivocal 'not for sale' mantra, waited for the paper's publication and cleared my Sunday afternoon schedule, preparing myself for the depressingly predictable follow-up calls from a variety of reporters which would prompt a plethora of Monday morning 'United *not* for sale' stories.

The following Sunday the *News of the World's* claws dug deeper into the Glazers' ownership. It had run with another so-called 'exclusive', its full-page headline screaming 'United Debt Storm.' The tabloid claimed:[73] "Manchester United will tomorrow be thrown into a fresh financial row when a controversial fans' report accuses the Glazer family of running up an astonishing £100 million interest bill. The report, which will be released to the City by the Independent Manchester United Supporters Trust, is understood to be described as 'wildly inaccurate' by the Old Trafford hierarchy. However, its release will re-open many questions for United supporters who have long had issues with the takeover by the Americans two years ago…MUST claim the £660m debt run up started by the club's American owners is spiralling out of control and is now "a ticking time-bomb". The Trust claim: The club's interest payments have INCREASED by a staggering £28m this year. The Glazer family have passed on rising costs by HIKING ticket prices by nearly 50 per cent. Some fans are taking LEGAL action. Other supporters have been FORCED to give up their season tickets.'

I had to take my hat off to the Supporters' Trust who were proving to be masters of spin, timing the story to perfection during the news

---

[73] United Debt Storm, *News Of The World*, 9 September 2007

vacuum of international fortnight when there were no Premier League fixtures, and when England's crucial Euro 2008 qualifier against Russia wasn't being played until the following Wednesday. The paper had called me the previous day but, while I was privately adamant that MUST's figures were wrong, I knew that to provide a comment would dignify this most sensationalist of articles. But by the Sunday morning – and following the inevitable flood of media calls – I found myself categorically rejecting the charge that the Glazer family faced a growing debt problem. I told Simon Stone from the Press Association:[74] 'The story is inaccurate. Nothing has changed. The debts continue to be comfortably serviced by the business, which is performing better than ever. As always there have been substantial funds for the manager to purchase players over the summer.'

Déjà Vu

Still, I was resigned that the charge sheet against the owners made 2007 feel like 2006 all over again. Just a few months into my full-time role I was already tiring of the clichéd 'Sold Trafford' headlines and I wasn't sure I was enjoying my dream job as much as I had hoped, wondering whether I was missing the diversity of agency life and the wide roster of clients.

The campaign against the Glazers, which had significantly escalated following the season ticket price rise and introduction of the vilified Automatic Cup Scheme, gained traction with the credit crunch which had derailed the planned debt refinancing and had led, wrongly, to the conclusion that the Glazers were therefore struggling with the club's finances. Add to this the Americans' continued silence and their not-so-frequent attendances at Old Trafford and there was an inescapable perception among some journalists and fans that the Glazers were not enjoying the experience, and that they wanted out.

---

[74] Glazers Hit Back Over Debt Claims, Press Association, 9 September 2007

Of course, the truth could not have been more different. Inside Old Trafford there existed a serene calm, built on the stable foundations laid by the triumvirate of Joel Glazer, David Gill and Sir Alex Ferguson. Moreover, the club and its fans had just celebrated winning the coveted Premier League title for the first time in four years. It seemed perverse to me that some fans couldn't appreciate this achievement, and couldn't even give credit to the Glazers for having provided some solidity to the club. There had been no rash actions after the team were dumped out of the Champions League in 2005; there was unequivocal support for the manager's player requests; and there was record growth in the club's off-field revenues without any public grandstanding.

Would fans of other clubs have been so contemptuous about their owners, months after winning a title? Definitely not. I even dared to contemplate that for United fans, many of whom were weaned on Sir Alex Ferguson's successes, perhaps winning was not everything? I only had to hark back to May 2005 when a MUST executive asserted he would rather see the team lose if it meant ridding the club of the Glazer 'leeches'. Maybe for some – albeit a small but media savvy minority – it wasn't really about loving United; it was more about hating the Glazers.

Lisbon

United's first game in the Champions League campaign was an away tie against Sporting Lisbon. I flew out to the Portuguese capital to meet some local journalists, including one from the country's paper of record, the *Diário de Notícias*. The trip marked my first tentative efforts to promote the club's strong business credentials abroad. Over a lunch of traditional salted cod and small custard tarts, washed down with strong espresso coffee, I happily expanded upon United's global reach and the stability provided by the Glazers' ownership, which did not seem to elicit controversy a thousand miles away from Manchester.

I always found it illuminating to discover from foreign reporters how Manchester United was perceived overseas. However, my dealings with the Portuguese press also prompted an unfortunate series of stories. The country's most famous player – Cristiano Ronaldo – was reputed to be seeking a move away from Manchester United (he'd joined from Sporting in 2003 as an eighteen year-old). While I would never comment on rumours about a player, the regular emails that I would receive from Lisbon-based journalists over the next 18 months – all enquiring after Ronaldo – were enough to justify speculative articles given weight by me as a Manchester United club representative saying 'no comment!'

On reflection, I would conclude that it was perhaps not the best use of my time to try and build relationships with the media in countries like Portugal, Italy and Spain, which already had their own iconic football clubs. Their interest in Manchester United seemed to be confined to idle gossip rather than serious business.

United bagged an away victory that night in a José Alvalade Stadium packed with green and white-shirted Lisbon supporters. Ironically it was Ronaldo that scored the winner, although his team's fourth consecutive 1-0 scoreline would prompt unfavourable comparisons with the pre-Wenger Arsenal sides, whose style of play would often elicit droning chants of 'one nil to the Arsenal' from opposing fans.

boring, boring Arsenal

Roman Abramovich

The football news the next morning was seismic. The most famous Portuguese man in Britain had dramatically resigned (and it wasn't Cristiano Ronaldo). Following his team's shock 1-1 draw in front of a paltry crowd at Stamford Bridge, José Mourinho had called it quits at Chelsea Football Club. The shock was palpable as I walked through the streets of football-mad Lisbon, with locals huddling around newspaper kiosks and billboards featuring the former Porto boss, absorbing the sudden news as if it were comparable to the assassination of a revered leader. Upon arriving back home in London, Mourinho's exit seemed to have caused as profound a consternation in the UK capital as it had in Lisbon, with Chelsea fans trying to come to terms with the departure of their 'Special One'.

It was clear from the outset that the club's owner had sanctioned Mourinho's departure. Abramovich had enjoyed a significantly better relationship with his club's fans than the Glazers; despite saying little in public, save for meeting a handful of journalists when he took over the club in 2003, Abramovich – unlike the Glazers – was seen by most Chelsea supporters as a benefactor to the club. His fabulous mining riches had bought two Premier League titles delivered by his managerial appointment of José Mourinho, fresh from his Champions League win at Porto. Abramovich, who was reported to have been inspired by the idea of owning a football club after seeing Manchester United beat Real Madrid at Old Trafford, clearly loved and understood the game and was undoubtedly committed to Chelsea. Indeed, it was his passionate antics in the Aston Villa directors' box the previous week, in which his dissatisfaction with his team's defeat had been caught on camera, that prompted speculation that the owner might be willing to dispense with his increasingly truculent manager. Mourinho had made no secret of his resentment towards Abramovich's interference, its apotheosis being the refusal to field Andriy Shevchenko, a Ukrainian striker who – against the manager's wishes – had been purchased by the owner for £31 million.

While many a football fan may have coveted Abramovich's financial largesse for his or her own club, Mourinho's departure illustrated that the Russian tycoon's cash came at a price: entitlement to treat his club as a plaything and the right to interfere in football matters. The Glazers' discretion and total deference to Sir Alex Ferguson's handling of team affairs (a few journalists even speculated that the Glazers feared him) were, by contrast, looking more virtuous.

Abramovich hastily installed Avram Grant as manager, his first test being a tantalising encounter with Manchester United at Old Trafford who, by mid-September, were starting to look like challengers to Arsenal at the top of the Premier League. The press lounge was packed, including a number of eminent sports columnists who had made the rare journey up to Manchester to study every movement made by the usually poker-faced Roman Abramovich, flanked by his Chelsea board colleagues in the away directors' box. But Manchester United compounded the west London team's woes with a convincing 2-0 win, the Old Trafford crowd revelling in the departure of Sir Alex's impudent rival.

At the final whistle it is commonplace for the directors' box to empty quickly as guests take advantage of the hospitality in the VIP lounge below. But Roman Abramovich, casually dressed in an open-necked shirt and a sports jacket, remained upstanding in the box, making a point of supportively clapping his defeated team and his new manager off-the-pitch. As Old Trafford quickly emptied it became clear that Abramovich had no intention to exit via the lounge, but was waiting for his security retinue to escort him out of the stadium via the players' tunnel. During this time the Chelsea owner had to contend with the boisterous taunts of home supporters around him as they made their exits. At one point one United fan was making particularly provocative gesticulations towards Abramovich and I feared for a fleeting moment that the scene could turn ugly. Instead, the Russian smiled and walked down towards his tormentor to speak with him, before shaking his hand and autographing his Manchester United flag. Abramovich continued to sign further autographs for the few straggling home fans before being escorted out of the stadium, leaving me with a surprisingly favourable impression of the man.

'A Rather Strange Thing...'

Also in the press box, watching Abramovich intently as he packed his bag, was the football commentator Alan Green, his Northern Irish twang making him one of BBC radio's most distinctive voices. Green had a fearsome reputation among his peers but I think it was the adrenalin of having seen United beat Chelsea that gave me the courage to introduce myself. I was, however, given short shrift but thought little of our brief encounter. The following week I received a cutting from the *Belfast Telegraph* which included Green's sports column. Like most commentators he had rounded on the Automatic Cup Scheme. He also added as a footnote:[75] 'A rather strange thing happened to me not long

---

[75] Alan Green: United fans crying foul on tickets; Glazers will suffer empty feeling, *The Belfast Telegraph*, 29 September 2007

after the final whistle sounded in the Chelsea game at Old Trafford last Sunday. Actually, it was quite bizarre. Someone I didn't recognise suddenly appeared at my shoulder. I was still frantically working so didn't need interrupting. "Hello," he said, "I represent the Glazer family in England. If you ever need to talk to me, don't hesitate." I didn't catch a name; I'm not sure one was offered, but I thanked him and politely made it plain that, unfortunately, I was rather busy. He stood by me for a few minutes before moving on for an 'introduction' to someone else. Why does this matter? Well, when I noticed that the attendance there for the Carling Cup tie on Wednesday night was 74,055 – a record for the competition outside of the final – it struck me that the Glazers are in severe need of a charm offensive towards their fans rather than the media.'

I bristled with embarrassment and shame at reading the article, although was relieved that his column was not nationally circulated. No way was Alan Green 'frantically working' when I approached him; I would have known better than to interrupt a busy broadcast journalist, I thought, my blood pressure rising. I was only trying to do my job, which was to engage with journalists. But I accepted the thrust of Green's argument, that the Automatic Cup Scheme had in one fell swoop alienated a proportion of supporters. While I would digest Green's point of view, I would remain saddened that journalists like him, who carried significant influence among supporters, had no interest in listening to the other side. His frequent vituperate attacks on the Glazers and their ownership of United in his radio broadcasts would remain 'uncontaminated' by any attempts at mitigation on my part.

While United's Carling Cup game against Coventry City would prompt a crescendo of journalist vitriol, epitomised by Alan Green's diatribe, there were contrary to predictions very few empty seats that night in Old Trafford. It was the dismal 2-0 defeat at the hands of the Championship side that would exercise supporters' minds. With Manchester United prematurely out of the Carling Cup for another year, attention on the ticket scheme would, thankfully, subside.

London Conference

Although it was only September, Manchester United was already putting together elaborate plans to commemorate the 50th anniversary of the Munich air disaster, which was due to be marked in February 2008. The tragedy occurred after the plane transporting the prodigiously talented United team – nicknamed the 'Busby Babes' – crashed after a failed take-off bid at a snowy Munich airport. It resulted in 23 fatalities that included players, club staff, journalists and supporters. I held a meeting with Ken Ramsden, the club secretary, who was overseeing the project. The disaster, which had prompted swathes of grief and sympathy around the world, would define Manchester United for the subsequent half-century. Its impact was felt particularly acutely by Ken who had joined the club in the raw aftermath. He told me how his mother, who was responsible for washing the players' kits, had the heartbreaking duty of polishing the players' coffins as they lay in the club gymnasium, having been flown back from Germany. Ken's deep sadness was still palpable, his considerable energies put into organising the anniversary clearly cathartic.

A few weeks later, inside an elegantly furnished suite of the Glazers' favoured Knightsbridge hotel, I briefed Avie and Joel on the club's Munich anniversary plans. From the outset they fully appreciated the occasion's gravity and were keen to do whatever was appropriate to mark the event, including a low-profile attendance in February.

Joel Glazer was in London to attend a business of sport conference that week hosted by the NFL to coincide with the inaugural American football league match between the Miami Dolphins and New York Giants at Wembley Stadium. The conference – held at the five-star Landmark Hotel in Marylebone, also a regular haunt of the Manchester United team when they stayed in London – marked the NFL's determination to project its global sports credentials by staging a high-profile and glitzy occasion. Although 'credit crunch' had entered the vernacular by now, the NFL conference was notable for the confidence and the immunity that the sports industry seemed to feel, despite the economic chill of the financial slowdown. This was, however, to markedly change by the following year. As well as Joel, the conference boasted a who's who of world sport, including other NFL owners, sport industry chief executives and a large press contingent, comprising all the country's main business of sports reporters. Joel Glazer had agreed to participate in the conference's main opening discussion on the 'Changing face of the global sports industry' which also included Tom Hicks, co-owner of Liverpool FC and Stan Kroenke, the recently-arrived investor in Arsenal.

We gathered in one of the Landmark's chandelier-lit ballrooms where a buffet breakfast was served. Joel, Ed Woodward and I sat around one table, picking at our mini croissants and bowls of fruit salad. Tom Hicks and his son Tom Jr sat some distance away, briskly thumbing through that morning's newspapers piled conspicuously high on top of his table. He seemed distracted by reports of Liverpool's 2-1 defeat to Besiktas the previous night in Istanbul, which had jeopardised his team's Champions League progression. This contrasted with Joel's relaxed and unobtrusive demeanour; the day before, Manchester United had assured their qualification for the knock-out stage after a comfortable 4-2 away win against Dynamo Kiev. A short while later, before an expectant audience, Joel, Hicks and Kroenke shared an elevated stage in a packed conference room, patiently waiting for the members of the press to leave the proceedings to provide for 'Chatham House' rules.

Actually, while the real energy of the conference lay in the frantic behind-the-scenes networking among the high powered delegates, the panel discussions that followed were usually a stilted affair with participants delivering anodyne remarks and carefully processed observations. This was particularly so for Joel Glazer who was noticeably happy to give up the floor to a more forthcoming Tom Hicks, who expounded upon his gushing enthusiasm for his ownership of the Anfield club. When the discussion addressed the prospect of the Premier League aping the NFL and seeking to play a competitive match outside England, Hicks quipped that he would be delighted to watch Liverpool play Manchester United one day in the States; Joel's face remained expressionless and he stayed silent. Indeed when Stan Kroenke mooted that he would like to see Arsenal play such a game, Joel provided perhaps the most thoughtful argument of the session noting that in the NFL not all teams play each other home and away, whereas in the Premier League they do and to have an overseas game would undermine the symmetrical integrity of the league. In the same vein, Joel argued strongly for the maintenance of the Premier League's collective TV rights model and assured delegates of his family's commitment to uphold Manchester United's traditions. As with his MUTV performance, more than two years before, I felt that Joel was a consummate communicator, with a pithy, straightforward manner that went down well with a sophisticated sporting audience. More's the pity, I thought, that the media were excluded from seeing him in action.

Joel was also in London on business to check out new premises for Manchester United's office, which his family were keen to expand. Lee Daley's short tenure as commercial director earlier in the year had focused the Glazers' minds on an opportunity to reassess the type of person they were looking for to spearhead United's commercial strategy. In fact, that person was already working for them and, with the credit crunch effectively putting on hold his efforts to refine the club's capital structure, Ed Woodward began to work more closely with the Glazer family on United's sponsorship direction. This coincided with the swift appointment of a new Manchester United commercial director, who was initially given the somewhat more grandiose title of 'director of global partnerships'. Richard Arnold had been a contemporary of Ed's at Bristol University and had been pipped to the post by Lee Daley's appointment the first time round. A confident, outgoing and quick-witted character, Richard also had a memorable claim to fame: in his previous employment he had been posted to Saudi Arabia where, as a keen rugby player, he had ended up representing the Saudi national team.

'Asia'

By the end of 2007, the cramped office in Belgravia had become a hive of activity, as Ed Woodward and Richard Arnold, in league with the

Glazers, forged a new method to generate sponsorship income. It was so brilliant in its simplicity that I would spend the best part of two years trying to keep it under wraps in order to maintain a proprietorial lead over the club's rivals.

Corporate sponsorship has long been a key revenue stream for all football clubs to tap into. The sport can use the passion and excitement it evokes among its loyal supporters to appeal to those firms keen to embellish their profile and reputation by associating with a particular team. Sponsorship revenues tend to be highly profitable – as much as 90p in the £1 – and there are relatively low costs involved in servicing a sponsor beyond the money originally invested to secure the initial contract.

Sponsorship works on two levels: advertising space and brand association. Conventionally, all football clubs provide billboard space for sponsors to promote their wares via players' and coaches' kits and, inside the stadium, on advertising hoardings around the pitch perimeter, and all in conspicuous view of television and newspaper cameras. By the time the Glazers had bought United, advertising had already reached a more sophisticated level with a more developed infrastructure allowing for an ever-growing platform for sponsors. The electronic 'digiboards' on the field perimeter wrapped around the West, North and East Stands are viewed by a global TV audience, enabling a constantly changing variety of sponsors that, by using state-of-the-art graphics, can be synchronised according to time zones. The club's growing sphere of publications – as well as the official website and the in-house MUTV channel – provided further lucrative advertising space.

The second level of sponsorship – the identification and exploitation of a club's 'brand' – is usually limited to the top football clubs. It was spearheaded by Manchester United after the launch of the Premier League in 1992, and was refined by the Glazers.

The Manchester United brand carried tremendous allure, yet it was incredibly elusive to define. Speaking of it loosely would also prompt contempt among some traditional supporters who resented how their club had been wrested away from them in pursuit of naked profiteering by outsiders like the Glazers. Even during off-the-record chats with journalists, I would only mention the 'brand' discreetly, acutely aware of its overtly commercial resonance which arguably countered the romanticism of the English game.

Manchester United's brand constituted of a number of separate parts, whose whole was considerably more valuable. Of course, the tangible club crest – which would sell a multitude of official (and counterfeit) merchandise – was highly evocative and had become one of the most recognised trademarked logos in the world, comfortably trumping its football club peers. This crest would excite true passion and irrevocable love from its supporters, who would wear the badge on their shirt or scarf on a match day and, during the rest of the week, would sport a key ring or even a credit card with the United crest on proud display.

However, among a domestic audience, the club could provoke an ambivalent reaction: pride among its loyal supporters, but animosity from rival fans. It would mean that more parochial sponsors would have to endure tacit boycotts from opposing fans. Among the reasons why Vodafone sought to end its deal with United was the fact that their mobile phone offer did not sit well with rival football supporters from Liverpool, Leeds and the blue half of Manchester. But it was United's *global* brand, which had begun to be extensively marketed during the Premier League era, which gave the club an edge over its English rivals. A sponsorship deal targeting a Korean or South African market was far less likely to carry the baggage and vitriol of an English link-up.

The club's crest also carried a 'luxury' premium among many countries overseas, thanks in part to its apparel partner, Nike, which since 2002 has used its high end stores and sophisticated promotional advertising campaigns to position football in general – and United in particular – as a high-end brand outside the UK.

The Glazers approached sponsorship laterally, understanding that potential sponsors were keen to embellish their image, as well as their profile, by associating with the world's best-supported sports team. This was illustrated by the 2006 shirt deal with AIG. Why would a hitherto barely recognised company in the UK want to sponsor an English football club when it didn't have a particular UK business to promote? Clearly, the partnership was not implemented primarily to raise its profile among Old Trafford's 70,000 home fans. Rather, the American insurance giant appreciated that United's global footprint matched its own, especially with its significant operations across Asia. AIG sought to grow the value of its own brand among clients and customers in Asia, who would see the logo emblazoned on players' shirts, thus allowing its executives to boast the corporation's association with the cachet and the success of Manchester United.

This concept was not new, since Formula 1 teams had pioneered sponsorship deals with corporate partners. While offering paddock access at a race, and television footage of the logo on a car driven at high speed, top Formula 1 teams like McLaren and Ferrari also provided sponsors with a year-round association with a glamorous brand that could be used by a sponsor away from the circuit to tap into its corporate audiences.

Under the Glazers, Manchester United's commercial appeal would not be confined to the growing number of logos it could squeeze onto the board behind the manager as he gave his post-match television interviews, but it was theoretically limited only by the club's resources to capture as many deals as possible.

Manchester United already had an undisputed reputation for sound commercial sense before the Glazers took over the club. Its groundbreaking 13-year, £300 million apparel deal with Nike (preceded by lucrative shirt sponsorships from Sharp and Vodafone) was recognised as the biggest in the business. Like other football clubs, United had succeeded in building many categories of sponsorship: official car, betting partner and travel agency partner. The club was also early to see the value of relationship marketing by offering sponsors the use of its huge database of loyal fans.

During my travels I was regularly asked: 'Why do United enjoy such a high global profile?' There was no simple answer: in my six years I learned at first hand that Manchester United's worldwide appeal surpassed football; its iconic status within British cultural life, I discovered, was on a par with the BBC, say, or even the royal family. Clearly, the successes the club had enjoyed over many decades were a key driver, in particular its European Cup triumphs. Manchester United's brand also embodied an exciting, attacking brand of football pioneered by Sir Matt Busby's Babes and taken to new heights during the 1960s, and subsequently the 1990 version led by Sir Alex Ferguson. Star players like George Best, David Beckham, Cristiano Ronaldo and Wayne Rooney became global brands themselves thanks to television coverage and frequent overseas tours.

The Munich air disaster also had a significant and lasting bearing on United's global support. Into their second European Cup campaign, the Busby Babes came to epitomise the virtues of an England team many years before Sir Alf Ramsey led the bona-fide national side to World Cup triumph. In 1958, the shocking news of the Munich crash – with the accompanying black and white still and moving footage of strewn wreckage – were widely disseminated due to advances in instant news gathering; this created an enduring wave of sympathy around the world for a club in mourning.

More recently, as England's most supported team, Manchester United would spearhead the growing appeal of the Premier League, which Sir Alex Ferguson's teams came to dominate following its inception in 1992. By the advent of the 21st century the club had signed a multitude of merchandising deals, had even tidied up its crest by controversially removing the words 'football club' from the logo and had set up a series of branded shops and cafes with local partners across the world. In 2001 the then chief executive Peter Kenyon had trumpeted a joint marketing partnership with United's globally recognised sporting counterpart – the New York Yankees baseball team – although I never divined how meaningful the tie-up was beyond the huge media bluster that the announcement prompted.

In 2005, when the Glazers bought Manchester United, there was considerable scepticism as to how the Americans could grow the club further commercially, the consensus being that the brand had already been sweated and – with Chelsea and Arsenal in the ascendancy – United's eminence was on the wane, in any case.

However, the Glazer family – perhaps benefiting from the big picture objectivity that being based afar provided – believed there was plenty of opportunity to advance the allure of Manchester United's brand around the world. Most obviously, they thought, in Asia and the Middle East where United was as synonymous with glamour and success as the Italian carmaker Ferrari, say, is to a non-automotive audience. Back in late 2005, inside the directors' private lounge at Old Trafford, I recall asking Joel Glazer a simple question regarding his family's intentions with Manchester United. 'Asia,' responded Joel with his habitual pithiness. 'That's where we see the growth potential, Tes. The club's barely scratched the surface over there. Manchester United is already huge there, but it could be so much bigger.'

333 Million

The Manchester United brand would not just be sweated; under the Glazers it would benefit from a 21st century luxury makeover.

The Glazers achieved this by changing the culture of how the club sought commercial partnerships. They did this by investing more resources into actively searching for new business leads rather than relying on the serendipity of corporations approaching the club. These ideas germinated into the Glazers' decision to establish a London-based commercial office to drive sales, which would then be handed over to a client relationship team based at Old Trafford, which would in turn service sponsors with access to hospitality and facilities, including occasional contact with the manager and the players.

There was a compelling logic to having a separate London office to Old Trafford. London was the country's indisputable commercial centre with a large talent pool and, logistically, it was a key international flight hub with regular connections to every business centre across the world. United's American owners also saw the value in fostering an operation whereby the sales culture would perhaps be more entrepreneurial than that of Old Trafford.

While there had been numerous estimates of the club's global fan base, the Glazers' technocratic approach to their ownership was marked by their seeking a more scientific insight, which would ultimately form the foundation for the club's commercial strategy. Everyone knew that Manchester United was global; the Glazers wanted hard facts to support this. In the first half of 2007 the club commissioned the market research consultancy TNS Sport to investigate the club's reach, implementing a programme that involved thousands of interviews in numerous core countries across every continent including the USA, China, South Africa, United Arab Emirates and the UK. These results were then interpreted using TV audience data, as well as information gleaned from the global use of the Manchester United website to extrapolate behaviour in a further 100-or-so countries. It was conceivably the most comprehensive research of its kind ever undertaken.

TNS supplied United with a huge body of insights into the club's – and its rivals' – global reach, even outlining how United fared against other sports and pastimes in local markets. The headline figures were outstanding: the research estimated that 1 in 20 of the world's population – or a staggering 333 million – said that Manchester United was their favourite team, the most of any club in the world; from that figure, some 139 million counted themselves to be active fans, substantially higher than a 2003 MORI poll estimate of 75 million. Given that TNS's research was conducted a full eight years after the club's last Champions League victory, and after a four-year period in which the club had gained just the one Premier League title, it was clear that the club had significant potential to expand.

Armed with the research – which drilled down to detailed information on fans' demographics and behaviour in specific countries – the commercial team realised that they could approach hard-headed corporate people who were less likely to be seduced by the glamour of Manchester United per se, but would probably be more impressed by the study's facts and figures which underlined the club's commercial appeal and cost effectiveness versus traditional marketing platforms like above-the-line advertising.

Going Mobile

As well as launching an impressive array of new sponsorship categories, such as an official club wine, a courier partner, even an office equipment provider, the Glazers pioneered a mobile communications strategy, which could be sold into individual territories around the world. While there had been wild predictions that football clubs could look forward to an explosion of revenues as fans tuned into information about their favourite team via their smartphones – especially in Asia – no club had yet succeeded in making this a commercially viable proposition.

The Glazers approached it from another direction and identified an opportunity whereby mobile phone companies might want to use the Manchester United brand to distinguish their offer from rivals'. Moreover, as mobile phone operators tended to market their services in country 'silos', there was a chance to market the club in distinct territories and reap the high margin revenues available on a country-by-country basis. A sponsorship deal would typically lead to the sponsor being granted permission to use the United logo on its promotional materials and website, as well as offering club video and newsfeeds to its mobile subscribers. In addition the sponsor would receive VIP access to Old Trafford for games and hospitality – ideal for entertaining clients and incentivising staff – and would be able to tap into the club's substantial fan database for email shots.

In late 2007 the club announced plans to play a New Year exhibition game in the Saudi capital of Riyadh. While providing Sir Alex's squad with a winter sunshine break, it also gave an opportunity for the club to test the mobile phone market; United's new commercial director, Richard Arnold, would be able to tap into his business network, having previously worked in the Kingdom for a western telecoms firm. I advised that we could improve Manchester United's business profile via media briefings and interviews. It was something the club already did on a piecemeal basis, but I saw an opportunity for being more strategic in targeting high-brow publications in countries where there was a strong awareness of the football club, but perhaps less knowledge of the commercial activity behind it.

My first foray was Saudi Arabia, although I didn't need to get on an aeroplane; rather the Piccadilly Line to Green Park on the Tube for a meeting at the Saudi embassy. The diplomatic immunity from the smoking ban allowed for an unwelcome fug of cigarette smoke to linger in the embassy's corridors as I made my way to the cultural attachés office. He was happy to put me in touch with one of his country's leading papers, the *Asharq Al-Awsat* and, after a subsequent exchange of emails and calls with the reporter, Phil Townsend and I made the arrangements for an interview with David Gill. By the following month we had succeeded in securing a prominent article in the paper to coincide with the club's visit. A simple cost benefit analysis revealed how much better value for money a business profile of the club presented to potential sponsors, as opposed to the expense of taking out a full-page advertisement.

Pall Mall

In early 2008 Ed Woodward moved Manchester United's expanded commercial office into larger premises, occupying the top floor of an imposing building on Pall Mall, one of London's most prestigious thoroughfares. As with Ed's previous office, security was paramount and the identity of 50 Pall Mall's new tenant was discreetly suppressed, with neither a nameplate on the outside door, nor a sign inside the capacious, marble-floored reception.

Apart from player photographs on the walls and the occasional pile of signed merchandise waiting to be shipped out, the dimly lit offices on the seventh floor were bog standard and were furnished with modern, nondescript desks and chairs. The airy boardroom, lined with an internal glass wall, was flanked by the equally modest private offices of Ed Woodward and Richard Arnold. If they cricked their necks through their small attic windows they could both enjoy impressive rooftop views of the Houses of Parliament.

One of the London office's new recruits was a talented young graphic designer, whose brief was to revamp the club's corporate presentations, including stunning digital brochures that drew upon the huge archive of footage from Manchester United's illustrious past. A steady stream of quick-witted, outgoing sales executives were also hired, who worked in small teams centred upon expanding the various category sponsors, including mobile phone companies. The sales team were complemented by a gang of clever but introverted desk researchers and analysts, who focused on digging up intelligence on prospective sales targets. Last but not least, the back office was completed by a crew of hard working PAs and office assistants who gave a new meaning to multi-tasking.

I do not recall a time, apart from perhaps the Christmas parties, when all the colleagues were all gathered together in London. I'm not even sure the office was ever large enough to accommodate the fast growing number of staff. More often than not Ed Woodward and Richard Arnold would be travelling back and forth to the States to meet the Glazers, while it was common not to see sales execs for weeks on end (though it was easy to tell when they were in the building as their battered executive luggage would often block up the narrow office aisles).

I always enjoyed the atmosphere at Pall Mall, which I visited frequently for my regular meetings with Ed Woodward. The office always hummed with good-humoured energy and banter; the entrepreneurial can-do culture akin to the activity of the Internet start-ups that, some ten years previously, had revolutionised London office life. A strong team ethic was deliberately shaped by Ed and Richard, who were naturally sociable animals and sought to imbue the fast growing number of London personnel with a 'work hard, play hard' ethos. Hence, they introduced the best practice of regular motivational talks, after work drinks-dos and, importantly, celebrating sponsorship wins through the ringing of an office bell. This would help compensate for the long and unsociable hours that the staff were often obliged to commit to, and served to minimise the risk of any breach of security given the sensitivity of some of the information that passed through the office.

Mounted on one wall was a whiteboard, which struggled to accommodate all the global itineraries of the sales staff. Excursions were made to every world city imaginable, and could typically comprise of a few days in Japan, followed by a whistle-stop flight to Brazil then onwards to the States and Mexico. Meanwhile, other sales execs would hop over to Scandinavia, before flying off to India and China. On first impressions these far-flung travel schedules may have looked glamorous but they were also gruelling, tearing the sales team from any semblance of home life for long periods at a time. This helped to forge strong bonds between the executives, most of whom had an international sales pedigree away from football and were already armed with an address book of diverse multi-industry contacts.

The main challenge for the Glazers was how to advance Manchester United's global reach – regarded as an estimated 1 in 20 people on the planet – while being limited by the club's relatively small resources. To put this into context, United's total annual revenues were approximately one hundredth those of another high-profile UK company – the retailer Tesco – but the club enjoyed a considerably higher global profile. Moreover, while United's brand reach was comparable with a luxury fashion house, it was still light years away from being able to enjoy the same-sized sales force. The Glazers understood this and, although they would commit millions into the Pall Mall operation, their sales resources were always going to be stretched, such was the seemingly limitless scope of pushing the United brand worldwide. By the time I had left the club, United had occupied the ground floor of 50 Pall Mall too, complete with a lovingly-crafted 'Old Trafford' replica table football game. More than 30 people were then working in the London office, with plans afoot to move to a more spacious HQ in Green Park to allow for continued exponential growth.

There was significant journalist interest in 50 Pall Mall, the existence of which I would barely admit, and would never elaborate upon. I got used to reading snide speculation about the 'secretive' London office, which only served to bond the tightly-knit workforce that was in the employ of one of the most famous companies on earth, but that had to work amid such cloak and dagger secrecy.

The Boardroom(s)

An example of the Glazers' ambition and attention to detail was their dissatisfaction with the existing lobby and boardroom on Pall Mall's seventh floor. While looking perfectly fine to my business-like eye, the brothers were keen that these areas should reflect the allure of

Manchester United to any visitor and potential sponsor. In place of a humdrum (albeit well-appointed) London office, they were keen to project a sophisticated ambience akin to an exclusive Ralph Lauren-styled clubhouse.

The work was slow and painstaking as the front office was completely remodelled using high-spec, money-no-issue materials: upon the dark wooden parquet flooring in the oak panelled lobby rested two deluxe red leather armchairs; they flanked a podium upon which was mounted the Manchester United Opus, an exquisitely-produced tome containing hundreds of silver leaf-edged pages of exclusive photos and articles. It would have been the ultimate coffee table book, had it not been too heavy for such a table. On the wall, behind the Opus, was a large United crest, resplendent in silver, in between two alcoves housing full-sized replica trophies.

The cream carpeted boardroom was now accessed through sliding wooden doors. Its huge oak table was surrounded by delicately-crafted chairs covered in the softest of suedes projecting an intimate warmth and sense of tradition that belied the state-of-the-art sound and vision system that had been discreetly installed. One wall incorporated a giant flat screen TV, used extensively by sales executives to show slick promotional films that demonstrated the club's rich football heritage.

Adding a true 'wow' factor was the decision by the Glazers to replicate the London boardroom at Old Trafford. They ordered a complete refurbishment of the executive suite behind the East Stand, the idea being that the Manchester United sales team, having taken part in initial discussions with marketing directors in the Pall Room boardroom, could now host them in similarly luxurious surroundings at Old Trafford on a match day. The suite, more spacious than its London counterpart, was replete with the same cream covered soft furnishings and carefully inlaid wood panelling and boasted a stunning view of the pitch. This was visible through a huge window that, at a touch of a button, split horizontally to reveal a gaping aperture, which allowed in the noise and atmosphere of a match day. Something the club could not control, though, were the outside fans near the box, who projected a less rarefied (and occasionally more profane) air during games. One sales executive told me that a potential sponsor he was hosting had had his beer pinched from his clutches by a particularly cheeky spectator.

'The Crowd was Dead'

There was an element of *déjà vu* to the New Year in 2008, since the team were flying high in the Premier League and were looking forward to another campaign in the knockout stages of the Champions League. In addition, Sir Alex Ferguson would make another of his regular supportive statements about the Glazer family, this time in his programme notes for the first home fixture of the year against Birmingham FC: 'At a number of clubs there have been problems with friction between managers and owners,' Sir Alex wrote, 'But you can see how smoothly the United ship is running as far as that is concerned, despite early hostility over the Glazer family's ownership, those protests were unfair because they weren't given a chance but the Glazers kept their cool and our owners have been nothing but supportive. Good teamwork starts at the top and I am happy to say, that is what we have at Old Trafford.'

However, it was Sir Alex's post-match comments after United's 1-0 victory that made the headlines the next day:[76] 'The crowd was dead,' he remarked. 'That was the quietest I have heard them. We needed them in this game…The players need the crowd to respond and vice versa but it was like a funeral it was so quiet and I don't think that helped us. We need them to motivate us.'

Indeed, after more than two years of attending matches at Old Trafford I was often struck by how quiet the crowd could be. I reckoned this was either due to anxiety among the masses when the team was not quite gelling, or when the Reds' domination of the opposition was so one-sided it almost became boring to those fans accustomed to 'champagne football'. Or, I wondered, was it a repercussion of the growing influx of monied middle classes?

---

[76] Alex: Our fans were dumbstruck, *The Sun*, 2 January 2008

Sir Alex's remarks meant that from then on, during every home match, Old Trafford's frequent periods of quiet would be interrupted by away fans chanting: 'Fergie's right, your fans are shite,' (which would usually stir the 70,000 or so United supporters into a gutsy riposte). Ferguson's comments also prompted a backlash from some fans who, already riled by his support of the owners, complained that 'real' supporters had been priced out of the game. This was a theme that newspaper columnists were keen to pounce upon. The *Daily Telegraph's* columnist, Henry Winter, pronounced:[77] 'For such an intelligent man, Sir Alex Ferguson should really see the link between the loss of noise at Old Trafford and the increase in ticket prices forced on Manchester United by the Glazer family. Strangely, United's august manager decries supporters while also praising the Glazers... The astonishing, greed-driven hike in ticket prices at Old Trafford has disenfranchised some of United's traditional support, the Salford lads who sing and chant. This is not rocket science, Sir Alex... Ferguson needs to call on the Glazers to re-think a pricing strategy which is damaging Old Trafford's atmosphere. No chance.'

But Old Trafford continued to enjoy capacity crowds with tickets at a competitively priced £25 a pop, with the club even having to turn down around 10,000 ticket requests for each home game. Moreover, internal research identified that the vast majority of season ticket holders, contrary to the myth they originated from the London and the home counties, actually came from the Manchester area. Plainly, the facts did not uphold the argument that ticket prices had priced out regular supporters, especially given the hefty discounts that were made available to youngsters and pensioners.

Where traditional support had probably changed irrevocably came long before the Glazers' takeover. The Taylor Report, commissioned following the Hillsborough disaster in 1989, ordered all Premier League stadia to become all-seated, thus making grounds indisputably safer but removing the passionate surges of standing fans. Old

---

[77] Alex Ferguson must listen to heartbroken fans, *The Daily Telegraph*, 5 January 2008

Trafford's much-vaunted Stretford End, for example, held 20,000 fans, which by all accounts had provided for a more raucous and feverish atmosphere in the stadium.

United Steals a March

In January 2008, while the Glazers were determined to keep a lid on the workings of the new commercial strategy, I sought to persuade them that we needed to expand press coverage of the club's improving business in order to increase awareness among potential commercial partners. As usual we had sat on the club's latest accounts – the 12 months to the end of June 2007 – for some considerable time, but we realised that some insight into the numbers (plus news of Richard Arnold's appointment) could create a strong business story. For good measure we also had the TNS-researched data to brief in, including the impressive '333 million followers' figure.

I again turned to the *Financial Times* newspaper. On the Friday night, ahead of our belated London office Christmas party, I put a call into Roger Blitz requesting an embargo for the following Monday's edition. I availed Roger of the club's record gross turnover figure of £245 million, which restored United as the top earning English club. Although I strenuously denied it at the time, internally we were peeved that Arsenal had claimed to have beaten Manchester United when it announced its £201 million full year turnover in September 2007, especially as it had included a sizeable non-recurring, non-football related property development windfall. I also gave Roger the 333 million Manchester United followers number, which to my surprise he was genuinely excited by.

The *Financial Times* duly splashed the story on the cover of its Companies & Markets section with a classic curtain-raiser headline of 'Man Utd to unveil turnover of £245m'[78]. It trailed the official release of the club's results later that week and prompted justifiably cross

---

[78] Man Utd to unveil turnover of £245m, *Financial Times*, 7 January 2008

Monday morning calls from other journalists, irked that they'd not been given the story. But I was also delighted with the following day's coverage, which saw all the broadsheets and tabloids getting excited at the prospect of Manchester United reclaiming its 'richest club' tag and publishing the 333 million fan base figure. The *Telegraph's* David Bond, not for the first time, had stolen a march from his rivals, by noting that:[79] 'United have developed plans to break up a chunk of their sponsorship rights and market them separately in countries around the world... The move is a departure from the traditional sponsorship programmes pursued by clubs with American owner Malcolm Glazer keen to exploit the club's global fan base after research found the club have a staggering 333 million supporters across the globe. Club executives believe that by offering limited rights to the United brand to companies in territories such as China and America, they will be able to significantly boost their revenues.'

However, the publication of United's results would be eclipsed by news of turmoil regarding the Premier League's other new owners. The once-reclusive Newcastle owner Mike Ashley, reputed to have been a Tottenham Hotspur fan, opted to watch his newly-purchased team from the stands rather than the directors' box, mingling with his club's supporters while sporting a black and white-striped Newcastle football shirt that clung tightly to his rotund torso. It was a highly public display of support that delighted some and appalled others. However, it was his decision to fire the Magpies' manager Sam Allardyce ahead of the team's trip to Old Trafford that suggested that Newcastle's desperate pursuit of glory would remain unrequited. Things were also continuing to go awry for Liverpool's owners with reports of an ongoing dispute with their manager, struggles to refinance their debt and talk of renewed interest by Dubai's DIC, which had been usurped by Hicks and Gillett's takeover a year previously. By the end of the month, Anfield's faithful would launch a mass protest at the game against Aston Villa beseeching the Americans to sell to Dubai.

---

[79] Man Utd aim to regain world richest club status, *The Daily Telegraph*, 8 January 2008

By contrast, Manchester United was basking in success both on and off the field. While its owners were nowhere to be seen, the club's chief executive David Gill would endorse Sir Alex's comments about the Glazers as well as the stability that the club continued to enjoy. The full year results showed Manchester United's operating profits (EBITDA) jumping 72 per cent to £80 million, comfortably covering the £42 million interest payments, while group turnover increased strongly to £210m and received largely positive press coverage. Gratifyingly, the record financial numbers were reported to have surpassed Arsenal's. In a series of media interviews, David Gill talked up the TNS research findings, and the *Times*' Oliver Kay commented:[80] 'Did he say 139 million core fans? Yes, almost double the figure outlined in the Glazers' business plan 18 months ago. What is more, a study today will claim that United have 333 million "followers" – more than 5 per cent of the world's population. Some will snort at the figures – and at the notion that such a tiny number of the fan base has visited Old Trafford – but no club in the world, except perhaps Real Madrid, are better at turning followers into fans and fans into customers. Say what you like about the Glazers – and most on the Stretford End have plenty to say – but they, too, are proving adept in this regard, having taken control of the commercial arm in recent months.'

However, while the results achieved precisely the sort of press coverage we had wanted, it was not long before a backlash was unleashed. Supporter groups seized on our crowing about United's commercial power as further evidence of the club's crude, relentless pursuit of the dollar and its disenfranchisement from its 'real' fans. David Gill and I fiercely maintained the truth that the debt was being comfortably serviced by the club's cash flow. However, news that the club was indebted to the devilish tune of some £666 million, in the context of growing credit crunch debt woes, drew increasing resentment from a core set of supporters. The more militant wing would daub slogans in red paint outside David Gill's home in the

---

[80] Record profits for Manchester United bring praise for unpopular Glazers, *The Times*, 11 January 2008

Cheshire village of Bowdon, just one month after the Glazers had had red ketchup thrown at them upon leaving a Manchester restaurant. While David and I would shrug off the attacks, such acts – which the press were happy to give the oxygen of publicity that the hooligan fringe craved – crystallised my ongoing realisation that for a small minority of supporters, a winning team was irrelevant.

The American *International Herald Tribune* captured the paradox of English football when it wrote:[81] 'United is top of the English league, and top of the world money markets so far as soccer is concerned. So, all's well with Manchester and the Glazer family that owns it? Not quite. The initial small pocket of dissidents is larger now that everything about being a United follower is more expensive – and with Malcolm Glazer and sons about as visible around northern England as UFOs, David Gill, the club's chief executive, an Englishman, bears the brunt of disaffection. His home was vandalized last week, and daubed with graffiti proclaiming: "Judas Gill – Glazers Out". No one disputes that England's Premier League has become the world leader in terms of high finance and global marketing... But do [new owners] understand what they are getting into? Do they understand the English, or the culture in which one's soccer team is very often an extension of one's pride and personality?'

The 50th Anniversary

After the Manchester United team returned from its five day trip to Saudi Arabia, the club set its focus on the impending most important day in the club's calendar that year: the 50th anniversary of the Munich air disaster. Press interest was huge, so much so that, a few weeks ahead of the anniversary, the club reserved an entire morning at Carrington for a series of media briefings and interviews. The interviewees were led by Sir Bobby Charlton and his fellow surviving teammates from the crash, including Bill Foulkes, Harry Gregg, Kenny Morgans and Albert

---

[81] English winter chills American investors, *International Herald Tribune*, 21 January 2008

Scanlon. As they relived their memories some former Busby Babes could only whisper their thoughts, while others struggled to hold back their tears. The ex-players' testimonies were utterly harrowing and were so vivid in their detail that each of these elderly men appeared to regress right before our eyes into the shocked survivors from that traumatic winter's day in 1958. Further fascinating insight came from the journalist David Meek, who would eloquently describe the tragedy's impact on the city and beyond in many media interviews. Meek had replaced the *Manchester Evening News* reporter, Tom Jackson – who was one of eight journalists to have perished – and went on to become Sir Alex Ferguson's ghost writer for the matchday programme.

I came away from the press briefings feeling profoundly moved. I also had a firm realisation as to why this disaster had such an enduring effect on Manchester United Football Club, and why the commemorations were being given such prominence. The briefings also seemed to stir something very special in the press members that day and would prompt some of the most thoughtful and inspiring journalism I would ever read about the club.

The memorial was held at 2:45pm on 6th February, a cold and cloudy Wednesday afternoon. The service took place in Old Trafford's Manchester Suite, which had been transformed into an intimate chapel, the platform dominated by the club's crest, uplit in red, and simple red and white roses flanking the modern wooden altar. The room was packed with around a thousand carefully invited guests, all wearing respectfully dark attire, the club's senior employees identifiable by their red club ties and crested blazers. The ownership was represented by Avie, Joel and Bryan Glazer who sat inconspicuously towards the front of the room. Following a captivating and beautifully-made black and white film evoking that fateful day, the service then marked the precise moment that, 50 years previously, the ill-fated Airspeed Ambassador crashed after its third attempt at take-off. At the stroke of four minutes past three, Manchester United club captain Gary Neville lit 23 small candles on the altar, representing the lives of each lost member of the United family.

The afternoon's proceedings were led by the club's chaplain, Reverend John Boyers, whose warm, genuine manner helped to lift a deeply sombre occasion into a thoroughly engaging one. In addition, moving tributes to the lives lost were paid by ex-players such as Harry Gregg and Nobby Stiles, the victims' evergreen images displayed in an iconic black and white photograph of the starting line-up against Red Star Belgrade, taken just 24 hours before the tragedy. The ceremony, which seemed to bond everyone together in sorrow and respect, culminated in the unveiling by David Gill of an elaborate memorial in the South Stand tunnel, at which the thousands of supporters who observed the anniversary from outside Old Trafford were able to pay their respects.

The Local Derby

As the day of the anniversary fell on a Wednesday, there had been intense discussion as to how the club would commemorate it on the nearest Old Trafford match day. By a quirk of fate, back in July 2007 the Premier League's fixtures computer had ordained that, on Saturday 10th February, United would line up against its derby rivals Manchester City. In the run-up to the match the club secretary, Ken Ramsden, had spent months liaising with his counterpart at City. While there was broad agreement that the match should be marked by both teams sporting nostalgic 1950s style shirts – which would be simple red and sky blue affairs unadorned with club crests, squad numbers or shirt advertising – there was considerable soul searching about how to mark the start of the event. Ken was adamant that there should be a respectful one minute's silence, rather than the modern custom of clapping, which had become favoured as it tended to drown out any inappropriate heckling. But, given the perceived threat of disruption from mindless fans, there were doubts whether the minute's silence would be observed. In fact it was bizarre how such a momentous occasion could be reduced to such a seemingly trivial talking point, with the press constantly questioning the club's stance:[82] 'Gill was

---

[82] Gill stands firm in face of charges that Manchester United are exploiting tragedy, *The Times*, 23 January 2008

defiant… "On the day of the City game, we have various elements planned and we will have a minute's silence," he said. "We believe quite firmly that this is a tragedy and, though we understand the modern move to applause, like we did for George Best, it is not appropriate in this particular circumstance. We believe it should be a minute's silence. We have discussed this and other aspects with City and we hope and believe that all supporters – including the 3,000 City fans – will respect that and act appropriately." Many believe his faith, and that of the club, to be misplaced, but United have not got to where they are by pandering to public opinion, and they are confident that they will be proved right.'

And Manchester United were proved right: the match's long preamble on a crisp sunny afternoon was choreographed to perfection. The managers, Sir Alex Ferguson and Sven-Göran Eriksson, were led onto the pitch in front of an eerily quiet Old Trafford by a lone piper playing *The Red Flag* while the digiboards on the pitch's perimeter replaced the usual adverts with the names of the victims. After a wreath laying ceremony in the centre circle, the players, with heads bowed and looking resplendent in their simple retro jerseys, were joined by everyone in the stadium for the minute's silence. The emotionally-charged 60-second silence was observed perfectly by home and away fans alike as they held aloft the free scarves provided to them by their clubs. Sadly, it was impossible not to be distracted by some members of the press box as they craned their necks to their right, seeking signs of any dissident City supporters.

While the occasion was one to treasure, the game itself was something best forgotten for the home support, with Eriksson's team getting the better over Ferguson's side for the second time that season. Perhaps the emotion had got the better of the United players that day.

39th Game

A major football talking point that week was a leaked proposal by the Premier League mooting the introduction of a regular 39th game, an extra round of matches played by all 20 teams but in overseas venues, just as the NFL had decided to host a competitive American football match at Wembley. Although the plans were tentative, with one suggestion involving 10 matches in five venues over one weekend, they were reported to have been supported by some clubs, in particular the smaller ones that lacked the overseas profile of Manchester United.

I first got wind of the proposal while up in Manchester for the Munich memorial service. By the time I was on the train down to London the next day the press were feverishly speculating that the 39th game was a done deal, some even presuming it was driven by the greed of the League's new foreign owners. Henry Winter typified the universal outrage of sports writers towards the idea incorporating his trademark scapegoating of the Glazers:[83] 'The Premier League plan is also an insult to all those loyal supporters who take great pride in having been to every match, home or away, in the league. For most, the 39th will prove an expense too far. Arsenal fans will not know whether they are going to the Emirates or the United Arab Emirates. Now we know why the Premier League is the new Klondike for American franchise-owners; why soccer agnostics like the Glazers are really here: it is to take an English institution and float it on the global market. Our game is now theirs.' Other commentators highlighted the likely discrepancies should the 10 extra games take place; conceivably a spectacle for the handful of cities hosting a Manchester United, Liverpool or Chelsea tie, but are Taiwanese fans, say, likely to throng to a match between Wigan Athletic and Blackburn Rovers?

Only a few months previously, Joel Glazer had asserted his objection to any change in the home and away balance of the Premier League status quo to a packed conference audience in London, and I suspected he would not have changed his mind. Speaking with Joel, I was struck by how conservative his family was in his handling of Manchester United affairs. 'No way would we want to disturb the tradition of the current system, it works and it's fair. We are traditionalists,' he explained to me. But sensing the controversial nature of the story and

---

[83] Premier League must not alienate ordinary fans, *The Daily Telegraph*, 8 February 2008

mindful of not wanting to be seen at loggerheads with the Premier League, we agreed to stay away from the pro-and-con argument, maintaining a radio silence on the issue. This was corroborated by my speaking with Phil Townsend, and we deliberately avoided taking any press calls on the subject.

After the initial furore and following a hostile media response, the Premier League's 39th game proposal, starved of unanimous support from its member clubs and football's world governing body FIFA, was quickly kicked into touch. I was then more forthcoming – off-the-record – in expressing the owners' original scepticism towards the plan. Moreover, contrary to the assumption that a club like United would in commercial terms be in favour of such a move, the truth was counter-intuitive. Having invested so much time and effort by taking the club all around the world on overseas tours, did United have that much to gain from the exposure provided by a tournament organised by the Premier League? Surely it was the smaller clubs who would benefit most from the proposal, especially those drawn against the likes of United, who could then bask in its reflected glory?

Barcelona

By the end of April Manchester United were on course to retaining the Premier League title and could look forward to a semi-final Champions League away tie against Barcelona, self-styled by its marketing men as 'more than a club' in the first of a double header. The Catalan capital was basking in beautiful warm spring weather, and romance was in the air as many of the centre's streets were closed off to cars to make way for stalls selling red roses and books, a time-honoured tradition to mark St George's Day.

I had been to Nou Camp a decade previously where I, like many a visitor to Old Trafford, had made a pilgrimage to one of the true cathedrals of club football. Back in 1999 I had witnessed Barça demolish Deportivo de La Coruña 4-0, with goals from legends like Figo, Rivaldo and Kluivert. I savoured the intensely partisan home crowd (who, if disgruntled, would wave their white handkerchiefs at every opportunity) and left in wonder, clutching my souvenir t-shirts and coffee mugs. Nine years down the line I was pinching myself as I stood alongside Ed Woodward inside the lobby of the team hotel on the outskirts of Barcelona. Ed had just been elevated to the Manchester United board and we nervously contemplated the semi-final, the winners guaranteed to play an English team – either Chelsea or Liverpool – in the final.

The press box was elevated high in the main stand giving a commanding view of the pitch and the sea of fans in Barça's blue and red, from where one could also see the distant cluster of travelling Manchester United fans herded into the outer reaches of the towering stand. They were up in the gods, perhaps enjoying the same vantage point from which they had witnessed United's 1999 Champions League victory against Bayern Munich. However, despite more than 95,000 spectators, the game failed to match the first few minutes' excitement; a third-minute penalty miss by Cristiano Ronaldo was jeered with even more schadenfreude-infested fervour by the home crowd, given his alleged desire to play for Real Madrid. This gave way to a stalemate that was dominated by an impressive display by United's hastily rearranged defence (Nemanja Vidic' had a late withdrawal due to illness) aided by a frequently tracking-back Wayne Rooney during some frantic moments. The resulting goalless draw provided for a finely-balanced rematch the following week at Old Trafford, with United fully aware that they would need to put in another flawless defensive performance.

666 Million

On my return from Barcelona I was charged with getting Red Football's accounts to the end of June 2007 into the media, it being the holding company of Manchester United in which the debt officially resided. There was little new in the accounts, as during my briefings over the past six months I had routinely guided on the debt numbers (apart from the 'good news' of an operating profit of £7 million after debt costs had been taken into account). However, I was acutely aware that the news coverage of the accounts would raise the risk of more limelight being shone onto the debt figure, officially standing at £666 million, which would invariably provoke a negative reaction, especially post-credit crunch.

As the accounts would have to be filed by the club at Companies House in London on an annual basis, we had the freedom to disseminate them to the media right up to the time when they were officially posted onto the Companies House website, at which point any member of the press (or public) had access to them. As with the previous year, I decided to speak only to the *Financial Times* to get the numbers reported as accurately as possible. Again, I briefed the paper on a Friday, hoping for as little coverage as possible in the following Saturday's edition. The tactic worked, with a relatively low key article in the business newspaper cryptically headlined 'Man Utd owners are going up,' noting:[84] 'The holding company that owns Manchester United saw both its interest costs and pre-tax profits rise last year, according to results the owners said put the Premier League champions on a more stable financial footing.'

While in the short run I was pleased with the relatively obscure FT article, the absence of any follow-up from other papers was unnerving. But with the second leg of the Champions League semi-final to look forward to, everyone's minds returned to the football pitch. Six days after Barcelona the atmosphere at Old Trafford was equally electric, nobody daring to contemplate the significance should United reach the final on the fiftieth anniversary of Munich and the fortieth of the club's first European Cup triumph against Benfica. Again, the game was a cagey affair, although a spectacular 14th minute goal from Paul Scholes, who had been suspended from the 1999 final, provided a fitting way for United to book their place in the first European final since that dramatic stoppage-time victory against Bayern Munich in the Nou Camp.

The next evening I was in my local North London pub watching the Chelsea versus Liverpool semi-final on television, relieved that United

---

[84] Man Utd owners are going up, *Financial Times*, 26 April 2008

had booked their passage into the final but completely ambivalent about the all England game's result. Half of me spitefully wished against Chelsea getting to Moscow, the other half dreaded the prospect of a Manchester United versus Liverpool showdown.

Within days the club announced an average 6.5 per cent rise in ticket prices, plus a modification to the controversial Automatic Cup Scheme, no longer making it obligatory for season ticket holders to purchase Carling Cup tickets. With United on the brink of securing a historic double, the news met a pleasingly muted response. However, it also became evident that I had managed too successfully to bury news of Red Football's financial results in the *Financial Times* at the end of April. Now that the results were live on the Companies House website, other newspapers would claim to have unearthed them, predictably leading with the £666 million debt figure and widely quoting the Manchester United Supporters Trust:[85] "'Fans celebrating the team's achievements are about to find out how much more they will be asked to pay for the pleasure of continuing to support United with their hard-earned cash," said Nick Towle, chairman of the Manchester United Supporters Trust. "United fans face another ticket price increase on top of big rises for the last three seasons. Another year of high finance costs due to the global credit crunch will mean more and more revenues will be soaked up in servicing debt payments – the new TV deal will not cover it, therefore ticket prices have to go up again and again. Fans are entitled to ask, 'At what long-term price is our current success being bought?'"

As Moscow beckoned, Manchester United's Premier League title chase went to the last Sunday, with the team having to secure a result at Wigan Athletic at least equal or better to Chelsea's outcome against Bolton Wanderers, given United's superior goal difference to their London rivals. A lively match in a packed JJB stadium, sealed by a wonderful goal by Ryan Giggs, provided United with a second successive title win, witnessed by the club's hierarchy including the Glazers.

---

[85] Fans' fear over United debt, *The Daily Telegraph*, 7 May 2008

Although Manchester United had been favourites to retain the title, the club's triumph that rainy Sunday afternoon in Wigan felt profound. The team had already managed to leapfrog a seemingly unassailable Arsenal a few months earlier, but Chelsea's subsequent challenge had felt more threatening. Had Chelsea managed to steal the title back from United, the Blues could have argued that United's title win in 2007 had been a blip interrupting the London side's four year stranglehold on the Premier League. As it was, United's 17th title win would manage to curb talk of Chelsea's dominance, although the true test was just ten days' – and some 1,600 miles – away.

With the season over it was time for the great and good in the football industry to attend the annual Football Writers' Association dinner at London's Royal Lancaster Hotel, also the venue of United's intimate party a year previously. We were there to celebrate the season just passed, which culminated with Cristiano Ronaldo deservingly winning the prestigious Footballer of the Year award, which he accepted with a remarkably graceful and well-versed speech. Despite the formal surroundings, the event was a relaxed occasion, fuelled by a constantly busy bar. It was strange to see so many football journalists all in one place, incongruously dressed in smart suits, most even wearing ties. They were joined in this very convivial atmosphere by many representatives from English football's hierarchy, including United's chief executive David Gill. For one night only, mutual suspicion was put on hold. I attended as an invitee of the *News of the World*; after all the grief the tabloid had given me during the past year, I reckoned I would happily accept its generosity as some kind of payback. As it happened, the evening was a pleasant one with the paper's journalists acting as gracious hosts.

Moscow

A few days later I was apprehensive about the trip to Moscow. The press had been full of nightmare stories about the city's notorious inhospitality and high crime rates. It was the first time that UEFA had ventured as far east as Moscow for the final and there were dire warnings of exorbitant costs and counterfeit tickets galore for those supporters intrepid enough to make the journey. Indeed, with two English clubs in the final, there had been last-gasp calls by some commentators to hold the event somewhere closer to home. But UEFA's spirit of adventure prevailed and provided for two extraordinary days.

Ordinarily I would DIY my trips to away Champions League matches by flying out of London using budget airlines like easyJet or Ryanair. But given the complex logistics of getting to Russia I felt relieved to be booked on the club's VIP trip on a specially chartered flight to Moscow which followed the team's departure by a day.

Manchester's airport that Tuesday morning was bustling with an exodus of United supporters bound for the Russian capital; some of whom I got chatting to were travelling without match tickets. After being fast tracked through the check-in and security, as I approached the departure gate I suddenly appreciated just how VIP my flight was. The club's directors and senior staff were dressed in their regulatory Paul Smith club suits and were joined by their elegantly dressed spouses and a large contingent of expensively attired players' wives and girlfriends. I realised I had committed the faux pas of dressing in my routine travel clothes of scruffy jeans, t-shirt and trainers, that didn't even sport the swoosh trademark of United's official kit supplier. To make matters worse I was also wearing a shabby yellow anorak in readiness of the Moscow rain that had been forecast. I felt truly embarrassed by my sartorial mishap and proceeded onto the aeroplane barely able to look anyone in the eye.

Our arrival in Moscow was chaotic and we all, regardless of our VIP status, had to wait an hour or so around the luggage carousel in a crowded and humid baggage hall where fans poured in from the many chartered flights from the UK. We eventually boarded a coach to our hotel, the Crowne Plaza, where the team had already set up camp. As we sped through the city's traffic, the long journey provided my first glimpse of the sheer scale of Moscow, its sprawling suburbs populated by ugly high-rise tower blocks.

The hotel was situated on the embankment of the Moskva River, in front of one of Moscow's busy ring roads. I delighted at looking down from my bedroom at the cars recklessly speeding past with one of the city's seven iconic, neo-classical Stalinist towers providing a contrasting Communist backdrop. I lost count of how many Rolls-Royce Phantoms and S-Class Mercedes-Benz I saw carving out a special lane for themselves, with their tinted glass windows and their whirring sirens and flashing blue beacons on their roofs, apparently signalling 'I'm an oligarch, get out of my way'.

Breaking away from the United entourage (and feeling safe and comfortable in my scruffy clothes) I took a long walk around the centre on the first afternoon, equally surprised and impressed by the beauty and cosmopolitan vibrancy of the city. That evening I joined my Manchester United colleagues Ed Woodward and Richard Arnold and their wives for a fabulous oriental meal in an alfresco restaurant, for which Joel Glazer – sitting with his wife Angela at a nearby table – kindly picked up the (presumably extortionate) tab.

By the day of the final a thick blanket of cloud had smothered Moscow, giving the city a sultry and humid air. The VIP trip included a post-breakfast coach excursion of the Russian capital; it was like any other coach tour except for the fact that our passengers included Sir Bobby Charlton, former Manchester United owner and chairman Martin Edwards and the football club's long serving directors Michael Edelson and Maurice Watkins (the four men behind Sir Alex Ferguson's appointment as manager). The tour guide's commentary, in faltering English, was memorably stochastic with unintentionally comic moments; at one point, for example, he proudly pointed at a new pipeline to heat Moscow's homes, which looked to my eye like a huge jungle of toxic pipes resting casually atop the pavement without a nod to health and safety.

I left the trip outside the Kremlin – which was more impressive and imposing than I had expected after watching years of Cold War news coverage – and walked for miles around the capital's vast centre. Here, crowds of United supporters and their Chelsea foes were good naturedly gathering around the UEFA-organised fan festivals and the entrances of Moscow's superlative underground stations. The kick-off was relatively late into the night, at 10:45pm local time, and by the early evening the hotel lobby was bustling with activity as well-wishers and onlookers gathered to see off the team. Of particular significance was the sight of Sir Alex Ferguson, David Gill and Joel Glazer huddled in a tight triangle, locked in good-hearted banter, a rare public sighting of the triumvirate and the core of the club's granite-like stability.

The Final

With all of us suited and booted, with tiny Manchester United crest badges tightly pinned to our lapels, we left the hotel with around four hours to spare before the kick-off and boarded the coach for the short trip along the riverside to the Luzhniki Stadium. Its entrance was guarded by an imposing statue of Lenin against the backdrop of two giant red banners, each carrying the crests of Manchester United and Chelsea. The Russian equivalent to Wembley, the Luzhniki Stadium had staged the Olympic Games in 1980 and, more tragically, had also hosted a UEFA Cup match in 1982 when an official number of 66 people were trampled to death. Its ageing exterior was elegantly ornate and was carefully dressed throughout in UEFA's red and gold livery, which had also been adorned on hoardings and flags across the city.

There was a VIP marquee to one side of the stadium and, after a very tight round of security checks, we were shown into the Petrovsky Lounge and were greeted by the actual Champions League trophy on display on a tall podium. The huge interior was beautifully dressed and glamorously lit, even incorporating separate chill-out areas for United and Chelsea delegations as well as further informal seating alongside a spectacular buffet of hors d'oeuvres and main meals, with a generously appointed free bar.

During the run-up to the game the marquee gradually filled with a who's who of world football; everywhere I turned I would see legendary players, many attending in their official capacity as UEFA ambassadors. With so much time to spare before kick-off, it proved a valuable networking opportunity and I introduced Joel, Avie and Bryan Glazer to numerous football dignitaries including FIFA president Sepp Blatter, who mumbled about how far he and Sir Bobby Charlton went back. But my claim to fame that night was meeting

UEFA president Michel Platini. He was a true football hero of mine, a point I was quick to impress upon him as he modestly responded with a nonchalant Gallic shrug.

Platini and Blatter would be joined by Chelsea owner Roman Abramovich and United club officials like David Gill and Sir Bobby Charlton in the stadium's plushest and most luxurious armchairs overlooking the centre of the pitch. Meanwhile the Glazers opted to join the rest of the club's VIP entourage, which included survivors of the 1958 air crash, in the normal hard plastic seats just to the left of UEFA's grandees. The view was still fantastic, although the running track around the pitch would make the game itself feel a touch remote. I found myself sitting next to Bryan Robson, his calm demeanour and frequent witty asides providing a nice antidote to this most tense of games. The match was preceded by a colourful opening ceremony with the obligatory troupe of dancers synchronised to pounding music over the inadequate speaker system. It climaxed with the impressive spectacle of thousands of red and gold balloons being released high into the Muscovite drizzle. And then without much fanfare – there wasn't even an announcement of the team line-up over the PA system – the match began. It got off to a cagey start but soon transcended into a pulsating battle, although I would have very little memory of the actual details, so engulfed was I with nerves and adrenalin.

At half time, with Chelsea having drawn level to neutralise Ronaldo's goal in the first half's dying moments, it felt like United may have squandered one chance too many to take the game. The second half, and the excruciating extra time that followed, saw a Herculean effort by United to contain a resurgent Chelsea and, by the time of the penalty shoot-out, it was anyone's guess which team would lift the cup. I did, however, seize on the memory of that warm August afternoon in 2007 when, as United had faced Chelsea in the Community Shield penalty shoot-out, I had confidently assured my fellow VIP spectators that Sir Alex's team would do it. However, as John Terry prepared himself for the tenth kick of the Moscow shoot-out I was steeling myself for a Chelsea win in front of the club's victorious Russian owner.

Of course, history would be fittingly kind to United, fifty years after the Munich air disaster and exactly four decades after the club's first European Cup triumph. Anelka's penalty was saved by Edwin van de Sar, giving Manchester United the result it so craved. Our initial shock soon broke out into frenzied mass jubilation, with much hugging throughout our section of the rain soaked stadium. Even the normally restrained Glazer brothers a few rows behind me joined in the scenes of pandemonium as we all expressed our intense joy and ecstasy. By the time of that last penalty kick, it was already the following day in Moscow; the celebrations continued into the earlier hours, having followed a wondrous trophy presentation that had been memorable for the explosion of golden ticker tape which had showered Ryan Giggs, Rio Ferdinand and their victorious team mates as they'd been presented with the huge silver cup.

There was no anti-climax: this victory felt as pure as anything I had ever experienced, which also came to crown Manchester United's reincarnation since the catastrophic event in 1958. For the Glazers, the victory meant this most maligned of families became the only people on earth to have won the two biggest titles in world club sport: first the NFL Super Bowl in 2003, now the UEFA Champions League in 2008, a feat perversely ignored by the world's media.

After a quick glass of champagne we were ushered back onto the coach. The sense of euphoria began to give way to some quiet reflection as we mostly sat in subdued shock, beginning to digest the considerable poignancy of the result. I remember too looking forward to attending the post-match party at the Crowne Plaza and even, with the same sense of impatient irritation as a schoolboy wanting to get home from games, feeling that we were having to wait for what seemed an eternity for the last person who hadn't yet made it to the coach. I didn't appreciate it then, but Sir Bobby Charlton had been delayed after being presented with a winner's medal and was busy congratulating the team, something I had totally missed in the exciting aftermath of the win.

The Party

Back at the hotel at 2am, with the players yet to arrive, there was time to shower and dress down for the party. Like the 2007 occasion in London, the principal focus was to celebrate the club's Premier League title regardless of the Moscow result and invitations were again strictly restricted to players, coaching staff, club owners and senior executives together with their partners. But in a happy contrast to London, which on reflection had been tamed by an FA Cup defeat that day to Chelsea, this party would be an unadulterated celebration, certainly the best party I'd ever been invited to, its exotic location and early-hours start providing a unique glamour and magic to the proceedings.

In contrast to the shimmering black theme of the previous party in London, the venue inside the Crowne Plaza was dominated by a brightly lit white dance floor with a live band whose performers were also dressed in white. The bar flowed with French champagne (rather than its sickly Russian equivalent, thankfully) and was used in abundance to toast the manager and players, who gradually arrived well into the Moscow morning. Many had come straight from their changing room celebrations and looked somewhat dishevelled in their rain-crumpled club suits, sporting their Champions League winning medals around their necks. At around 5am a huge breakfast buffet was laid on with chefs cooking up delicious made-to-order omelettes for their ravenous guests. While we ate, David Gill and Sir Alex Ferguson gave touching speeches, interrupted frequently by loud cheering, everyone intoxicated by the sense of historic occasion.

As with the previous year's party, at various points we took turns to congregate at one end of the room, where the club's two major trophies stood on a narrow white table with a red and black curtained background, providing the photo opportunity of a lifetime. Alas, my official photo would also prove to be bittersweet souvenir. While Sir Alex and Ed Woodward joined my side, the photo would be gate-crashed at the last moment by Carlos Tévez who pushed into the middle. For sure, he was entitled to do so especially as he was the first penalty goal scorer that epic night. But Tévez would gracelessly turn his back on the club just one year later.

At one point Joel Glazer introduced me to an Englishman with whom he had roomed as a college student. Joel's friend was an ardent Tottenham Hotspur fan, and it was while speaking to him that I quickly realised that he was the person that Joel had once cited as being partly responsible for switching him onto the Premier League. At last, the missing link! It was great to have eventually met him, especially as we had grown up at a similar time in London so could reminisce about seventies' and eighties' football.

Another special encounter that evening was to share a special toast with Phil Townsend. We were able to mark another key milestone of having worked closely together for the best part of three years. Phil had been a diehard United fan long before he took up the job, but it was the first Champions League win since either of us had worked at the club, and we were both especially moved by its Munich-related poignancy. 'Enjoy every moment of this result Tes,' Phil sagely advised me. 'Who knows whether we'll still be around when we win this title again?'

The Morning After

Although the dance floor was still busy with many of the players in full swing, I left the party at around 7.30am and went to sleep to the hum of the rush hour traffic outside. After only an hour or so I was awake again, the previous night's adrenalin still swirling. Downstairs, the hotel's palm tree-studded foyer was starting to get busy again and I could also see the presence of many television crews and reporters. I was one of the early birds to file to the club's breakfast suite alongside a few of the coaching staff. Gradually more personnel appeared including Sir Alex Ferguson who was still warmly congratulating – and being congratulated by – his close-knit circle of colleagues.

Phil Townsend was also down early, having to consult Sir Alex about a pressing issue: an open-top bus parade in Manchester. Normally, the team's Premier League success would have merited a civic opportunity for the club's Manchester fans to laud the victory; the Champions League triumph on the 50th anniversary of Munich should have made the event an automatic and truly historic one. However, just a week before, violence had broken out in Manchester as Rangers fans had rioted in the city following the team's UEFA Cup Final defeat to Zenit St Petersburg, and discussions between the police and club had already deemed that United would not get the opportunity for a parade. The sense of injustice was palpable and it was up to Phil to confirm the news to the media; it would dominate that morning's interviews with David Gill and would sadly detract from the club's success.

One of my most enduring memories of the trip – indeed of my whole time working for the club – occurred just before we departed for Moscow airport. After the late breakfast I loitered in an ante room, next to the breakfast lounge, where the players' kit was being packed. Sir Alex, beaming like the Cheshire Cat, was sat alone literally on top of the padded silver crate, inside of which was the Champions' League trophy. I proceeded to sit next to him on another case and, while I do not precisely recall our conversation (my brain felt pretty addled by this point) it certainly had nothing to do with football or the events of last night. It was, however, a remarkably special ten minutes or so of inconsequential small talk with someone truly content and in the moment. His infectious state of bliss was not even disturbed when a worried looking young member of the squad, with his winners' medal around his neck, approached Sir Alex to declare: 'Boss, I've lost my passport.' 'Oh dear, why have you gone and done that, lad?' asked the manager in the softest, most benign of tones, offering genuine empathy to the bemused player before volunteering to him a check-list of practical advice on how to find it.

A little later club staff assembled for the departure. We followed a safe distance behind the players, who could bask in the global media gaze and enjoy the rapturous applause from the many onlookers and hotel staff. We forged a corridor created by a red cordon on each side across the large hotel lobby and walked out, greeted by camera flashes as we stepped aboard the waiting coaches. A long coach ride later we arrived at a packed Moscow Airport, although our club entourage was spirited to a brand new private terminal from where we waited for the flight. The plane was delayed, however, and it felt strange how, despite being privy to such a momentous scenario alongside the Champions

League winning players (most of whom were by now dozing off to their iPods) I just wanted to get home and get some sleep.

Even on board the plane we were delayed, but the atmosphere was notably happy and sociable. The players and coaching staff sat, as always, towards the front of the plane, with Sir Alex and David Gill enjoying the prized seats with extra legroom. I sat towards the rear; to my immediate left was one of Sir Alex's sons and his family. Just in front of him was Carlos Tévez, busily nurturing his young baby. A few metres from me, across the gangway, I noticed a slumbering security man with the Champions' League trophy strapped in its own seat next to him.

By the time we touched down in Manchester, night had already descended. After two effectively sleepless days I felt shattered, although we had to wait a little longer while the players streamed through the plane to get off via the rear exit for the photo opportunity of their arrival with the Cup. The long flight back gave me time to ruminate on a historic few days, surely among the greatest in the club's history. The city of Moscow, despite the dank weather, seemed to revel in the occasion and scored well among those supporters lucky enough to have made the trip. Indeed, on reflection, the May 2008 final would represent a high water mark not just for United but perhaps for a simpler era not yet ravaged by the global credit crunch.

There Goes my Summer

Back in London there was little respite after the past few days' excitement. The Glazers wanted to seize on the Champions League final to gauge how widely reported United's triumph was in order to assess the value of sponsoring United globally. This was in particular reference to the shirt sponsorship; although the club was only two years into its AIG contract, Ed Woodward and Richard Arnold were already gearing up the London commercial office to start the renewal process. So we initiated a full-scale analysis of press coverage across the world and I contacted various third parties to help us glean the most accurate assessment of what kind of exposure – and how much value – a logo on a Manchester United shirt could really command.

While I still felt fuelled by the achievement in Moscow – especially its synchronicity with the Munich commemorations – from scanning through the mountain of press coverage I did not feel that Manchester United had received the plaudits it deserved. This may have been due to the very late conclusion of the final (which meant that UK newspapers could barely do justice to the epic game the following morning), the damp squib of the club being denied an open-top bus parade, or even the players' immediate return to international duty for the European Championships. In any case, the aftermath of victory felt unrequited and was as unsatisfactory as my lingering exhaustion and hangover.

Moreover, speculation over the future of the final's goal scorer, Cristiano Ronaldo, would threaten to usurp United's triumph. Stories of Ronaldo's impending departure to Real Madrid had already circulated for a year or so, but within hours of the team's arrival from Moscow, the Spanish football newspaper *Marca* splashed that a deal valuing the Portuguese winger for a world record £70 million had been agreed with the Madrid side. Moreover, despite Sir Alex and David Gill's constant denials, the Spanish press were mischievously suggesting that Real Madrid had done a deal directly with the Glazers. It was nonsense that I sought to quickly quash and, following a call to Joel Glazer, issued a short statement to the press: 'As Sir Alex and David Gill have already said, Ronaldo is not for sale.'

The following week the club put out a further unequivocal 'Ronaldo not for sale' statement, even threatening to report Real Madrid to FIFA for illegally tapping up its star player: 'Manchester United has watched with growing irritation the comments attributed to Real Madrid over their alleged desire to sign Cristiano Ronaldo. The facts are: 1) The player is on a long-term contract and his registration is held by Manchester United; 2) The player is not for sale… No one should be in any doubt that Manchester United will do everything in its power to keep its best players.'

But it would be Sir Alex Ferguson's carefully chosen words that would ratchet up the story to an ever greater intensity and rope the

Glazers ever more closely to Ronaldo's fate at the club:[86] 'The thing people miss the point about is that I've had a couple of meetings with the Glazers,' said Ferguson. 'Their attitude [to Real] is "To hell with them." They would sit a player in the stand. There's absolutely no doubt about it. They'd do it just to prove a point and not to give in to these people. They've got balls, I can tell you. I've been delighted with them in that respect... They [the Glazers] have been good to this club. They've been brilliant owners,' he said. 'All the nonsense about them taking the club over and putting it in debt... every takeover is done by debt. If I wanted to buy Marks & Spencer do you think I could just go under the floorboards and pull out £3 billion? No, I'd go to the Bank of Scotland.'

'There goes my summer' I thought to myself ruefully. Indeed, speculation over Ronaldo's future would grow into a full-blown saga by early June, with Moscow a seemingly distant memory, drip fed by Ronaldo's nuanced press comments at the Euro 2008 championships. I knew from the outset from Joel Glazer that Ronaldo was not for sale, and the manager's colourful insistence that the owners would rather see him rot in the stands obliged me to field scores of enquiries with the simple message that the club would not sell him. Seen in the context of the memorable £666 million debt burden it was obvious that Real Madrid, the player's agent and the media were content to conjecture that the Glazers might have been tempted by a knock-out price for the unsettled winger. A point I acknowledged might be tempting for journalists to believe, before stressing the more humdrum truth: Sir Alex was in charge of his squad and the owners backed him 100 per cent.

The *Guardian* commented:[87] 'The question now is whether United will stay true to their word and refuse to let player pressure affect their decision. Ferguson has spoken highly about the club's owners, the Glazers, recently and this, in many ways, will be one of the biggest challenges the Americans have faced since taking over the club three

---

[86] Fergie: I'll drop Ronaldo rather than sell to Real, *The Sunday Times*, 1 June 2008
[87] Ronaldo comes clean: I want Real move, *The Guardian*, 6 June 2008

years ago. Real clearly believe they have the money to be able to finance the deal and it remains to be seen whether the Glazers can turn that down. If, however, United dig in their heels, the alternative is keeping hold of a player who has made it clear he no longer wishes to be a part of Ferguson's team, and that in turn throws up the possibility of Ronaldo refusing to return to Manchester... Ronaldo's sale would be a devastating blow to the club's hopes of establishing themselves as the best team in Europe over the next few years. By backing down, United also stand to lose face and, for the self-styled biggest club in the world, there might be no amount of money that could make up for that.'

South Africa

As one of the main cheerleaders behind the 'biggest club in the world' epithet I looked forward to flying out to South Africa, where the squad had already embarked on a short pre-season tour, with Mike Phelan having taken over as assistant manager from Carlos Queiroz, who went on to manage Portugal's national football team. Before leaving for Johannesburg I worked with Pall Mall's graphic designer to produce a 'Facts & Figures' brochure, which comprised an at-a-glance statistics-rich guide to the club's global reach, supported by some great photography. It became an invaluable aid and keepsake for journalists around the world, something that we would refine each year into a polished little publication.

While United's trip to South Africa, its third in 15 years, reflected the club's well-trodden habit of flying overseas and playing friendly matches, I was aware of a creeping cynicism among foreign journalists that Premier League clubs were more attracted by the exhibition fees rather than wanting to build meaningful ties with the host country. United were sensitive to this accusation and a huge effort was made for the club to demonstrate empathy and lay down roots with its hosts through initiatives like coaching schools and support for charitable concerns on the ground, particularly via its partnership with UNICEF. In this vein, I discovered that my overtures to the local business media would be greeted favourably. Many of those at the other end of the phone were genuinely shocked that someone from Manchester United was making the effort to reach out to foreign journalists, and I hoped there would be an opportunity to build interest in the club beyond its fleeting visit to that city.

South Africa was a favoured destination for the club; the night flight and negligible time difference minimised disruption to players from jet lag. The facilities were usually first-class and there was a passionate following for football, especially the Premier League with most games beamed live on satellite television. Although I quickly learned that Manchester United enjoyed a deeply ingrained popularity, star African players like Didier Drogba and Emmanuel Adebayor had served to greatly lift the popularity of rivals Chelsea and Arsenal respectively. While the South African sports media also took a huge interest in United, I was charged with raising the club's business profile, mindful that the London commercial team was already busy building a network in Africa armed with insights from the TNS market research. Hotspots had been identified in South Africa (with an estimated 15 million United supporters) and Nigeria, where United would pay a whistle-stop visit.

I based myself in the Michelangelo Hotel in the heart of Sandton, Johannesburg's main business district. It was a vibrant if sanitised shopping mall hub, where security was tight and any semblance of Africa was kept at bay. That said, South Africa's reputation for great value food and wine held up well; I was able to indulge in one of the many perks my job brought by arranging my meetings with journalists in the bustling canteen-like Butcher Shop and Grill restaurant to sample its divine steaks on each of my cholesterol-busting five day visit. The preliminary meetings with the country's main business outlets – which included *Business Day*, *Finweek* and the *Sunday Times* – went well. They offered up the opportunity to provide background on the club's rationale for being in South Africa (training camp a priority, reaching out to fans but also looking to grow club's commercial activities) and even how the credit crunch might be impacting affairs (an opportunity rather than threat). I was really impressed by their understanding of the football business and only wished that my dealings with the English press could be as smooth.

On the second evening, the team arrived from hot and humid Durban into the high altitude cool of Johannesburg where Vodacom, the South African telecoms group that was sponsoring the soccer tournament which United were participating in, held a gala dinner to officially welcome the club. This black tie event was an extravagant affair, with thousands of guests paying a large fee to be under the same roof as Sir Alex Ferguson, his squad and the Champions League and Premier League trophies, both of which were on proud display. It brought home to me the passion that Manchester United sparked not just in the townships, but also among some of South Africa's wealthiest elite.

At the gala I met Gary Bailey, the former Manchester United goalkeeper who had won two FA Cup medals with the club during the early eighties and who was now a Premier League football presenter in South Africa. Phil Townsend and I hosted Gary for lunch the next day where we looked to glean insights into the club's popularity in Africa, although much of the conversation dwelled on Gary's tales from the time before Ferguson had taken over as manager. The following day I proceeded to invite journalists to an interview with David Gill, although I did insist on one rule: no mention of the speculation surrounding Cristiano Ronaldo which had by this time become extremely boring – and irritating – to everyone concerned with the club.

The team were located in the northern outskirts of Johannesburg; The Palazzo Montecasino was a huge modern hotel, styled as a mock Italian palace, situated next to the largest indoor entertainment complex I had ever seen. Its casino, cinemas and restaurants were clustered into a mini-city sheltered by a huge sky dome; this kept Johannesburg's cold winter night chill out while also providing a hermetically sealed 'gun safe' environment within one of the world's highest murder rate zones.

Understandably the hotel provided tight round-the-clock security; autograph-hunting fans were barred from entering its grounds, so the players felt free to wander around its lobbies, cafes and gardens. Much of the time, however, they seemed content to be quarantined to their rooms which were located on the same guarded long corridor, their doors, as was customary, left open to foster a 'community' spirit.

Johannesburg was the first time I would glean an insight into the players' touring lives, which proved to be incredibly regimented with their movements, training schedules, diet and even dress code carefully controlled. On tour, players routinely wore identical Nike training outfits, artfully chosen by the club's gregarious kit man, Albert Morgan. Because of the prevailing security concerns, players were not free to wander outside their hotels so, despite travelling to some of the most interesting locations on earth, a typical day would be mainly confined to their luxury accommodation or the coaches that would transport them to and from training sessions and charity fundraising events. A players' typical day on a non-match day would comprise: breakfast in a hotel's private lounge; a session in the hotel gymnasium; lunch; attendance at a sponsorship or charitable press event; two-hour training session; buffet dinner in private room; bed.

In the meantime the manager, senior club executives and ambassadors would have a busy itinerary spent glad-handing local dignitaries and sponsors, with the chief executive David Gill mostly taking responsibility for media interviews. David's first press meeting under my supervision was with the business television station CNBC Africa. The Palazzo Montecasino provided us with the use of its Presidential Suite, an ostentatious mini palace in its own right which apparently – and appropriately – was a personal favourite of the Zimbabwe president Robert Mugabe. That interview was followed by a sit-down with the print journalists, joined by photographers, in a humbler but still striking meeting room. David was noticeably more relaxed and forthcoming with the South African reporters than their UK counterparts, and the interviews went beyond their allotted time. He was also impressed by how business-like and informed their line of questioning was, and appreciated their adherence to the request not to mention the 'R' word.

Manchester United's third and final game in South Africa was a rematch against the country's biggest team, the Kaiser Chiefs, in Pretoria's Loftus Versfeld Stadium. The atmosphere inside the packed stadium, on that crisp Saturday afternoon, was boisterous and vibrant, the nearest I had got to the 'real' Africa during my trip. The passionate crowd, a huge number sporting Manchester United shirts (both authentic and fake) cheered in equal measure for both United and the Soweto-based team. Manchester United's easy 4-0 victory was received with the accustomed reverence and acclaim accorded to their superstar status. Then the team were whisked off in a private jet to the more uncharted hospitality of Nigeria's capital Abuja where the team played a mock '39th game' against fellow English Premier League club Portsmouth.

The next day, having stayed back in Johannesburg, I was able to read through with some satisfaction a number of articles that had followed on from my relationship-building efforts and from David Gill's interviews. Headlines like 'Man United: The money angle', 'Everything seems to be adding up for Manchester United', and 'Red Devils mean business in SA' reflected supportive business coverage in the country's main news media. This, I hoped, would provide insight into United's global brand strength to the region's business community (and potential sponsors) as much as the club's football prowess, which had already been amply covered in the back pages. Indeed, the success of my South Africa trip would serve as a prototype for future overseas media relations trips, although I would struggle to find journalists as straightforward to deal with (and as fluent in the nuances of football and the English language) as the Johannesburg press.

Part Five
2008 / 09 Season

With the off-season consumed by speculation over Cristiano Ronaldo's future, there was relatively muted discussion over United's actual transfer activity, which involved the signings of Brazilian twin defenders Fábio and Rafael. There were, however, continued reports of Sir Alex Ferguson's interest in Tottenham Hotspur's 27 year-old striker Dimitar Berbatov, which the London club had sought to rebuff.

A New Press Launch

As the new season approached, the London commercial team was in full swing and already some lucrative new deals were in the pipeline. Traditionally an announcement of a new commercial partner lay with the sponsor, but we were keen to offer Manchester United's publicity firepower as part of the deal, spearheaded by a formal press conference launch led by the manager and a selection of players. However, while there would be no problem attracting the media to such an event, the club's Phil Townsend and I were extremely wary of inviting the UK football press, who we confidently predicted would use the access to ask Ferguson or the players salient football questions rather than pay attention to the actual commercial deal.

So Phil and I worked with David Gill and Richard Arnold to design a new type of press launch which sought to serve the overseas sponsor's aim for maximum publicity in their home market, minimising the risk of the press conference being usurped by any unedifying questioning from UK football reporters.

The first new type of launch to be rolled out was the announcement of Saudi Telecom, a result of drawn-out negotiations by Richard Arnold's dedicated mobile sales team. Saudi Telecom had agreed to pay the club a fee later reported to be worth £10 million over five years for the right to use the club trademark on its marketing materials, and for its specially-subscribed mobile customers to access video clips and United content solely in the Saudi kingdom. The media strategy would be confined to my placing it on record in the British press, but otherwise encouraging the Saudi media – herded by the sponsor's rather than United's press team – to report on the deal. This approach seemed particularly prudent given the sports media's then rabid interest in the club's reputed pursuit of Berbatov; also because of the likely identity of one of the players earmarked for the launch event.

On the morning of the first day of the new Premier League season the *Sunday Times*, thanks to some carefully provided guidance, reported exclusively on the deal illustrated with a photo of Evra, Rooney and Sir Alex on walkabout from their visit to the historic part of Riyadh at the start of the year.[88] At Old Trafford, where United were up against Newcastle United, the club's London sales and Manchester servicing teams lavished Saudi Telecom executives with the best corporate hospitality the stadium could offer, followed by a private dinner at the Lowry Hotel. Sadly, though, the team's 1-1 draw earlier that day as well as the teetotal nature of the dinner provided for a rather subdued and formal atmosphere.

The following day at Old Trafford we hosted the press event. Adjacent to the press conference room, in the directors' VIP lounge, Sir Alex and David Gill met and greeted Saudi Telecom officials with a formal exchange of gifts and a smiling photo opportunity. They were joined by United players Owen Hargreaves and, in his first public appearance since all the furore surrounding his future, one Cristiano Ronaldo, who, in my opinion, did not look very happy to be there. Inside the press conference room I was pleased that the atmosphere

---

[88] Red Devils Score – Manchester United sign £10m phone deal with Saudi Telecom, *The Sunday Times*, 17 August 2008

managed to emit a considerable air of expectation; it was filled with Saudi journalists flown in by the telecoms company and was augmented by United's own large press arm (this included journalists from MUTV, the club's matchday programme and the official website). Phil Townsend and I noticed that the conspicuous absence of British football reporters made for a much more relaxed atmosphere, as Ferguson and Gill were confident of receiving no curve ball questions on Berbatov or indeed Ronaldo from the overseas or in-house media. We were also relieved that Saudi Telecom's VIPs, who had flown a long way for the event, were extended the courtesy of actually being asked questions too, unthinkable if football writers had dominated the questions session.

However, I had also briefed David Gill to remain tight-lipped about the club's commercial strategy; one key advantage to inviting only selected foreign media was the opportunity to maintain a shroud of secrecy over the booming Pall Mall venture. The event was rounded up by a photo-call with Sir Alex Ferguson, David Gill, the players and the Saudi Telecom execs on the Old Trafford pitch. Usually this would provide some impromptu special memories for those on one of Manchester United's stadium tours; it was always remarkable to see the excitement on the tour party's faces as they came so unexpectedly near to their heroes.

Phil and I reviewed the considerable positive coverage of the launch in the Saudi press, coupled with the intentionally muted coverage elsewhere, and agreed that this approach would provide a template for all future sponsorship announcements. We would also be careful to ensure that sponsors would be responsible for press invitations to journalists from their own country, which would happily keep us off the hook from accusations that the club had blocked the UK football press from attending.

Blue Moon Rising

The last day of the summer transfer window proved unusually eventful as Manchester United pursued Dimitar Berbatov, despite the

Tottenham Hotspur board's apparent refusal to enter official negotiations. However, a frenetic day for footballing news was eclipsed by an announcement confirming that Thaksin Shinawatra had trousered more than £100 million profit by selling Manchester City to Abu Dhabi's Sheikh Mansour bin Zayed Al Nahyan, described as one of the world's richest men. The deal, reputed to be around £200 million, was supposedly turned around in just three weeks and was brokered by Amanda Staveley, the financier who had worked on the DIC's bid for Liverpool. To get some perspective, Sheikh Mansour's £200 million outlay for City amounted to approximately just 1/100th of his reputed personal oil wealth of around £20 billion. Or, as Oasis songwriter Noel Gallagher, an ardent Manchester City fan, succinctly put it: 'It'll be nice to know that every gallon of petrol that a Manchester United fan buys is going into our transfer kitty.'[89]

For the time being, United fans at Old Trafford would continue to hang their Stretford End banner which so publicly taunted City's supporters with a rolling tally of years since the club had last won a trophy (at the last count 32). But the Arab-owned club's transfer kitty would sorely test Manchester United within hours of the announcement. With the time ticking before the transfer window closed, United were hoping to complete their signing of Dimitar Berbatov, but Manchester City came in with a higher counterbid which would force United to pay more than the original £28 million that Spurs had held out for that summer. Moreover, this did not appear to be mere sabre-rattling by City's new owner, as that very same day City splashed out with a British record signing of £32.5 million for Robinho, the Brazilian forward from Real Madrid. That heady Monday, the front man for Manchester City's new owner, Sulaiman Al Fahim, told a UAE business website that the newly-endowed City would even consider a swoop for Cristiano Ronaldo:[90] 'Ronaldo has said he wants to play for the biggest club in the world, so we will see in January if he is serious. Real Madrid were estimating his value at

---

[89] Abu Dhabi: the Sheikh's real goal, *The Sunday Times*, 7 September 2008
[90] Abu Dhabi boss plans $240mn Ronaldo swoop, arabianbusiness.com, 2 September 2008

$160 million but for a player like that, to actually get him, will cost a lot more, I would think $240 million. But why not? We are going to be the biggest club in the world, bigger than both Real Madrid and Manchester United.'

While overnight reports of the seemingly farcical antics surrounding the Berbatov and Robinho signings galvanised football supporters, the following morning's press sought to gauge the meaning of City's takeover. The *International Herald Tribune* captured the pulse of the new football landscape;[91] 'So deep, in fact, that in the space of one day the Gulf state had changed the perception of the soccer industry, and possibly begun a change in the power structure of Manchester's sporting duopoly. For more than 50 years, United has been a giant of the game, and is the English and European champion; City is a club with its own virtues, but soldiering on through relative poverty among those. Now, it seems, the balance could change.'

United had got their man in Berbatov and I did not sense any alarm among United's owners or senior executives in regard to City's new owners. Rather, another rich owner affirmed the Premier League's attraction, wherein Manchester United continued to enjoy its hegemony. A status that had been achieved through thick and thin over the previous 50 years of exposure and success, and was something that could certainly not be superseded quickly. Such was the fervour that football aroused in Manchester, there was indeed a generous appreciation that United could benefit from a revived competition with the Blue half of a city that deserved two big teams. But the big money that City had available to secure Robinho, and perhaps even Cristiano Ronaldo too, did mark a paradigm shift for the so-called 'Big Four' football clubs. Manchester United, Chelsea, Arsenal and, in particular, cash-strapped Liverpool, might no longer be able to feel sure of their entitlement to a place at the lucrative Champions League table. However, this was by no means felt immediately in a business where results on the pitch dictated the mood off it. City's eventual

---

[91] Blast of petrodollars sweeps out Thaksin, *International Herald Tribune*, 2 September 2008

tenth place at the end of the 2008/09 season suggested that the world's richest-backed club would continue to be a work in progress.

AIG RIP?

From the start of the summer, despite two years still outstanding on the AIG shirt deal, the Manchester United London office had started to explore how to discreetly market the attraction of United's shirt to potential sponsors without antagonising the incumbent. This was triggered by news in June of the ousting of Martin Sullivan, the English boss of AIG, and reports of significant financial losses at the American insurer. I was charged by Ed Woodward and the club's owners to tentatively – and surreptitiously – talk up the merits of United's shirt deal among business correspondents, in particular to convey the 'true' value of the AIG deal. The total value of the deal was closer to £19 million per year (when United's tie-up with AIG's financial services arm was factored in) rather than the £14 million usually cited to benchmark prospective sponsors' expectations.

However, by mid-September my caution proved to be academic as the collapse of Lehman Brothers would augur the hitherto unthinkable fall of the world's largest insurance company. The news of billion dollar losses unleashed understandable press speculation that AIG would no longer honour its sponsorship of the United jersey. However, it was difficult for anyone at United to glean any clear commitment from AIG over the relatively minuscule £20 million-or-so outstanding on the shirt deal, while AIG was engulfed in a raging fight for its own survival.

Coming after the months of speculation over Ronaldo's future, AIG's crisis was a further reminder to me how quickly events would move in the world of football, consigning the celebrations of Moscow to a dim and distant memory. Just a few months on from that jubilant night I was now preoccupied with the impact that a tainted brand like AIG could now have upon United's profile. Beyond this, given that AIG had already paid up front for the right to have their logo on the shirt for the remainder of the season, questions remained as to whether AIG would pay for its final year and whether we could publicly go in search of a new sponsor. These questions became more pressing as it soon transpired that the US government would have to save the beleaguered – but too big to fail – insurance giant from extinction.

AIG's bail out by the US taxpayer prompted opprobrium towards its previously profligate spending on sports sponsorship. So febrile was the atmosphere following the Lehman Brothers' collapse, for the first time I began to track angry speeches on Capitol Hill, wondering whether politicians – indeed the recently elected President Obama – might have the power to break a binding contract with the club, even though there was no clause to unilaterally terminate the deal.

Amid all the uncertainty I rolled out my tried and tested 'business as usual' mantra to journalists, which did not exactly fit with their doom and gloom narrative. Behind the scenes we were as curious as anybody as to whether AIG would be able to see out the credit crunch, but were optimistic that United could look forward to a better deal in spite of obvious concerns about the state of the economy. There was a strong conviction that the threat of the credit crunch represented an opportunity for United, whose commercial team had hedged against the risk of a downturn in the western economies by spending a lot of effort cultivating the Middle East and far east markets, which were relatively buoyant. The sharp depreciation of sterling had made any overseas sponsorship deal with United better value too. Also, while there were reports of other clubs and sports struggling to maintain sponsors, Manchester United could capitalise on its safe haven status as corporate sponsors pursued a flight to quality.

A further announcement that Hublot, the luxury Swiss watchmaker, had signed a three-year multi-million pound sponsorship deal with Manchester United – on top of new partnerships with the Seoul Metropolitan Government, Diageo and Budweiser – provided further optimism that the club could withstand the deteriorating economic environment in the UK. During that autumn, Ed Woodward and Richard Arnold began to formalise the shirt sponsorship process. The Glazers were keen to widen the search from the rushed process after Vodafone's withdrawal in 2005; three years on, United's owners would sharpen their technocratic approach to the process, keen to draw on the findings of the TNS research to target hundreds of companies across the world in the countries where United enjoyed a strong footprint.

'Shirt Sponsorship'

Analysts in the London office compiled a long list of corporations, including sponsors of other football clubs and sports rights. No stone was to be left unturned. In the meantime the Glazers wanted to inject a 'wow' factor into their pitch to chief executives and marketing officers. A mock shirt was created for each company on the list, with a replica of the company's logo carefully printed in white on the front of an extra-large Nike Manchester United shirt, thoughtfully designed to flatter the more rotund recipient. That shirt was carefully packed into a quality black box that had been expensively embossed with a silver logo and branded 'Shirt Sponsorship'. Inside the box was a bespoke hardback brochure featuring dynamic pictures of United players sporting the logo of the targeted company, the message being: 'No need to imagine what it would be like for Rooney to wear your company's shirt…we've already done it for you.' This approach was painstaking and required a dedicated team of graphic artists and administrative staff in London working round the clock to get the boxes ready for dispatch.

The boxes cost a small fortune to produce, but the Glazers were keen to proactively present the Manchester United brand with as much care and attention to potential sponsors as, say, Apple or Gucci does in packaging its products to customers.

By the end of November the club was getting clear signals from AIG that, while it would abandon its high-profile US based sponsorships which included the New York Yankees, the company would honour its remaining 18 months on the Manchester United contract. It wouldn't obviously be seeking to renew the deal. Press speculation was already rife that a string of companies such as Saudi Telecom and Korea's LG were lined up to take over from AIG. Thus, before the year was out, the green light was given for United to start its extraordinary mail shot. This initiative was surrounded by the obligatory veil of secrecy; the club wanted to retain an element of surprise (as well as the allure of exclusivity) although, if truth be told, many hundreds of sample shirts were to be dispatched.

By early 2009 all the boxes had been sent out and London sales executives began to work their phones to set up preliminary meetings with the companies that had received the shirt on spec and who wanted to pursue a dialogue. This led to a core sales team scouring the globe for a series of sales meetings. Armed with Apple Mac laptops loaded with sophisticated statistic-rich PowerPoint presentations and fast-paced videos of the team in action, sales teams were buoyed by the belief that, even if a shirt deal weren't forthcoming, perhaps a chance to foster a business relationship would be. Indeed, it could lead to another type of sponsorship opportunity.

It was inevitable that United's novel way of seeking a new shirt sponsor would find its way into the public domain. Early on we had received anecdotal evidence that the sample shirts were being proudly worn by either the recipients or their children, and some pictures of their new owners were being posted onto the Internet. It seemed a variety of companies were leveraging the opportunity of receiving the pack to raise their own media profile; this was particularly annoying for me, as I had to deal with a constant round of speculation from overseas media – from Kuala Lumpur to Kuwait – but it was a useful testimony to the power of the Manchester United brand.

Tokyo

As winners of the UEFA Champions League, Manchester United qualified for an opportunity to play against other continental confederation cup winners for the FIFA Club World Cup in Yokohama, Japan. I flew out to Tokyo to replicate the relationship-building with the local business media that I had done in South Africa, and duly arranged interviews with the club's chief executive David Gill. However, the huge Tokyo media market proved a harder nut to crack, not least because of the significant language barrier; my Japanese did not extend beyond the most rudimentary sushi menu.

While the team were based in Yokohama – a fast train ride from Tokyo – I arranged to stay in the capital's vibrant Shinjuku district. As in Johannesburg, I set about approaching the country's main business newspaper journalists, who held huge sway in a country still hooked on the printed word, some of whom were receptive about finding out more about the club. Although Tokyo seemed affluent, after speaking with the journalists I was struck by how the lengthy period of economic stagnation had gripped Japan, and how this extended into their suspicion of the club's debt, inviting intrigue as to why it was optimistic that it could grow its commercial revenues against strong global headwinds. While Japan had spawned United's very first shirt sponsor – the electronics firm Sharp – I didn't feel that the country represented particularly rich pickings for the commercial team, especially since our internal research showed that United's appeal in Japan was uniquely fickle. It was generally contingent upon the allure of a star player like David Beckham or Cristiano Ronaldo rather than loyalty to the club as a whole.

I introduced David Gill to journalists from two newspapers, the *Nikkei* (Japan's equivalent to the *Financial Times*) and the *Sankei Shimbun*. We met in a cavernous banqueting room at the team's rather soulless hotel, the Pan Pacific Yokohama Bay Hotel, outside which a small group of around 30 Japanese fans, mostly female and clutching photos of Ronaldo, had created a vigil in order to catch a glimpse of their idols going to and from training. After the customary exchange of business cards and polite bowing, the interview was surprisingly robust with the journalists illustrating their thorough knowledge of United and indeed the global success of the Premier League. David appreciated the informed line of questioning and his candour and bullishness about the club's recession-proof prospects served to produce two high-profile interviews in both newspapers in the ensuing days.

My last evening in Tokyo was spent at the International Stadium of Yokohama attending the semi-final between United and Gamba Osaka. My rush hour commuter train to Yokohama was packed with impeccably well-behaved supporters and families, many of whom had taken the trouble to sport whatever original Manchester United clothing or accessory they could. Outside the stadium were a surprisingly large number of heavily-built Englishmen flogging counterfeit United merchandise. Inside, the atmosphere was as safe and benign as one could imagine. Although the opposing team were Japanese, the 68,000-odd spectators all seemed to be rooting for United as well as Gamba. And because this was Japan, where the audience seemed half male, half female, it was the women's shrill cries just as much as the men's yells that rang loudly around the stadium.

United would outclass Gamba on that cold night, although the 5-3 final score suggested the team were either a touch complacent or, like me, still suffering from *Lost in Translation* jet lag or a combination of both. However that evening was most memorable for Sir Alex Ferguson's post-match press conference, when he slammed suggestions that he had agreed a deal with Real Madrid to sell Ronaldo: 'You don't think we'd get into a contract with that mob, do you? Jesus Christ. I wouldn't sell them a virus. So that's a no – there is no agreement between the clubs.'

On my return to England, with the Christmas tree newly installed in the living room corner, I watched Manchester United winning the Club World Cup against Ecuador's Liga de Quito on TV. While the trophy would not carry the prestige of United's brace of titles won earlier that year, it was the first time that an English club had lifted FIFA's club trophy. Just as United were the first to win the European Cup, the club's pioneering spirit had written a new chapter of football history.

No Press Release; No Press Briefing; No Press Interviews

Manchester United began 2009 as reigning Champions League, Premier League and now Club World Cup champions. A historic quadruple was also on the cards; the team were in all three domestic competitions and could look forward to the knock-out rounds in Europe.

United fans could also afford a wry smile at their newly-enriched neighbour's efforts to try and prise Kaka from AC Milan for a reported

£150 million and the promise of a £500,000 salary package per week. Manchester City's chief executive Garry Cook – in response to the news that Kaka was not for sale – was not very gracious, memorably claiming that the Milan club had 'bottled' the deal.

January usually signified the time of year that we routinely published the club's annual accounts. The latest set, which had sat in my email inbox since the autumn, applied to the 12 months to June 2008. The results showed a record turnover of £256 million, up 22 per cent from the previous year; this reflected domestic and European success which had in turn led to a surge in television monies, pushing operating profits above £80 million for the first time. However, the results also revealed accounting losses partly because of the debt interest charge, but also reflecting the large write-down of goodwill, a legacy of the takeover but something that had absolutely no bearing on the club's cash-rich finances.

By early March, Manchester United had displaced Liverpool at the top of the Premier League and had faced the first test in its pursuit of a potential quadruple, namely the Carling Cup final at Wembley. After a truly spiritless encounter against Tottenham Hotspur, United comfortably won a penalty shoot-out to lift the trophy. The lack of many football highlights led to the media latching onto United's hero of the hour, goalkeeper Ben Foster, who attributed his bravura performance to his touchline review of Spurs' spot-kick habits via an iPod.

However, the unconvincing form on display at Wembley was to be severely tested two weeks' later, when Liverpool looked to have revived their challenge with a 4-1 win at Old Trafford. United then slumped to a 2-0 away defeat to Fulham at Craven Cottage, the splendidly antiquated ground reverberating to a home team that had capitalised upon two red cards shown to Paul Scholes and Wayne Rooney, as well as a petulant performance from Cristiano Ronaldo. Manchester United still clung on to the top position in the League, but the odds began to widen as to whether they could retain their title.

Similarly, as the world's financial markets slumped, journalists began to pick up on the poor performance of Manchester United debt which had been traded, albeit infrequently, since the takeover. Of course, all debt prices had slumped and it was completely irrelevant to the daily workings of the club, but it served as another stick with which to beat the Glazer family; The *Guardian's* David Conn delivered the last word via his trademark exasperation at the Glazers' complex financial dealings:[92] 'The discovery that this debt in Manchester United is now a commodity on the screens of City traders drives home the still-staggering facts of the takeover. Here was a great, pre-eminent football club that prided itself on being well-run, owed not a penny to anybody, financed Sir Alex Ferguson's awesome achievements and rebuilt Old Trafford entirely with cash, yet was loaded up with £667m of debt, massively more than any other football club ever, solely to pay for the Glazer family, whom nobody wanted, to take over the club.'

UEFA were also making noises about wanting to clean up the football finances of elite clubs and to impose greater financial discipline. Following a string of critical pronouncements about debt by its president Michel Platini, the media inferred that UEFA actions could spell bad news for the Glazers' Manchester United. In fact the club, which continued to generate growing revenues (of which wages accounted for a sustainable 50 per cent) was a key supporter of Financial Fair Play (FFP). Alongside other well-managed clubs like Arsenal, United hoped that FFP would curb the profligate spending by clubs like Chelsea and Manchester City, which could not support their way without being underwritten by the largesse of their billionaire owners. Although the devil would be in the detail, Manchester United proceeded to work cooperatively with UEFA to reshape a landscape that would limit spending on players to income generated by clubs, rather than their sugar daddy benefactors. It was a move that could have potentially cemented United's edge over richer newcomers.

While Manchester United were able to restore their composure after the humiliations of Liverpool and Fulham with a string of spirited victories – the true sign of a great team – the media continued to wax

---

[92] United's massive debts now at mercy of the market, *The Guardian*, 25 March 2009

pessimistically about the club's prospects away from the pitch. There was general consternation as to why United should carry on with AIG, given the insurance giant's bailout by US taxpayers. Jim White, the *Telegraph* columnist commented: [93] 'AIG is considered the most inflammatory three letter phrase in the English language; to sport it in public would be a criminally provocative act. So violent has reaction to the company become that AIG staff were this week advised not to wear any clothing carrying the corporate brand. Meanwhile, the chief executive Edward Liddy has suggested that the name is now "so wounded and disgraced" the only way forward is to change it. In short, it means that if the Glazer family hope to reduce some of their gargantuan borrowings by flogging a few shirts in the States, then they had better get busy with the scissors.'

By the start of April, having sat on the 2007/08 accounts for a few months, the clock was now ticking for United to have to file them in the public domain with Companies House in London. Previously I had sought to spin the accounts by releasing them earlier in the year to selective journalists, bolstered by an interview with David Gill. However, this time, David had no appetite to engage with the press given the constant speculation surrounding Ronaldo's future. So, a decision was made to simply lodge the accounts, alert the media and stand back. My email to the press provided the notification that the accounts had been filed, accompanied by a terse message: 'There will be no press release; there will be no press briefing; there will be no press interviews'.

Suffice to say I received a torrent of bemused phone calls from hard-pressed journalists who were not only angry that we had not guided them in line with previous years, but were also genuinely requesting help to decipher the hundreds of pages of complex accounts which applied not only to Manchester United but to Red Football and Red Football Joint Venture too. My response was defensive: 'I understand where you're coming from, but that's how we're doing the accounts

---

[93] It's the damned brand United: Old Trafford tarnished by AIG, *The Daily Telegraph*, 27 March 2009

this year.' Paul Kelso of the *Daily Telegraph* summed up his and his fellow colleagues' frustration with our awkwardness with a predictable sideswipe at the overall debt figure:[94] 'In a move that suggests a degree of disdain for supporters who have taken a keen interest in the club's finances since the Glazers took control in 2005, United and the family chose not to comment on results that showed debt with the ultimate parent company had spiralled to £699 million. Instead they were left to draw their own conclusions from a trawl through the occasionally Byzantine structure of England's dominant club... last night fans were left to reflect on confirmation of the Glazers' legacy to United; a burden of debt that leaves even the most commercially astute and successful of clubs running to keep up.'

'Fergie, Fergie, Sign Him Up'

The club's attempt at an historic quadruple trophy clean sweep came to an end with another lacklustre display at Wembley in a goalless FA Cup semi-final against Everton, which the Merseysiders won on penalties. But United did manage to cruise to another Champions League final following a resounding semi-final defeat of Arsenal, which United won with some élan in the second away-leg at a shocked Emirates Stadium after going 3-0 up after just 11 minutes.

The Premier League was drawing to a climax, too, with Manchester United requiring only a draw against Arsenal in their last game of the season at Old Trafford to beat off Liverpool and secure the title for the third consecutive year. The match proved a tight affair with Arsenal obviously seeking to avenge their Champions League humiliation of a fortnight earlier. However the defining moment of the game came with the 66th minute substitution of Carlos Tévez for Ji-Sung Park. Tévez waved to the crowd, which was reciprocated with a standing ovation. In my mind this was bizarre, as this was a player who, in pre-match interviews, had shown brazen disloyalty and had hinted that he might

---

[94] £699m debt raises United concern, *The Daily Telegraph*, 10 April 2009

well leave the club. The game petered out into a goalless draw, providing Manchester United with its eleventh Premier League title, and equalling Liverpool's 18 top-flight trophy haul. Apparently it was only the second occasion that Sir Alex Ferguson's team had clinched the title at Old Trafford; his ebullience, which I witnessed at close quarters from the players' tunnel at the end of the game, was plain to see.

However, when Ferguson gave his customary post-match, end of season speech of thanks to the home supporters who had stayed on to watch the squad receive their medals and parade the Premier League trophy, I witnessed something quite unbelievable. Sir Alex was actually being jeered and his words were being drowned out by a voluble proportion of the crowd who incessantly chanted, 'Fergie, sign him up, Fergie, Fergie, sign him up,' a common refrain at matches in the previous few weeks among those wanting the club to extend Carlos Tévez's contract beyond the two years he had already spent at Old Trafford.

While it was tempting to dismiss the chants as just cheeky ribbing of the manager, the atmosphere inside the stadium struck me as being more foreboding. Those chants marked a degree of dissent towards a manager who had just steered the club towards a historic title. Indeed, those scenes from that warm, sunny afternoon would haunt me for the rest of my time at the club, symbolising the moment when some supporters' delight at winning on the pitch had become eclipsed by their mounting frustration with actions off it.

Even with the club in touching distance of Rome and the game's highest honour, the mood of some United fans had become ever more contemptuous of the Glazers. Whether it was the daily diet of United's 'crippling debt' across the press (compounded by, I suspected, our ham-fisted refusal in April to comment on the accounts), the feeling of resignation among fans that Ronaldo wanted to move to Spain, or their despair at reports that Tévez also wanted a transfer, it was the distant American owners who remained the focal point for supporters' deep frustrations. Sir Alex Ferguson and David Gill were mere proxies for their anger.

Just after the Premier League title win, the club announced that season ticket prices would rise by £1 per match for the next campaign. This would further antagonise many supporters. While the rise was modest, it bucked the trend of other big clubs which had frozen or even reduced their prices as the recession bit harder. Despite the rise, the cheapest ticket for an Old Trafford seat would cost £27 and the most expensive would cost less than £50, still good value when compared with most of Manchester United's rivals (tickets to watch Newcastle United, for example, ranged between £25 and £60). Nevertheless, the Manchester United Supporters' Trust's comments were widely reported in the press: 'It has been said in the past that the owners of the club will squeeze United supporters until the pips squeak, and this is clearly the case.'

While the owners had continued to give free rein to Sir Alex over transfers, Ferguson and David Gill reportedly balked at paying the previously agreed £32 million to Carlos Tévez' 'owners'. This led to an acrimonious stand-off, with Manchester City happy to step into the breach and, in any case, trump United's offer. But for United, the Tévez saga represented something purer: a player dissatisfied with Sir Alex's tried-and-tested rotation system would become dispensable regardless of his merits. No player was bigger than the club.

Aon

All the off-the-pitch issues would thankfully melt into insignificance, at least for a few days, as Manchester United prepared for its second successive Champions League final, against Barcelona in Rome. That's what I had thought, but on the flight out of Manchester a fatigued looking commercial director Richard Arnold ushered me to join him in a quiet section of the plane where he revealed the identity of the club's new shirt sponsor. The media had for weeks speculated that an announcement was imminent, and the insurance giant Prudential and the banking group Standard Chartered had seemed to be in pole position. Indeed, both organisations' marketing big-wigs had enjoyed the club's matchday hospitality in the directors' box as negotiations had slowly progressed.

But Richard Arnold's unusually dishevelled state was down to him having just switched planes from a flight from Chicago, where United's new sponsor Aon Corporation was based. The deal had been finalised only hours before and was due to be signed off in Rome by Aon's bosses who were last-minute invitees to the game. The obvious question I asked Richard was the value of the deal, which, to my relief, would trump the incumbent AIG despite the deepening global recession. I felt pleased, too, that a tiresome chapter of constant speculation was coming to a close. I did, however, begin to feel preoccupied with the midwife-like responsibility of having to deliver the news to the wider world.

The Aon deal had been a direct result of the London office's speculative mailout. A sample shirt had landed unsolicited on the desk of Aon's new marketing head, Phil Clement, who was subsequently approached by the sales team with the offer of a presentation. The eventual tie-up with Aon, following many transatlantic air miles, reflected the same logic of United's partnership with AIG; a sponsor with a huge global footprint that wished to enhance its profile and glamorise its brand through an association with Manchester United. Clement would go on to explain that he saw the sponsorship as an opportunity to unite Aon's disparate international workforce of 36,000 people under the identity of a globally-recognised Manchester United 'umbrella'. Aon had indeed been vying with several prospective sponsors including Standard Chartered, who would end up branding Liverpool FC's shirts. While Standard Chartered was willing to pay more than Aon for the privilege, the bank stipulated that Manchester United should hit performance targets. This was anathema to United who preferred to see their revenues come without strings attached.

Roma

It came as no surprise that Rome proved to be a wonderful city to host the Champions League final. A festive atmosphere permeated the city's narrow antiquated streets, while the sun shone brightly on hordes of largely good-natured Manchester United supporters who were gathered in the many bars and cafés around the Bernini fountains in the stunning Piazza Navona. However, for the club, I felt the build-up to the game was an altogether different – and less satisfying – experience compared with that a year previously in Moscow. The team were housed in a classically beautiful hotel, the Exedra, located on the traffic-clogged Piazza della Repubblica, one of the city's grandest squares in central Rome. But the VIP party that I had travelled with was located in a resort-style hotel on the city's outskirts, which gave a fractured feel to the entourage compared with the tight grouping of Moscow. Indeed, I couldn't help thinking that the team would have benefited from staying in the relative idyll of my suburban hotel, which seemed a more relaxing environment in which to prepare for their biggest game of the year.

On the afternoon of the final I fought my way through the noisy crowd amassed outside the entrance of the Exedra to go downstairs to a sparse underground conference suite, which revealed excavated Roman bath ruins below its toughened glass floor. There, Manchester United's hierarchy, Joel, Avie and Bryan Glazer together with David Gill, – all suited and booted for the final, and wearing identical red club ties – were standing with their counterparts from Aon. As soon as the club photographer arrived it was straight to business to capture the moment when United and Aon's chief executives put pen to paper and toasted their partnership with champagne. Maybe it was the secret cellar location in the centre of Rome, but the slightly awkward gathering of a dozen or so power-dressed alpha males from two corporations signing off a multi-million dollar deal seemed reminiscent of a scene from a Mafia film.

Shortly afterwards I managed to push through the crowds in the lobby to see off the players as they braved the chaotic scene outside the hotel and boarded their coach en route to the final. I then travelled with our new Aon executive friends in one of a fleet of Mercedes people carriers with tinted windows, which proceeded to whisk us to the stadium at breakneck speed, taking full advantage of the slipstream provided by the police escort surrounding the coach carrying the Barcelona team.

'A Bad Day at the Office'

Perhaps it wasn't fair to compare, but the whole experience at the Stadio Olimpico felt like the antithesis of the superlative matchday experience of Moscow's Olympic Luzhniki stadium. Accessing the ground was marred by incompetent and heavy-handed staff, and the VIP hospitality – organised inside a drab marquee – felt cheap and tacky. Watching the actual match was spoiled by a succession of distracting arguments between people claiming that others were sitting in the wrong seats. As for the game, for anyone rooting for United it was to be a chastening experience. Despite a promising first ten minutes from the Reds, the rest of the match represented an excruciating surrender of the Champions League title to a masterful display by Barcelona, with goals from Samuel Eto'o and Lionel Messi.

There was a sense of deep disappointment at the team's performance and the coach trip back to the hotel felt eerily quiet and despondent. After the convivial night in London 2007, and the ecstatic celebrations of Moscow in 2008, the 2009 party in Rome – held regardless of that night's result to mark the club's third successive Premier League victory – felt more like a wake. After navigating the scrum to get into the tiny elevator to reach the hotel's rooftop terrace, the party exhibited the club's scale and generosity of previous seasons with a live band and a huge buffet. But after an initial lift from a glass of champagne, it quickly tailed off into an anti-climactic occasion; nobody seemed to want to be there. Even the table that bore the Premier League, Club World Cup and Carling Cup trophies had few takers for souvenir photographs. At one point I sat down next to a clearly dejected Sir Bobby Charlton, who delivered an apposite verdict: 'A bad day at the office, simple as that. The players barely turned up today.'

During the party I managed to talk shop with the Glazer brothers, who remained stoic in defeat. My mind was already focused on the Aon deal, and we talked for a while about my ideas for communicating it to the outside world. At one point, as we looked over to a particular player choosing a dessert from the buffet, Joel hinted that there may be also some news about the footballer in question that I would need to think about.

The next morning's flight back from Rome again felt like a polar opposite experience when compared with Moscow. As we boarded the plane, the glum players and coaching staff were already strapped in towards the front of the plane. As I advanced towards the rear I could not even summon the courage to look a dejected Sir Alex Ferguson in the eye. Phil Townsend's advice to savour every moment of that Champions League triumph against Chelsea felt more prescient than ever: it took the ruinous disappointment in Rome to truly appreciate the marvel of Moscow.

After Barcelona's triumph I would have to get used to reading gushing hagiographies of its self-styled '*Més que un club*' ethos (translated as 'More than a club'). This centred on its cooperative model whereby paid-up supporters each owned a slice of the organisation. Barcelona was indeed a special club, with its style of football, its illustrious history and its magnificent stadium arguably a match for what United had to offer. However, I grew frustrated that Barça's model was used as a stick with which to beat the Glazers' ownership of United. To me, Barcelona was rooted in a Spanish tradition which saw football clubs being owned cooperatively and being underwritten by local banks and government bodies. This was in direct contrast to top-flight clubs in England, where ownership reflected the prevailing *laissez-faire* market principle where clubs lay in the hands of private entities and the government did not interfere.

Indeed, I would regularly remind misty-eyed journalists (off-the-record, of course) that the club carried hundreds of millions of pounds of opaque borrowings, and that its revenues were underpinned by a controversial decision to sell its TV rights – along with Real Madrid – separately from its rivals in La Liga. This ensured that Barça could scoop some €140 million per year, 12 times the amount that smaller Spanish top-flight clubs received. This sustained a competitive imbalance between the country's top two clubs and the rest of La Liga's hapless challengers. Contrast this with the Premier League's collective approach to TV rights whereby Manchester United's €70 million was only one and a half times that of the bottom club in the Premier League.

Aon Announcement

The aftermath of Rome was dominated by deliberations with Aon, including many drafts of the press release that would publicise the announcement. Annoyingly, the news leaked via an early example of an online blog – penned by an overexcited member of Aon staff, apparently – which was duly picked up by the *Sunday Mirror* who naturally ran with the story. Nevertheless, there was little follow-up by other news outlets, which allowed us to maintain an element of surprise. However, come the day of the announcement there was widespread speculation that Aon was indeed the new sponsor. As it happened, the actual timing of the announcement was held up by administrative niceties, as United needed to officially inform AIG first before ensuring that the final year's payment due from the beleaguered insurer had cleared United's account. There was even a tiny amount of apprehension at United that AIG could have technically objected to the publicising of the deal one year before it was activated, given that Aon operated in the same insurance space.

As the self-imposed announcement deadline came and went we were still frenetically tweaking the press release, which was subject to review from participants across the world. Bryan Glazer, with minutes to spare before we went live, had the last word with a small change to the headline. Indeed, those nervous moments before going live took a strange twist when United's Phil Townsend, with whom I had been closely liaising, called me from his holiday in Italy to tell me he had just had a car accident; thankfully nobody was injured but, ironically, he would have to spend the next few hours sorting out the insurance formalities. As soon as we had received AIG's approval – and confirmation that its final year payment had been banked – we were ready to officially release the statement. Although the deal had by now been widely leaked across the Internet, it still felt like a real milestone – and a relief –to finally put United's exhaustive shirt sponsorship search to rest after nearly a year's effort.

While it represented a rare good news story for United, I suspected the real winners that day were Aon. The company had gained worldwide exposure with news of the deal, with thousands of stories referring to Aon as 'the world's largest insurance broker' (*Independent*) and 'American insurance giant' (*Daily Telegraph*). It was the sort of publicity that Phil Clement at Aon could only have dreamt of reading. Aon could also look forward to a free one-year honeymoon before their logo was to be emblazoned upon the players' chests. While we never guided a definitive figure on the value of the deal, the £80 million touted widely in the press would still represent a record figure. However, even before the ink had dried on the contract signed in Rome, there was a view inside the club that Aon had got itself a bargain, negotiated when markets were at their credit crunch low and when the outlook seemed even more uncertain. The deal with Aon reflected the Glazers' natural caution in wanting a deal done, especially as Aon were willing to front up a significant portion of cash. The *Times* cited Tony Allen, a brand consultant, who commented:[95] 'It may be paying about £20 million a year, but Aon looks to be getting a very good deal. Manchester United have 333 million fans worldwide – and 190 million in Asia alone – while their matches are watched around the world by even more people, because not every viewer is a fan. Paying £80 million over four years for a leading association with the United brand and that kind of exposure is cheap by other measures and universally appealing because of the massive and growing popularity of football. Try to reach a similar-sized audience through advertising alone and it will cost far more than £20 million. Consider that a leading supermarket might spend £10 million on its advertising in an average year in the United Kingdom and that's only for one country.'

Adiós Ronaldo

Just one week after its reported £80 million deal with Aon, Manchester United would bankroll a further £80 million with the world-record

[95] Sponsorship deal offers Aon huge exposure for minimum risk, *The Times*, 4 June 2009

transfer of Cristiano Ronaldo to Real Madrid. Although speculation had been rife for the best part of two years that Ronaldo had wanted a move to Madrid, the actual moment when United confirmed his exit proved to be big news. Contrary to the public perception of Ronaldo as a moody prima donna, his currency at the club had been high; he was popular among players and staff and, of course, had grown into a prolific goal scoring match winner. However, having won every top-flight medal and player award football had to bestow during an illustrious six year career, club insiders found it understandable – and inevitable – that he should want to move on one day, given that he hadn't any local family roots and, presumably, didn't particularly fancy the Manchester weather. More importantly, despite having persuaded him to stay one year previously, Sir Alex Ferguson was resigned to losing his Portuguese protégé.

The stakes surrounding Ronaldo's sale were high. Manchester United had forged a reputation of not being a 'selling' club; players were sold on its terms rather than at the behest of another club. Therefore to acquiesce to Real Madrid's demands could be seen as weak, an admission that United no longer owned the bragging rights to being the richest club in Europe. Widespread reports of the Glazers' £700 million debt and their holding company's multimillion pound losses served to conflate the suspicion that Manchester United indeed could no longer hold onto both the Madeira-born winger and, just as damning, Carlos Tévez.

But the truth was more mundane: Ronaldo wanted to move on and the Manchester United owners, after a long spell of soul searching by manager Sir Alex Ferguson, would accept this. Significantly, too, Real Madrid had a new president in Florentino Pérez with whom United could just about bring itself to do business, unlike his predecessor, Ramón Calderón, whom the club had accused of making illegal approaches to lure Ronaldo. The world record £80 million, to be paid (very unusually for the football business) in one mighty single instalment, provided some solace for Ronaldo's 185 pounds-or-so of flesh.

The news of Ronaldo's departure captivated the world's media, particularly since that, after two years of speculation, it was reported to have taken just two hours and a handful of phone calls – including one to Sir Alex Ferguson while holidaying in France – to complete the deal. Normally a player transfer was handled by the club's communications team and I, happily, had nothing to do with it. However, I did not anticipate that Ronaldo's exit would be so inextricably linked with the Glazers' ownership, thus prompting an intense bout of enquiries about the club's motives to sell him, exactly what the club would do with the proceeds, and whether any of the cash would be used to pay down the debt.

With the club's communications department giving short shrift to media enquiries, I found myself at the sharp end of journalist calls. Unusually for a major announcement, Phil Townsend and I hadn't prepared and signed off a list of key messages and quotes to feed into the media as we would normally have done; this reflected how quickly the Ronaldo transfer had been expedited. So I was left to 'wing it' and rely on my own judgement to navigate the minefield of questions. The most obvious issue was to project the club's gracious disposition towards Ronaldo, as anything less would have sounded churlish and would have been dangerously amplified by the press. I knew Ronaldo would be missed; he was a popular figure at Carrington and certainly his calibre as a player and his loyal service to United meant the club would have never wanted to close the door on him for good. As far as the proceeds were concerned, I suspected that it was premature to make any specific utterances – not least because the debt was traded and its holders would scrutinise any rash comments on 'splashing the cash' – so I stuck with my four years' tried and tested formula. I duly scribbled a statement and fed it into the press: 'The decision reflects Cristiano's desire to move on after six years of distinguished service for the club during which time he has won everything, and the manager has accepted his decision. The Glazer family, as owners, have always supported the manager consistently since their takeover of the club and that is again the situation in this case.'

Interestingly, other commentators would be less admiring of Ronaldo, referring to his frequent petulance on the pitch and dredging up memories of his infamous wink to the Portuguese bench following Rooney's red card in the 2006 World Cup, both of which stuck in the craw of many observers. It was interesting to note that Jim O'Neill, a prominent City economist and for a short time a member of the Manchester United PLC board just before the Glazers' takeover, was quoted as saying:[96] 'I think he was not as good as they think, and it is good business for United. Hopefully we can get a couple of really genuine world class players with the proceeds to accompany Rooney et al!'

Given that Ronaldo no longer wanted to play for United, the record transfer was obviously good business for the club. However, there were questions about the impact of his exit upon Manchester United's business away from the pitch, especially its commercial drive. The *Daily Telegraph's* Paul Kelso speculated:[97] 'A private concern inside the club might also be that Ronaldo's departure might make commercial deals like the Aon sponsorship harder to pull off. Ronaldo has become the most marketable player in the game, and the relationship has suited key sponsors such as Nike, who produce United's kit and the player's boots... United fans will have to find a new idol, with many hoping that the Glazers will grant Ferguson the resources to buy one.' Certainly Ronaldo featured prominently in the club's promotional materials, and the aftermath of his departure saw London's graphic design team busily air-brushing his image from the club's forward-looking marketing collateral. But while there was a little concern about his exit, the Manchester United club – and yes, its brand – were so much more potent than any single player, be it Best, Cantona or Ronaldo. In fact, apart from Japan (where its young female fans appeared to take the Portuguese player – and therefore Manchester United – to their hearts just as they had done with David Beckham) it did not feel that Ronaldo was as immersed in Manchester United folklore as, say, a Ryan Giggs or a Gary Neville, suggesting that his commercial appeal may have been more ephemeral.

While I sought to be as diplomatic as possible when speaking to journalists about Ronaldo's exit, an analogy did occur to me from my

[96] Ronaldo-nomics, *Financial Times*, 12 June 2009
[97] Two deals worth £160m in a week is music to Glazers' ears, *The Daily Telegraph*, 12 June 2009

own observations of the player, especially post-Moscow 2008. I shared this in confidence with Oliver Kay of the *Times,* who honoured its off-the-record status in his comment piece the next morning:[98] 'The hole left by Ronaldo's departure is enormous. United have lost not only a world-class forward but their only genuinely prolific goal scorer. But his heart was never truly in it. It was never going to last. One figure from Old Trafford characterised it yesterday as "a rocky marriage, but the sex was great." It is a splendid analogy.' My 'rocky marriage' analogy even became BBC Online's Quote of the Day. As ever, my rare claim to fame would be cloaked in strict anonymity.

My Paranoia

The next day, after ploughing through the saturation coverage in the press, I had hoped that the Ronaldo story had finally reached closure. As usual, my wishful thinking had underestimated the media's insatiable scrutiny into the club's affairs. That afternoon I received a call from Simon Stone who covered Manchester United for the Press Association. He was one of the most decent journalists I dealt with and someone whom I spoke to – indeed consulted – on a frequent basis. It transpired that the Manchester United Supporters' Trust had issued a statement urging the Glazers to 'make a statement of intent that ALL incoming transfer funds will be made available to Sir Alex Ferguson.' Simon wanted to explore whether the Ronaldo money had indeed been ring fenced for the manager's disposal.

One of the main features of the media is its desire to see everything in black or white especially when it comes to football finances and the Holy Grail: the transfer budget. The truth was that the £80 million proceeds had gone into Manchester United's cash pot from which expenditure on every aspect of the club, including transfers, could be drawn. But while there was obviously no specific cash pile in Sir Alex's office which he would jealously hoard, he knew – and was constantly

---

[98] Eighty million reasons why Ronaldo sale made sense, *The Times,* 12 June 2009

assured by the Glazers via chief executive David Gill– that there was never a defined transfer budget. Rather, Ferguson would always be supported by the owners with his transfer requests. A running in-joke I had with Ed Woodward during our in-house media training sessions was to ban him from using the archaic term 'fungible' when explaining player expenditure. But as far as transfers were concerned 'fungible' was precisely the correct word to use to convey the fact that Manchester United's transfer budget was never set in stone, and that the club's finances were much more fluid and flexible than the press would have people believe.

In my subsequent telephone conversation with Simon Stone I explained that the money had always been there to support the manager's transfer budget, and that the Ronaldo money hadn't changed anything. 'But what about MUST's claim that the £80 million would be used to pay down the debt?' enquired Simon. 'The debt remains serviceable from current cash flows,' I replied. 'It's nonsense to argue that the manager will be deprived of any transfer funds that he wants to use, as the last four years have proved.'

Our friendly – and as always off-the-record – conversation continued a little longer; at the end Simon said that he was not sure what quotes he'd like to use but, as usual, would get back to me to check whether he could attribute any to a Glazer spokesman. A few hours later my BlackBerry vibrated, pointing to an online story by Simon quoting me as saying: 'Only the paranoia of some supporters would lead you to believe the owners are not going to continue investing in the team. A substantial number of world-class players have been brought to the club in the past few years and that will still be the case. Sir Alex Ferguson is in total control of his squad. He is empowered to make whatever decisions he thinks are in the best interests of Manchester United. That continues to be the case. The fact is that Cristiano Ronaldo decided, after six years, that it was time to move on and the manager said OK. The idea that Manchester United are motivated by a debt burden is just not true. It is not an issue.'

I couldn't believe my eyes. While I had made those remarks off-the-record, and had genuinely stood by them, there was no way that I would have sanctioned the word 'paranoia' to be published. Privately

I did believe that MUST and its supporters were indeed paralysed by paranoia in regard to their excessive pessimism over the club's finances. But I instinctively knew that it was too emotive and judgemental a word to use in the public domain. I hurriedly put a call to Simon complaining that he had never called me to check; he apologised for any misunderstanding and assured me he would rewrite and republish the story with the 'paranoia' reference omitted. However, by that Friday evening my unintended 'paranoia' comment was circulating around the Internet and was sourced to his original story. By the following morning it had made it into the printed national newspapers and I was crestfallen. I wasn't cross with Simon Stone, who had made a genuine mistake, but was angry with myself for daring to use such a loose term within such an incessantly febrile atmosphere.

Beijing

The following week, and travelling half way round the world on a trip to a smoggy Beijing, my arrival at its gleaming airport was delayed as Chinese officials checked each and every passenger off the flight to ensure that no-one was carrying the H5N1 'Bird Flu' virus. The Ronaldo story was still the only topic that seemed to excite, even among the local Chinese journalists that I encountered in my routine relationship-building meetings. And when an emotional Sir Bobby Charlton rose to speak at a well-attended press conference held in an elaborately decorated hall on the Communist Party's compound it was his comments, the first utterances from a Manchester United official since Ronaldo's exit, which would reverberate:[99] 'It's a lot of money, it's crazy really,' said Charlton. 'If you want to be in the race, you have to pay the price, it seems sometimes a little bit vulgar. That is business, I'm afraid, we have responsibilities to our company and to all the fans that support Manchester United, and it was decided that Ronaldo could go. But it's a little bit soul-searching, you never know if you've

---

[99] Ronaldo price vulgar – Charlton, BBC Online, 18 June 2009

made the right decision until the start of the season. It's an enormous amount and we will make sure we use it properly and our club will be better for it.'

The four-day trip to China, ahead of the team's visit later that summer to play a pre-season game, was illuminating; while football evidently did not dominate Chinese sporting life (the imposing Workers' Gymnasium in the centre of Beijing highlighted the popularity of table tennis, for example) the words 'Manchester United' were enough to open all the doors I wanted, the club's recognition among the Chinese I encountered easily surpassing rivals football teams. In Beijing I also enjoyed spending time in the company of Sir Bobby Charlton, his softly spoken and down-to-earth manner belying his global fame. Always feeling in awe of the presence of a true legend, I nervously steered our conversation to more mundane talking points like his extensive travels. However, it was Sir Bobby who would naturally revert to his true comfort zone: football and Manchester United, topics which he expanded on freely with the enthusiasm and sparkle of a teenage fanatic.

By July it was clear that the issue of the 'Ronaldo money' was not going to go away, especially after Sir Alex Ferguson's decision to let Carlos Tévez depart the club too. Speaking at a press conference at Carrington to introduce the club's three new summer signings, Michael Owen, Antonio Valencia and Gabriel Obertan, Sir Alex rejected calls for him to splash the cash:[100] 'I can only placate fans one way and that's by not being stupid. We have that wonderful sum of money from Real Madrid [£80 million for Ronaldo], but we are not going to throw it away and spend it in situations when an extra zero is being placed on the end of transfer fees…We have always had to pay a bit extra but, this summer, we were not prepared to do that and I think we have concluded our business.' But Sir Alex's parsimony would be inferred as the Glazers' tightening of the purse strings. The *Times* commented[101]: 'His reluctance to spend more than a quarter of the £80

---

[100] Ferguson preaches prudence, *The Daily Telegraph*, 14 July 2009
[101] Ferguson puts away chequebook and ushers in sensible era at Old Trafford, *The Times*, 14 July 2009

million fee for Ronaldo is certain to fuel the persistent anti-Glazer feeling among the club's supporters.'

The Asia Tour

I was looking forward to my first pre-season tour to Asia with the club, which meant that, since there was no major football tournament that summer, a full squad would be in attendance. The purpose of Manchester United's tours was threefold. The priority was to provide the squad with a close knit training camp and some non-competitive games in order to prepare the team for the forthcoming season (explaining why the manager always had the sign-off on the destinations and itinerary). Secondly, pre-season tours enabled the players and the club to forge closer links with its many millions of foreign supporters. The last but not least reason was to explore commercial opportunities, both by leveraging the club's presence overseas to promote an existing sponsor, or to eke out new commercial partners in a destination against the backdrop of the hoopla that all tours created. This effort would be stepped up given the Glazers' commercial strategy to seek out territorial deals.

The itinerary, meticulously scoped out on a multi-coloured matrix, would take the squad to five countries in just 14 days: Malaysia, Indonesia, South Korea, China and then a tournament in Germany. An 80-strong entourage included the players and coaching staff, the chief executive David Gill, the father and son duo of club photographers, a phalanx of security guards, the communications team, tour organisers, the MU Foundation chief executive, the club's Soccer School coaches, reporters and crew from in-house television channel MUTV, the club's website journalist and blogger, representatives from Nike and UNICEF and even an executive with the full-time responsibility of investigating any club's trademark infringements in the host countries' many markets. Also on board was a member of the London commercial team who had been charged with helping to organise next year's 2010 tour, which the Glazers had decided they wanted the club to control rather than outsource to a local sports events agency. Other members of the London sales team would also parachute into the various tour destinations at different stages. My role was broadly defined to try and replicate what I had achieved previously in South Africa, Japan and China; namely to seek out prominent business journalists and cultivate supportive press coverage to underpin the club's commercial efforts. I was also keen to sample at first hand the mania of Asian fans that I had heard so much about, which had become an important feature of the Manchester United global story I was charged with telling. In addition, the tour would serve as a gauge whether the club had been diminished at all by Ronaldo's exit, especially as his face still adorned the official tour artwork that had been designed and printed before June.

Logistics were planned and executed with military precision. Before departure everyone was kitted out with a Nike branded suitcase filled with sets of club crested t-shirts, shorts, trainers and other clothing items, all tailor-made exclusively for the tour. We were also provided with individually-numbered luggage tags, which would ensure our bags' magically seamless super-VIP transportation from the hotel room in one country direct to the hotel room of another without our ever having to handle the bags ourselves.

I also packed a large bag of goodies to distribute to foreign media: Manchester United lapel pin badges, upmarket cuff links and key rings (made by United's official clothing partner Paul Smith) and a wad of an updated 'Facts and Figures', now revised into a smart A6-sized booklet. I was also supplied with a smart black crested silk tie which I was required to wear whenever in transit.

Pyjama Party

I reported as instructed at Terminal 2 at Manchester airport to see a specially cordoned off check-in desk with local TV cameramen, photographers and expectant fans waiting to see the team arrive. With my passport processed and baggage through – curiously the only time of the thoroughly pampered trip when we had to check-in ourselves – I sped through the busy summer holiday rush with my VIP boarding pass to a specially laid-on lounge in the departures terminal. This area gradually filled with the cliquey clusters of players, coaching staff and executives; but all United in smart club suits and ties.

The plane was specially chartered for the whole trip. At first sight it was impressive; the whole interior was composed of cream leather business class seating with swathes of walnut burr veneer inlaid on the tables. One of my favourite memories was to observe everyone simultaneously ditching their smart suits before departure for the complimentary first class pyjamas, trying their best to get changed in an incredibly confined space. (The handful of women on board were allowed the courtesy of getting changed in the privacy of the on-board toilets). It meant that for the next 12 hours or so everyone on the flight – the players and Sir Alex included – was identically and very incongruously dressed in grey brushed cotton pyjamas. Indeed, the convivial atmosphere reminded me of the anticipation and excitement I felt before a long school trip; Sir Alex Ferguson and David Gill, seated together as usual in their specially reserved exit row with the extra legroom, added a benign school masterly air to the proceedings.

As it was 'our' plane, the usual conventions were conspicuously dispatched with. I neither recall a pre-flight safety drill nor any orders to buckle up. Soon into the flight we were supplied with our own hard drive movie players and were attended to by a team of glamorous and attentive Greek stewardesses, bringing course after course of food and refreshments (healthy and light for the travelling squad of course) served upon trays draped with crisp starched napkins and a freshly cut rose. However, it also became clear that the seats, while initially spacious and luxurious, were not geared for sleeping in: the leather seats were too slippery and they didn't recline as generously as the contemporary flat beds in business or first class that most of the plane's passengers had become accustomed to. That said, some of the players did manage to get some quality kip by ingeniously resorting to sleeping on the 180-degree flat floors in the large cavities between the seats.

While most towards the dim rear of the plane seemed to be asleep, many of us stayed up for much of the flight given that our body clocks were still insisting it wasn't yet bedtime in the UK. By the time we were soaring high over central Asia the flight began to take on the feel of a pyjama party, as that morning's VIP lounge's cliques seemed to melt into a more sociable unit, some of the non-playing staff happily lubricated by the plentiful supply of free alcoholic beverages.

Jakarta Bomb

We arrived the following morning, local time, in Kuala Lumpur. As the plane touched down onto the tarmac many of us were already receiving texts and emails on our mobile devices alerting us to reports of a number of bombs in Jakarta locations. This included the Ritz-Carlton, the hotel we were planning to move onto for the second leg of the tour in a couple of days' time. With our pyjamas off and our club attire back on, we disembarked the plane and, spared of the formalities of customs and assured that our luggage was heading separately to our hotel bedrooms, walked straight through a quiet terminal building which had evidently been cleared for our arrival. But as we approached the sliding doors of the exit there was a sudden, large roar from a group of excited banner-waving Malaysian supporters, proclaiming their love for Manchester United (and their worship in particular for Wayne Rooney and the newly-acquired Michael Owen). They proceeded to thrust their cameras into every outriding member of the tour party. It was my first taste of the 'ManUmania' that I had heard so much about; the fans' enthusiasm really startled me, such was its scale and intensity. As a lifelong Beatles fan, I felt suddenly able to comprehend the fanaticism that greeted the Fab Four whenever they travelled overseas during their touring pomp: exhilarating but also a little disconcerting.

While the main party headed for the coaches parked outside, Sir Alex, David Gill, Phil Townsend and I climbed onto a third coach along with the local tour organiser, whereupon a calm conversation began about whether the tour to Indonesia should still proceed. At that juncture, news of the bomb was sketchy and I proceeded to boot up my laptop and started to scour the Internet for any new information that I could feed into the impromptu 'crisis' team meeting. The surreal aspect was heightened by our coaches enjoying a routine police escort comprising several motorcycle outriders, their continuous loud *CHiPS-style* sirens blaring, clearing the road ahead of us as we sped our way into the centre of Kuala Lumpur. It was remarkable to see how many locals, stuck in their vehicles, summarily parked up on the motorway to allow us to pass before cheerily waving us on: the power of Manchester United.

Our hotel, the Mandarin Oriental, overlooked the stunning Petronas Towers, one of Asia's great landmarks. Like the terminal building, it was besieged by hundreds of enthusiastic but well-behaved supporters and onlookers. Most sported some form of Manchester United paraphernalia, and each was armed with a camera device; their screams modulated by the players' appearances as they stepped off the coach. As soon as we squeezed into the hotel we were ushered into a meeting room where Sir Bobby Charlton, who had arrived in the city before us, was waiting. A representative of the local British embassy also joined the ad hoc crisis team around the table. I continued to monitor online press coverage of the bomb and piped up when fatalities were confirmed. We soon came to the sad conclusion that the trip to Jakarta would have to be scrapped. A great feeling of disappointment and resignation hung around the table, especially as United had never played in Indonesia before and there was a genuine appetite among Sir Alex and the club's hierarchy to take the team to a new frontier promising millions of passionate fans. But with United's first press conference less than an hour away, the discussion focused upon what needed to be communicated to the media, in particular how important it was to pay careful attention to protocol and not risk offending our Indonesian hosts. It felt exceptional to be privy to the discussions between the club's footballing hierarchy over such an extraordinary issue, only to be reminded just how calm dealings between the club's board members always seemed to be, even against a backdrop of such fast moving and chaotic events.

The press conference was held in the hotel's capacious banqueting hall. The amassed journalists, including several UK football reporters who had travelled ahead of us to cover United's tour, were already assuming the Indonesia leg would be cancelled so their agenda had moved onto what the club had planned to do instead. On the sidelines after the press conference I was surrounded by a group of newswire journalists from Reuters, Bloomberg and Malaysia's main news agency. The questioning, depressingly, centred upon Ronaldo's exit and the speculation as to whether the proceeds would be drawn to pay down the debt. Wary of giving more air to this most vexed of subjects, I gave my usual briefing on the stipulation that my words were for background guidance only and could not be used for publication.

The Merry-Go-Round

Later that afternoon our coaches left in convoy towards the Bukit Jalil National Stadium for the players' first training session. A strict protocol prevailed, and was to be observed throughout the tour: coach number one contained the players and coaching staff, while coach two tailed its illustrious passengers with the club's ancillary employees, including me, on-board. Our police escort noisily alerted drivers and pedestrians of our passage and again the coaches were greeted with onlookers waving and cheering, which we somewhat self-consciously sought to reciprocate. The coaches rushed straight into the stadium wherein a crowd of some 20,000 supporters, in spite of the hot and sultry evening, were waiting to glimpse their idols performing routine training drills.

Meanwhile, other members of the club entourage kicked off a fortnight of continuous events, which had been carefully choreographed by United support staff – some of whom had flown ahead to help with planning – and which usually attracted huge interest from local media. The likes of David Gill and club ambassadors Sir Bobby Charlton and Bryan Robson attended a merry-go-round of photo opportunities and meet-and-greets with local sponsors and dignitaries, often accompanied with the Premier League trophy. At the same time, the ebullient chief executive of United's charity foundation, John Shiels, would be involved in a programme of tremendously worthy activities which aimed to reach out to local underprivileged children, many of whom were football mad. Nike would also lend their weight to a series of expensively-staged promotional 'Fan Fest' activities involving the players, which drew in thousands of spectators in the city centres of the tour destinations. In the meantime I managed to meet as many local journalists as possible, eventually introducing some to David Gill and commercial director Richard Arnold for business-orientated interviews.

Wearing the Crest with Pride

Many of the events had a strong hint of glamour, often involving lavish dinners and cocktail parties, although as the tour unfolded and the fatigue and jet lag accumulated it wasn't unusual to wonder exactly which country we were in now, or indeed to crave something simple to eat like egg and chips. While it was customary for everyone at the business end of the club to put in 15-hour days during the tour, there was also a strong sociable dimension and it was commonplace to see the late bar populated by United staff (everyone apart from the manager and the players, that is). The club's generosity was legendary, although a few members of the party, after a few too many drinks, would cheekily charge their bar tab to David Gill's room number!

During the tour I did something that I would never have imagined doing back in the UK; I wore the Manchester United crest with pride at every event (amusingly, I was occasionally asked to sign autographs by fans who probably should have known better). In England, prior to working for United, I would never wear anything identifying myself as a fan on a match day, and would always eschew the showy tribalism of club football. And despite the fact that I now rooted for Manchester United in my professional capacity, it would certainly have been anathema to wear a United crest out and about in England. But on tour in Asia I found myself comfortable wearing the club badge just about anywhere, gaining first-hand insight into its status rather than the tribal calling card it seemed to provoke back in the UK.

As I had witnessed in the previous year's South Africa tour, the players' routine was strictly regimented to a schedule of training, resting and eating. But in Asia this was interspersed with an obligation to conduct a succession of press interviews as well as appearances at various sponsor and charity events, which they usually did with good humour.

Staying in luxury five star hotels with large, opulent – and very public – lobbies meant that the players often had to be chaperoned by security staff to protect them from the scores of fans who maintained a constant vigil. In Kuala Lumpur the security concerns centred mostly on autograph hunters who would wait on each floor to 'trap' a player in the elevator, providing enough time for an autograph and photo before the lift settled at the next floor, when the fan would get out and try his or her luck in the other three elevators. In the Mandarin, where the club entourage was housed towards the top of the 30-storey hotel, this could be a highly frustrating affair. By the time we got to Seoul, fans seemed to have taken this elevator-hogging to an even more annoying level, with coordinated sets of supporters occupying every floor to ensure maximum inconvenience to the players and any hotel residents unlucky enough to be in their midst. In Hangzhou, we were all taken aback by the passion and fervour shown by the legions of ever-present Chinese fans, who would swarm inside the hotel lobby and around the club's publicly visible dining area, tracking every single movement of each player.

En route to Kuala Lumpur, I teased some of the players by suggesting that they should venture out and sample a bit of the local culture while they were on tour. By the first day on the ground I appreciated why this would not be possible. Every player commanded huge amounts of adulation and adoration from their devoted Asian following, and it would have been reckless for any United star to have left their hotel without a large security retinue; more to avoid being mobbed rather than the risk of a malevolent attacker, I suspected.

Hysterical Scenes

What struck me during the Asia tour was the depth of knowledge and passion for Manchester United. These were not fly-by-night supporters chasing the glamour of a particular player. Most fans I encountered were incredibly knowledgeable about United, their love for the club following in the footsteps of their fathers or uncles, and facilitated by Internet access.

Manchester United's first match of the tour, versus a Malaysia XI, attracted a sell-out crowd who enthusiastically cheered on the Reds and their opponents in equal measure. Despite taking place on a particularly hot and steamy night, it was a surprisingly rousing game that ended in a 2-2 draw. In light of the Jakarta bomb, the club decided to stay on in Kuala Lumpur and, a couple of days later, played a re-match against the country's best players in a stadium that was, extraordinarily, still half-full.

After the unexpected relaxation of the extra days in Malaysia the tour's pace soon became unrelenting, and I found my busy and tiring schedule being compounded by the fuzz of jet lag and fatigue. Still, there were few grounds for complaint; the facilities were superlative and we couldn't have been more spoon fed: every aspect of the tour was precision-planned for us, the only 'hardship' being to constantly unpack and pack our luggage late at night (although once we left the bags outside our door we would be sure to see them again in the hotel room of our next destination). Our VIP status also meant that we were spared the usual formalities of check-in and passport control; sometimes our police escorted coaches would even drive us directly onto the airport apron to the bottom of the aircraft stairs. And while our chartered plane may not have been conducive for sleep, seeing the same crew and the creamy leather interior provided a comforting level of familiarity which many of us would welcome.

In Seoul, ahead of the third tour match, I accompanied United's South Korean player, Ji-Sung Park, in an unmarked car to a promotional event on the banks of the city's Han river. I was already aware that Park was a superstar in his home country, but it was frightening to witness the hysteria from thousands of young Koreans from the moment he stepped out of the hotel elevator. Our vehicle was mobbed – and literally rocked – by screaming fans hoping to get a glimpse of their idol; it seemed as intense as any film footage of the Beatles trying to escape crowds after a concert. While the down-to-earth Ji-Sung took this fanatical adulation in his stride, he made a point of telling me how much he enjoyed the relative anonymity of living and working in England.

The stadium in Seoul was packed with expectant fans and featured a large Fan Fest before the game at which sponsors like Kumho Tires,

Smirnoff and Nike hosted events to attract the huge numbers of United supporters. The game against FC Seoul was an enjoyably tight affair which United won 3-2, the noisy atmosphere reaching a deafening crescendo when Ji-Sung Park came on as a substitute towards the end. It transpired that thousands of these raucous fans would be waiting outside the stadium after the game and, as our two coaches left the ground, a normally orderly Seoul seemed to descend into chaos. Local fans hurled themselves at the coaches just to touch the vehicles' windows, behind which sat bemused players and staff. It seemed a miracle to me that nobody was seriously injured.

'Glazer Spokesman Kills United Manager'

In a hot and humid Hangzhou, a city in eastern China, crowds of supporters followed us everywhere and even appeared to camp outside our lakeside hotel. Disappointingly, the game's attendance had been tightly restricted by the authorities, which meant that United's 8-2 victory over a local team was played in front of largely empty concrete stands in the Huanglong Stadium. After the match our coaches drove us directly to the airport, its stark, empty terminal seemingly reserved for our departure. However, the crowds outside the airport entrance were again enormous, and we all struggled to climb off the coach into the sea of red-shirted Manchester United fans. I happened to be one of the first off the coach and, faced with a gauntlet of wildly screaming fans, I panicked and froze, not feeling able to push through. The next thing I heard was one of our security men shouting at me to keep moving; I tentatively carried on walking, only to feel my wheeled hand luggage clumsily tripping someone up behind me. I immediately turned to look over my shoulder and saw that it was, in fact, Sir Alex Ferguson himself who had become entangled with my case. Horrified, I was immediately seized with fear and remorse. However, I had to keep moving until I turned a corner and, upon reaching a quiet area reserved for our slowly assembling tour party, I paused and waited for Sir Alex to approach me, wondering whether he was okay and how cross he might be. I apologised to him profusely and enquired after his welfare; fortunately he was not hurt and he was immediately forgiving. Still feeling in a state of shock I sat down in the departure terminal, idly contemplating the headline: 'Glazer Spokesman Kills United Manager'.

The wait in the Hangzhou airport departure gate proved to be equally surreal. While there were no other passengers, it was full of officials identifiable by their uniforms (although I couldn't tell apart the airport security staff from the conscripted military personnel). The squad members streamed through and took their seats, looking particularly tired after their match in the smoggy heat of the stadium. Like moths to a flame, the officials crowded around each player, awkwardly crouching at their sides to pose for hundreds of 'selfie' photographs. What struck me as bizarre was how brazen they were in contrast to the statue-like stillness of the players, who seemed utterly indifferent to the latest onslaught into their personal space.

By the time we had arrived in Munich, most of us were feeling completely addled after two weeks of continuous travel. United's matches during this German leg of the tour were to take place at the Allianz Arena on the outskirts of the city, which had been recently built to host the 2006 World Cup and which was now home to tournament hosts Bayern Munich, with Louis van Gaal recently installed as the new manager. It was one of the best – if not the best – stadium I had ever seen. Its near 70,000 capacity also included a terrace for standing supporters which enveloped the lush green pitch and provided for wonderfully intense acoustics. Everyone seemed to be properly catered for at the stadium; wonderful beer and sausages for the masses, while the tiers of expansive executive lounges provided a superlative experience for Munich's affluent corporate diners, too. It was good to have the opportunity to acclimatise in Germany, with the frenzied crowds and oppressive heat of eastern Asia being replaced with cool Teutonic order. My scheduled flight back to London was in economy class where – shock, horror – I even had to carry my own bags. My return back down to earth actually felt a novelty after two weeks of constant pampering; something, unlike some of the real VIP passengers on the tour, I knew I would never be able to take for granted.

'Mercenaries, Toilets and Carpets'

The tour – the Jakarta bomb notwithstanding – had gone well, faithfully adhering to the very tight schedule. The reception to the team had been overwhelming and, I thought, showed no negative impact from Ronaldo's absence. I also felt a sense of satisfaction that my role had helped to stimulate useful press coverage and cement media relationships. That said, I'd had to endure one particularly stressful episode. At the end of that first press conference – within hours of our arrival in Kuala Lumpur – I had briefed journalists, as usual, on the impact of Ronaldo's exit. It was, I had thought, strictly off-the-record. A few days later, however, I got wind that the Reuters journalist had written up my briefing, and had even cited my name. While I was sure that the renowned news agency, which I had proudly worked for during my journalist days, had transgressed our agreement (I felt consoled that the other two news outlets did not run a story, and the Reuters journalist was to apologise to me for any misunderstanding) I was overwhelmed by embarrassment, not least because my loose tongue was reported verbatim. In the wake of my 'paranoia' comments, it would be my second media gaffe in as many months. My instinct was to just wish it away; while the story had been picked up by other online news websites, I vainly clung onto the hope that it would be buried by other tour news.

My uneasy calm was halted, however, by the time we had arrived in Seoul. To my dismay, I discovered that, a few days after the original Reuters story, my comments had been extensively reported in the UK's main newspapers which had also mentioned me by name. The headlines focusing upon – like the 'paranoia' incident – my use of a word with emotional connotations: 'mercenary'. The *Times* splashed: 'Sir Alex Ferguson not interested in signing "mercenaries"'; the *Daily Mail:* 'Mercenary wasters are not welcome at Manchester United, say Glazers,' and the *Daily Telegraph:* 'Manchester United won't sign mercenaries despite £80m Cristiano Ronaldo sale.'

My words, to be fair, were reported accurately, but too accurately for comfort: 'The delay [in signings] is because the manager has not been able to locate the players that he believes fit the Manchester

United mindset; ones that are motivated to play for United. You don't want mercenaries, to pay over the odds for players not willing to give their all for the club. Our operating profits are climbing and we continue to secure significant sponsorship deals. On a normal business level, United is in a very strong position and, so far, unaffected by the downturn. It would be foolish to say there would be no impact, period, because you never know what's going to happen down the line. But our season-ticket sales stand up to comparisons in previous years. I've been saying that one should expect an impact on our corporate sales, but every club is faced with that. Having said that, the manager has a significant amount of money to invest if he wants to. We do have a debt to service and carry a significant amount of debt but our interest payments are around £43.3 million a year, while our operating profit was £80 million, topped by an extra £25 million from transfer profits. So we are talking about a net amount of about £60 million. That's cash that can be reinvested in the squad, doing up the toilets or new carpets. The point is, there is money coming into United. One thing that is certain, because of globalisation and the growing middle classes in India and the Far East, is that the appeal of football is set to grow. We are part of that story.'

What I had sought to explain in my briefing was that it was not the United way to chase after players whose heart was not into playing in a red shirt, and that all club cash was interchangeable. But I truly winced at seeing my reference to mercenaries, toilets and carpets in print – all true but never words I would have deliberately cited for publication – and suspected that my admission that the club had 'a significant amount of debt' would come back to haunt me too. Also my 'spokesman' anonymity which I had cultivated for more than four years was blown: I even had a series of emails from long lost friends, bemused at seeing my name associated with Manchester United. Chastened by the experience, I was wary too of the reaction from my United colleagues. When I encountered David Gill in the lobby of the Shilla Hotel in Seoul – someone who himself had been routinely bruised by the vagaries of the media – he smiled wryly and said 'welcome to the club.'

Part Six
2009 / 10 Season

The 2009/10 season, my last full one with the club, was to yield one trophy, the Carling Cup. No mean feat for most clubs, but by the standards of Manchester United – which had just produced a sequence of three Premier League title wins and one Champions League triumph – it would represent the same modest haul as the Glazers' first full season in charge of the club. And although the team were just pipped by one point to the title by Chelsea, and were to reach the quarter final of the Champions League, the season would become synonymous with the supporter protests against the Glazer family.

Project Free Kick

During the autumn of 2009, with the credit markets beginning to show distinct signs of improvement, Joel Glazer and Ed Woodward were occupied with a further attempt to refinance Manchester United's debt. Unlike the previous abortive move in 2007 to go for an amendment to the existing borrowings, the Glazers began to look to the corporate debt market for funding, which had been a beneficiary of the banks' reluctance to lend during the credit crunch. Moreover, a potential conversion of the debt into a bond provided some operational advantages to the club in addition to the obvious certainty of a fixed interest rate payout – the coupon – that a bond would provide. In particular, there would be fewer strings attached to the running of the club than the covenants imposed by a bank loan. However, launching a bond would require a huge amount of disclosure, supported by a sales roadshow and the obvious transaction risk of failure; this was evidenced by the operator of the

Donington Park racetrack which was forced to pull its bond issue plans at that time.

By mid-November 'Project Free Kick' had gathered pace and I was put in touch with the bankers at JPMorgan and lawyers at Allen & Overy, the same advisors whom the Glazers had used since the 2005 takeover. As ever, I warned Ed Woodward that his extensive discussions with potential investors would eventually leak and that any talk of launching a bond would be inferred by the sports press as a desperate move by the owners to shore up their finances. Moreover, Allen & Overy were adamant that that any leak could jeopardise the entire deal as United's owners planned to market the bond in the US, which carried strict restrictions what a company could say or do.

However, just as soon as we were getting ready to go live, the window to an apparently benign bond market abruptly shut. News broke that the state of Dubai was struggling with its debt burden and might even default, which sent the world's markets sharply lower. Soon after the decision to put Project Free Kick on ice, a Manchester football journalist from the *Times*, James Ducker, contacted me to say that he had heard that United were struggling with a refinancing. Desperate to keep Free Kick a secret I entered into a tortuous set of telephone discussions with James and ended up splitting the thinnest of hairs with him. As he had not mentioned the 'B' word I could, strictly speaking (and under enormous pressure from the lawyers) keep our powder dry and say that no refinancing was planned. I had managed to buy a little more time, but by early December a tenacious Ducker was confident enough to go with his source's claim and he called me to say that his editor was running the story. Still, with no mention of a prospective bond from James, I could sleep well and felt comfortable reading his splash the following morning:[102] 'The Glazer family, the owners of Manchester United, are struggling to refinance their enormous debts amid concerns about the impact they are having on the club. The Times understands that the Americans have been trying unsuccessfully to secure a refinancing package for part of the club's

---

[102] Glazers feeling strain of United debts, *The Times*, 5 December 2009

£699 million debt for months, having failed in 2007 and last year, because of the bleak global economic climate.'

Just as in 2006 and 2007 when United's owners had looked into refinancing the debt, there was spurious speculation that the Glazers might be wanting to offload United, the *News of the World* appearing to have dusted off one of its own stories and headlines from 2007:[103] 'A consortium of Far East businessmen have put together a £1 billion deal to buy Manchester United. The group of six billionaires have spent three months on a deal they hope is too good for Malcolm Glazer to reject.' The story triggered further speculation in other more authoritative newspapers, which I responded with my well versed 'not for sale' rebuttal. In fact I was not too displeased with the red herring of a 'United for Sale' in the papers; anything that put journalists off the scent of highly sensitive preparations for a bond was fine by me.

While Ed Woodward's efforts were focused on the club's finances, his London colleagues were still busy drumming up commercial opportunities. During my frequent visits to Ed's office to discuss the bond with him, I noticed that the floor space was beginning to fill with piles of boxes, just as it had been during the shirt sponsorship mailout a year previously. This time, commercial director Richard Arnold had settled on another gimmick to support his sales team's speculative outreach to potential sponsors: a black leather football with the logos of both Manchester United and the recipient company, the ball encased in a luxury silk surround and cocooned in a black box embossed with the silver club crest. As ever, Ed and Richard insisted on an assiduous focus upon detail in order to project the quality of the Manchester United brand to prospective partners.

'Historic' Defeat

On New Year's Day 2010 I was left a voicemail by a business reporter on the *Sunday Times* saying his paper was going to report that United

---

[103] £1 Billion Chinese Take A Way, *News of the World*, 13 December 2009

was in advanced plans to market a bond in the region of £500 million to refinance the debt and that potential investors were being approached. Finally, I thought, the cat was out of the bag as the bond had been explicitly cited. But, mindful that the journalist had assumed I would be on holiday I knew there was no point in returning the call and trying to wriggle out of the truth. The paper gave due prominence to its story the next day, speculating:[104] 'Sources familiar with the situation say the amount that Manchester United will seek to raise depends on the appetite shown by investors. At present the figure is between £500 million and £600 million. If demand is strong, the club could seek more. It is unclear whether the proceeds of a bond issue would be used to repay the controversial PIK debt or the £520 million that is secured against the club.'

The *Sunday Times* story was picked up extensively by the media who were also focused on that afternoon's big FA Cup third round tie, an old-fashioned clash between Manchester United and the club's historically fierce rivals Leeds United. Leeds now found themselves two divisions below United following an ignominious exit from top-flight football that had been widely blamed on its spiralling debts. In front of a sell-out Old Trafford crowd, and beamed live on television across the globe, United proceeded to lose a riveting game to a Leeds side that managed to outplay the reigning Premier League champions. The result provided two unwelcome milestones for Sir Alex Ferguson's 23-year reign: it was the first time his side had lost this early in the FA Cup and it was the first occasion that his team had been eliminated by a lower division side.

United's ignoble defeat, combined with the news that the club might be seeking to launch a bond, created a press backlash that was as intense as that which followed the early exit from the 2005 Champions League. The Manchester United Supporters' Trust called for the Glazers to sell up: [105] 'We warned from the beginning that the Glazer takeover would saddle the club with huge debts and now we can see

---

[104] Manchester United examine £600m bond issue, *The Sunday Times*, 3 January 2010
[105] United start to suffer in City's shadow, *The Guardian*, 6 January 2010

them biting. If it were a race, then United are dragging their owners behind them like a tractor, while City's owners are providing rocket fuel.' That 'rocket fuel' referred to the news that Manchester City, comfortably through to the fourth round of the FA Cup, had benefitted from nearly £400 million in investment by its owner Sheikh Mansour, although the sudden dismissal of City's manager Mark Hughes suggested that the Sheikh's patience for trophy success would be less generous. The contrast between the two Manchester clubs would be heightened by a semi-final Carling Cup clash that was due to take place within days of the FA Cup third round, but was postponed due to snow.

The Bond Memorandum

The mood was febrile, and that week I was swamped by calls from journalists wanting to get any insight into the bond, many with valid questions that I would have loved to respond to. However I had to stonewall every enquiry, a frustrating scenario given that I wasn't even able to provide the faintest of guidance that the bond process was being pursued because of Manchester United's financial *strength*, rather than spelling the widely-reported gloom and doom for the club. While no green light had yet been given for the bond to proceed, I was involved in frantic activity making preparations for the launch. As well as dusting off the press release and investor presentation from November, the other key document needing my input was the Offering Memorandum. Also known as the bond prospectus, it was a huge 322-page tome which was probably the most thorough exposition of its kind relating to the multifaceted business issues affecting a top football club. The Memorandum would also reveal in forensic detail how Manchester United went about its business, outlining the many risks that any prospective investor deciding whether to buy a bond would need to be aware of. It was a big step for any private business, but especially so for the Glazer-owned club which had spent nearly five years jealously guarding its secrecy, abetted by my role as their 'gatekeeper'.

The Memorandum was first drafted in the previous autumn but had now become subject to continuous revision as negotiations unfolded between a club that wanted to preserve its privacy, and its lawyers who advised full disclosure to safeguard the organisation from any legal reprisal from potentially unhappy investors. To me, the Memorandum represented a mixed blessing: on the one hand, given the many sensitive issues that it addressed (much of it couched in dispassionate legalese) it would probably attract negative publicity. On the other hand, it felt cathartic that – after so many years spent running rings around inquisitive journalists – finally the truth would be out.

While I had managed to advise on several minor amendments to the document, I was mindful of the pressure from the lawyers and I felt largely powerless to contend with the deliberately 'warts and all' contents of the Memorandum. But I took the precaution of drawing up a paper which I sent to the owners identifying what I thought to be the issues that the press would seize upon, thus readying us for what I predicted to be a furore. Joel Glazer's reaction was as sanguine as ever, reminding me how the outcry and protests following previously leaked business plans had eventually subsided.

However there was a litany of subjects (when taken out of context of the full-disclosure, legally-tight document that the Memorandum stood up to be) that would likely serve as a call to arms for those already entrenched against the Glazers' ownership. The £70 million of club cash made available to pay down the PIK, for example; the admission that the club 'cannot assure you that our business will generate sufficient cash flow from operations or that future borrowings will be available to us in an amount sufficient to enable us to pay our indebtedness, including the Notes, or to fund our other liquidity needs'; the disclosure of a mind-boggling £38.6 million loss from the club's interest rate swap, and the boast that 'we have been able to consistently increase matchday ticket prices for both general admission and seasonal hospitality seats at levels above the rate of inflation, particularly following the most recent expansion of Old Trafford.'

Another potentially contentious aspect of the densely-written document lay in one of the shortest sections, outlined in a mere three paragraphs on page 86, entitled 'Related Party Transactions Loans to directors.' It detailed that a £10 million loan had been made to the Glazer siblings as well as confirmation that millions of pounds in management and consultancy fees had been paid out to them since the takeover. This was wholly justifiable to my mind – and was by no means controversial for common or garden business owners – but, in the volatile atmosphere of January 2010, it was likely to provoke anger and derision among some fans.

Towards the end of the first week in January, finishing touches to the documentation were made. The schedule for the roadshow was also being finalised, which would take Ed Woodward and his London office colleague Jamie Reigle – chaperoned by JPMorgan – on a gruelling two-week tour of the world's financial capitals to present the bond to prospective investors. The itinerary included the briefest of flying visits to Hong Kong, Singapore, Paris, Edinburgh, London, Amsterdam, Frankfurt, New York, Boston and Los Angeles.

Manchester United's Norwich Hub

Meanwhile, I was holed up in my home in not-so-exotic Norwich, where I coordinated the club's communications strategy from my terraced house, in the most humble of spare bedrooms. Overlooking the dangling washing lines of my neighbours, my study also doubled up as an impromptu playroom for my young daughters: a more incongruous place to launch a mega-million pound global news event was hard to imagine.

That weekend was spent refining the press release, which the lawyers were adamant should detail the bare minimum, notwithstanding a prominent boilerplate statement in bold typeface warning that 'None of the notes or the guarantees to be issued in the offering have been or will be registered under the U.S. Securities Act of 1933 and may not be offered or sold in the United States.' Liaising with Ed Woodward, who had just arrived in Hong Kong, we agreed that we would go live on Monday morning his local time, or 22:30pm Norwich time.

So from the suburban quiet of my spare room, amid Lego detritus, and with the simplest press of a button from my shabby coffee-stained keyboard, I let two news agencies in Hong Kong – and thereby the world – know of our intentions to sell £500 million worth of bonds to replace the existing debt carried by Manchester United.

The plan had been to send the press release to all the journalists in my contacts file the following morning together with the club's latest set of accounts, which were lodged in the Memorandum but had become an afterthought superseded by all the bond deliberations. So I spent a largely sleepless night drafting a press release of the results which needed the board's sign-off in the morning. This led to a succession of frantic calls and emails between Joel Glazer in Washington DC, David Gill in Manchester, Ed Woodward in Hong Kong and communications director Phil Townsend who was in Qatar accompanying the team on a short training camp: Manchester United: a global enterprise.

Before I had even managed to distribute the press release and results I began to get deluged by journalist calls. I didn't take any of them. I was governed by a strict gagging order from the lawyers, restricting me from saying anything beyond the legally sanctioned words in the press release, lest Manchester United was being seen as trying to inappropriately solicit investors to the bond. This proved frustrating; I wasn't even able to clarify why we were looking to launch the bond (primarily a means to take advantage of the club's financial riches to achieve a more stable capital structure) which meant that the knee-jerk nonsense propagated by the supporter groups – and some in the media – that the prospect of a 'junk' bond reflected financial difficulties for the club quickly took root without any chance of rebuttal.

PR Own Goal

Later that morning, following distribution of the bond and results press releases, I found myself sitting in my pyjamas watching possibly the world's biggest story of the day unfolding on my computer screen and giving tightly-controlled 'no comment' statements to the incessant journalist calls that continued to flood in. Still, I said to myself, at least the Memorandum, the circulation of which was to be strictly confined to prospective institutional investors, hadn't surfaced; then all hell would break loose. The Memorandum would expose the inner workings of the club, its risks and fears catalogued in black and white legalese. Gold dust for journalists, for so long frustrated by our awkward dealings with them.

Then Tariq Panja from Bloomberg called me to say he had the Memorandum; it had been sent to him by a City source as a PDF file. Over the next few hours other reporters called to say they had it too. There are moments in life when you can run, but you know you can't hide. This was one of them, my resignation to the likely storm of negative press coverage coming my way evoking the closing scenes from the famous series of Hamlet cigar television advertisements in the 1970s.

It's fair to say that a tsunami rather than a mere storm of blanket press coverage greeted the news of the bond and disclosure of the Memorandum during the following days. While Ed Woodward and Jamie Reigle would report back with very positive investor meetings and even concrete orders taken by the book runners from enthusiastic Far East investors, I could only reciprocate with tales of intense furore: a PR own goal. Our public relations were made worse, I feared, by our inability to mitigate let alone rebut the thousands of words written in the document in Manchester United's name. This fed a truck load of misleading speculation that money would leave the club to pay down the payment-in-kind loans, or even that a sale and leaseback of Old Trafford and the Carrington training ground was imminent. The *Daily Mail* encapsulated the mood of panic:[106] 'They boast of having 469 million followers around the world but then warn that they may have to sell their own stadium. They are the most valuable football club in the world – worth £1.2 billion according to Forbes – but have no money of their own to buy players. This is Manchester United 2010;

---

[106] Have Glazers put United on the road to meltdown? *Daily Mail*, 14 January 2010

Manchester United the Glazer way. Fears of financial meltdown have stalked the dreams of supporters since the Glazer family took their club into private ownership in 2005. Now – as they tour the world trying to raise £500 million to ease the burden of debts worth £699 million – United's owners have put down in black and white just what their four-and-half turbulent years have done to England's most famous football club.'

But while the press coverage's tenor reflected a degree of incredulity towards the club's efforts at further financial engineering, many reports were balanced by citations from business commentators and analysts who believed that the bond would get off the ground despite the club deciding against paying for a rating from a credit agency like Standard & Poor's and Moody's, relying instead on the high recognition of United's reliable cash flows and strong brand allure among the investment community. Indeed, by the end of the first week (with David Gill joining Ed Woodward in London to present United's roadshow, accompanied by replica Premier League and Champions League trophies) it felt as though the pendulum was beginning to swing back in favour of United, corroborated by a report in the *Daily Telegraph*:[107] 'This is a well-run company whose owners have demonstrated it can get bigger and more successful,' said one banker with knowledge of the sports market. 'People will be attracted by the emotional link to United as well, but this is not a flaky investment. There is more risk in football than many other industries, but United are better protected than any other club.'

The first game since the bond launch, a Saturday 3pm home match against Burnley, would serve as a focal point for further media interest. The manager was due to give his routine press conference on the preceding Friday morning and I was acutely aware that it could be hijacked by questions to Sir Alex about the bond. So, in consultation with Allen & Overy, I drafted a short statement which I forwarded on to the communications team in Manchester to read aloud before Sir Alex spoke, prohibiting members of the press from asking any

---

[107] United hit the road in GBP500m pitch, *The Daily Telegraph*, 14 January 2010

questions relating to the bond for 'regulatory requirements.' The tactic worked and closed off one obvious route to take the story forward. However, with the issue having dominated the news agenda for five days, the club's supporter groups, enraged by the bond and Memorandum, astutely saw the opportunity to fuel the news agenda by calling for a meeting ahead of the Burnley game.

While the team cruised to a 3-0 victory against Burnley, towards the end of the game there were significant protests inside the stadium, including some anti-Glazer chants. There was even an attempt by some fans – intercepted by stadium security staff – to unfurl a 'Love United Hate Glazer' banner similar in look to the thousands of stickers that had been plastered all over Manchester around the time of the takeover. 'Yet no matter how strenuously Manchester United attempt to keep a lid on comment about the club's financial situation,' the *Daily Telegraph* pronounced[108], 'they cannot control the 75,000 voices of those supporters who continue to pay to watch Ferguson's team and the mutinous air within the stadium during the closing stages of this game, when a series of vitriolic chants against the Glazer family, the club's owners, rang around the ground, would have had the bond salesmen squirming in their seats. After all, there was little mention of revolting fans in the prospectus. This was the first time that Old Trafford had rung out to such condemnatory chants.'

Spooked by their Noisy Neighbours

The level of vitriol reflected the passionate zeal of those vociferous United fans who were tired of reading endless stories about the club's debt and cash payments to the owners. Yet it also represented, to my mind, an explosion of anger and frustration at the growing dissonance between an ever-reclusive ownership and the Old Trafford fan base, which had not been entirely sated with trophy success. Supporters also seemed spooked by the prospect of Manchester City – their 'noisy

---

[108] Glazer protest beats censor, *The Daily Telegraph*, 18 January 2010

neighbours' – gaining further ground in the Premier League. Indeed, as the weeks unfolded and United went on to clock up sizeable home victories over lesser opponents such as Hull City, Portsmouth and West Ham United, it became noticeable to me how the mutinous protests would take on a seemingly rehearsed theatrical quality of their own, and would only escalate once the team enjoyed a two or three goal lead over their opponents. It made the stadium resemble another British institution: the pantomime. 'Now that we know we're going to win, we can relax and focus on our hatred of the real bogeymen, the Glazers'.

Into the second week of the bond roadshow, which saw Ed Woodward and his executive colleagues continuing to trot the globe, press coverage in the UK was unabated in its vehement attacks against the Glazers. Much of it was centred upon content dug up in the Memorandum; journalists were quick to extrapolate and exaggerate the many, often hypothetical, provisions laid bare in the document as statements of fact. This was the case in the *Daily Telegraph,* which ran with the 'revelation' that:[109] 'The Glazer family could take out more than £600 million from Manchester United's revenues over the next seven years in dividends, interest payments and fees arising from the club's bond issue.' Indeed, anti-Glazer press sentiment that week felt even rawer than usual following news of US food giant Kraft's controversial gobbling up of English chocolate stalwart Cadburys. Was nothing sacred?

United fans found their anxieties reaching new heights during the first leg of the Carling Cup semi-final against Manchester City at the City of Manchester Stadium. Although the Carling Cup had never been a priority for United, this tie, coming so soon after the ignominious FA Cup defeat to Leeds, was to reach epic proportions since City were looking to the fixture as a route to win their first silverware in three decades. A truly pulsating game saw the Reds surrendering an early Ryan Giggs lead to two goals from former player Carlos Tévez.

---

[109] Glazer bond issue fuels fans' fury, *The Daily Telegraph*, 19 January 2010

Contemplating 'Failure'

The next day my own anxiety also reached new heights after the accidental submission of United's parent company, Red Football Joint Venture accounts, to Companies House, which became available for all to see. The owners had certainly not sanctioned the accounts to be published – we normally did so in the spring time – and I had categorically advised against disclosure of the latest debt figure amid the furore over the bond. Yet a clerical error in Manchester gave the green light to their erroneous release and I was inundated with calls from journalists, the accounts displayed on their computer screens revealing that the overall debt (including the rolled up interest from the payment-in-kind notes) had increased from £699 million to £717 million. That was perilously close to the original £790 million buy-out figure, suggesting that the Glazers' original cash injection of around £270 million had diminished to around £70 million, the rest having been swallowed up by the PIK interest.

Later that morning I snatched a conversation with Ed Woodward who was travelling between investor meetings in the States. We agreed that we should have a back-up communications plan in case the bond was not a success; I didn't even dare summon the word 'failure'. In need of some fresh air, I drove an hour-or-so into the desolate north Norfolk countryside, comfortably out of mobile phone reach with the rest of the world, and proceeded on a long walk in the beautiful winter sunshine. While my previous role in a PR agency had made me accustomed to clients failing to succeed with their daring business plans, in this instance I had come to feel personally and inextricably intertwined with United's fortunes, and I felt churned up as I contemplated events not going our way. Moreover, having exposed the club to such intense scrutiny with the Memorandum, I felt that not getting the bond through would have an irrevocably harmful effect on the Glazers' business reputation, and the ensuing fallout would be a public relations nightmare for me. Later that afternoon I drafted a short memo to Ed outlining that the priority was to manage internal communications in order to assuage any alarm and panic among Manchester United staff and commercial partners. Externally I advised that we had no choice but to pull up the drawbridge until the commotion started to settle down.

Over the Line

The probability of launching the bond by the end of that week was made suddenly worse from a completely unforeseen quarter: the President of the United States of America. Barack Obama shocked the financial world with a speech calling for tight restrictions on banks' so-called 'casino' activities. His remarks sent the world's stock markets into a tailspin the next day, which impacted upon the corporate bond markets too. As one of the many millions who had cheered Obama's ascent to the White House, I suddenly found myself bizarrely conflicted between his laudable sentiments and my innate (and overriding) desire to see the bond over the line.

By the evening of Thursday 21 January I was ignoring a flurry of press calls speculating that the bond was a done deal. However, my call into Ed Woodward suggested otherwise, with evidence that Obama's remarks had prospective investors getting twitchy about the direction the overall market might be heading. While the order book was satisfyingly full, thanks in particular to surprisingly strong demand from American investors, United's syndicate of advisory banks had to finalise the final coupon rate on the bond; the higher the yield it offered the more cash interest outlay the club would have to bear. The following morning, with papers reporting that the bond had been launched,[110] I stayed in touch with Ed for a nervous six hours-or-so, the time difference meaning that Ed and his advisors would be working through the night in America while I constantly texted him with London's latest stock market prices. By the late afternoon, with the US markets now trading, the final pricing of the bond had been clinched to the Glazers' satisfaction and approval, albeit with an

---

[110] Glazers buy time as bond issue raises £500m for United debts, *The Times*, 22 January 2010

interest rate towards the higher end of expectations. This pointed to an overall annual charge of some £45 million to service it, taking out the previous tiered debt structure.

The bond had been a success: more than twice oversubscribed despite being launched against a considerable press backlash and intensifying market headwinds. The fact that sophisticated investors around the world had seen fit to buy into the £500 million bond represented a vindication of the Glazers' ownership, Manchester United's business model and Ed Woodward (and his team's) unstinting salesmanship. The *Independent* went on to write:[111] 'A year ago, the deal could have cost them twice as much…Those fans calling for Sir Alex Ferguson to walk out in protest are missing the point. Unpalatable as it might seem, there were few options other than the bond left to Manchester United. Its successful sale puts the club in an infinitely better financial position than it was in a month ago.'

But the bond sale's success proved to be double-edged, too, given the upheaval it had triggered among supporters. Still, I felt a massive sense of relief; having exiled myself for the best part of two weeks in the spare room of my Norwich house I felt I had aged about two years. Joel Glazer called me later that Friday evening, his unfailingly calm voice giving nothing away about his emotions. 'Thanks Tes, it's been quite an interesting couple of weeks. I'm happy we're over the line,' he said. 'Sure Joel,' I replied, 'I'm delighted we got there but it's not without some collateral damage to your reputations. That bond Memorandum is like an albatross around our necks.' Joel chuckled. 'Well, it's all out there now, there's nothing else negative for the press to write about.'

Green-and-Gold

The ire of Manchester United's disgruntled supporters was to take on a new lease of life when fans were called on by supporter groups to

---

[111] Reds' bond issue may be a blessing in disguise, *The Independent*, 23 January 2010

adopt the colours of Manchester United's antecedents, Newton Heath, who had sported yellow and green stripes. The 'green-and-gold' movement was arguably the public relations coup of the year, a powerful, colourful and imaginative way for fans to symbolise their anger and despondency towards the Glazers' ownership in a highly visible manner, fully aware that these images would reach millions of television viewers worldwide. Disconcertingly, the green and gold livery was identical to Norwich City's colours, providing me with no escape from the campaign in the coming months, whether I was working in Manchester or 190 miles away at my home in Norfolk.

A day after the successful launch of the bond, Manchester United hosted Hull City at Old Trafford. While a four-goal scoring spree from Wayne Rooney would demolish the opposition, it was the sight of hundreds of fans in the Stretford End, wrapped in their Newton Heath scarves and chanting 'We love United, we hate the Glazers' for 90 minutes that gripped the attention of the press box. To paraphrase the 1969 Thunderclap Newman classic – which had become firmly lodged in my head at the time – something was undeniably in the air, but could it actually escalate into revolution?

Sir Alex Ferguson had already pre-empted the mutinous atmosphere by addressing the supporters via a powerful statement in his matchday programme notes: 'The family of Manchester United is under pressure as a result of all the issues and controversies surrounding the ownership and financial situation of our club. Everyone is entitled to their opinion, and to express disapproval if they don't like what they see around them. I'm not slow to express disapproval myself if there is something I don't agree with – even in the boardroom with the directors. But once I walk out of the meeting, I get on with my job as manager of the team. Some of our fans are clearly unhappy with the financial position, but we mustn't allow the situation to become divisive. The danger, as I see it, is that we could be presented as being split, which could be harmful and inaccurate because I believe the vast majority of United fans are behind us. We must remain loyal to the cause of Manchester United. This is not about stifling criticism; it's simply a plea to stand together rather than take action that will damage ourselves more than anyone else. Manchester

United is bigger than me, the players, the directors, officials, and the fans and, particularly at this critical stage of our season, we need to pull in the same direction.'

Duncan Drasdo from MUST, the Supporters' Trust, responded:[112] 'He talks about the Manchester United family and he's right, all strands of the family must come together to accelerate the change of ownership because we certainly don't see the Glazers as part of the United family. I thought Fergie's words smacked of a conciliatory gesture to the supporters and that he understood our concerns. He has not defended the Glazers in his notes!'

All of a sudden MUST had rediscovered its voice; after years of dire warnings about the Glazers' ownership, it had seized on the fallout from the bond sale Memorandum as an opportunity to challenge the Americans' ownership. MUST's well-oiled propaganda machine would swing into action, quick to speculate about any divisions, albeit imagined, between the Glazers and the other two key players in the club's powerful triumvirate, Sir Alex and David Gill.

MUST would forge new links with seemingly powerful allies, too. Jim O'Neill, who had briefly sat on the PLC board prior to the 2005 takeover and who counted Sir Alex as a friend, criticised the club's finances in comments to a newswire while on the sidelines of a conference in China:[113] 'There's too much leverage going on with Manchester United, it's not a good thing. I'm not a buyer of the bond.' O'Neill's view was hardly exceptional given his steadfast opposition to the takeover. Indeed, I'd had the pleasure of Jim O'Neill's down-to-earth company twice during the second half of 2009, when he had implored me to ask my bosses to remove the hedge funded payment-in-kind notes. O'Neill's sincerity as a United supporter was unimpeachable, but on this occasion his employer, Goldman Sachs, was among the syndicate of banks that had just advised on United's bond sale.

---

[112] Green and gold United protest gathers momentum, *Manchester Evening News*, 25 January 2010

[113] Goldman's O'Neill, Lifelong Manchester United Fan, Spurns Bonds, Bloomberg, 25 January 2010

Joel Glazer's response was less equivocal. Wanting to avoid a public spat, Joel and I agreed that it would not be appropriate to make any comment. However, the Glazers would use their close contacts with the bank's New York hierarchy to make their displeasure privately known.

The Second Leg

After losing away to Manchester City in the first leg of the Carling Cup semi-final, United faced a hotly anticipated return match at Old Trafford the following week. As usual, I travelled up to Manchester on the Pendolino and arrived at Piccadilly train station. However, the instant I stepped onto the platform I was taken aback by the amount of men, women and children wearing green-and-gold scarves. As I walked through the city centre, I could sense the magnitude of this local derby among Mancunians, but could also sense the tension. That afternoon, over a cup of tea in the editor's office of the *Manchester Evening News*, I learned from Maria McGeoghan exactly how inflamed the atmosphere had become. She told me that one of the city's police chiefs had been sitting in my seat the previous day, and had requested that the paper approach the game in a sensitive and responsible manner in order to avert any further tension between the Red and Blue halves of the city in the run-up to the match.

Later that day I had further conversations with Manchester-based reporters and was told in no uncertain terms that United's fans were in rebellious mood, petrified of losing their bragging rights to their nouveaux riches rivals. Indeed, it was difficult to overestimate fans' stirrings that month: the anger at the Leeds FA Cup loss; the outrage prompted by the Memorandum; City's play for Manchester's top dog status; even rumours that Wayne Rooney might be poached by a wealthy Spanish club. The Glazers, just as their predecessors at the helm of the Manchester United board, seemed appropriate scapegoats for their club's perceived malaise.

Outside Old Trafford, the many burly green-and-gold scarf hawkers might have wondered whether Sir Matt Busby Way was indeed paved with real gold, as crowds of red-shirted fans queued up – patiently clutching their £5 notes – to buy their new polyester scarves. An unsuspecting visitor might have presumed that United's colours were indeed Norwich City's. That evening I couldn't muster the will to sit in the press box; being in the 'lion's den' should United have lost would have been unbearable, so I chose instead to sit in the South Stand.

The atmosphere proved to be scintillating, matching the intensity of the biggest games that I had been privileged to attend at Old Trafford. Despite half of the home fans appearing to be clad in green-and- gold shirts, the game itself was so absorbing that United supporters kept their anti-Glazer chants at bay and stayed true to their love of the team, screaming their gutsy support throughout. Even at 2-0 up nobody was taking a United victory for granted. When Tevez – who else – clawed a goal back for the Blues in the 76th minute, extra-time seemed to be looming. The Old Trafford faithful had to endure a nerve-wracking 15 minutes before, in the second minute of stoppage time, Wayne Rooney scored with a powerful header, thus sealing the tie, vanquishing City and sending United to Wembley. Delight and delirium prevailed; perhaps now the supporters' despair at the ownership would now be put on hold, I wishful thought.

Football Focus

That week, the BBC sports reporter Dan Roan approached Phil Townsend and me to comment on the prospect of growing supporter dissent, especially in relation to the perceived lack of spending of the Ronaldo transfer cash. Post-bond, supporter groups were arguing that the money was now earmarked to pay down the Glazers' payment-in-kind borrowings. Phil and I discussed the merits of contributing, particularly as it represented the first time that we could break our silence since the bond issue. Given the reach of a BBC report, we decided to cooperate and submitted a statement, signed off by David Gill and Joel Glazer:

'Manchester United is the most profitable football club in the world. Last year, on a record turnover of £278 million, the club made a record cash profit of £91 million. Interest payments were £41 million and wages accounted for less than half of the turnover. The recent bond issue has been very successful and provides the club with certainty in its interest payments, as well as great flexibility with the removal of bank covenants. The cash from the sale of Cristiano Ronaldo is available for Sir Alex to spend and it will be spent on players who are available for purchase and who the manager thinks can improve the squad, not to prove to pundits that it exists.'

I was looking forward to watching Dan Roan's report, having spent considerable time briefing him off-the-record with our 'business as usual' mantra. It was to feature in *Football Focus*, a long-established, must-see television programme which traditionally raised the curtain to the football weekend. However, I was appalled to find that the much-trumpeted report would centre around the thoughts of financier Keith Harris, who had helped broker several high-profile deals in football including Roman Abramovich's purchase of Chelsea and Thaksin Shinawatra's acquisition of Manchester City. Interviewed in his London office (with an autographed photograph of United legend Denis Law together with team-mate George Best behind him) Harris used his appearance to pour scorn on the Glazers, revealing that a group of unnamed investors dubbed the 'Red Knights' were being lined up to buy out the Glazers. He remarked:[114] 'It's too early to say how much would have to be raised. I would hope that there would be sufficient money in addition to that to show the Glazers they could take a profit and put the ownership into more caring hands,' said the media savvy Harris. Then he provided a memorably cute line: 'Seventy-five pence of every pound that [Manchester United] fans are spending is now going to the Glazers either for themselves or to pay debts.' The lunchtime programme's report also featured a fan outside Old Trafford who commented: 'The club is now technically bankrupt in many ways.'

I felt incensed by the one-sided nature of the report and felt that our statement had been given the most cursory of treatments. Harris'

---

[114] Interview with Keith Harris, *Football Focus*, BBC, 30 January 2010

'seventy-five pence' sound bite was total nonsense, and to include the outrageous accusation that the club was 'technically bankrupt' struck me as irresponsible if not defamatory. Of course, this wasn't the first (or last) time that I had felt the truth was being ridden roughshod by sensationalist journalism, but this was the BBC, I thought; they're supposed to be balanced. I had become disciplined at not responding to press coverage that irked me, mirroring the Glazers' consistently phlegmatic approach to arguably the fiercest media culture on the globe. Imagine if they had been inclined to seek legal redress against every stinging article? They would surely have been preoccupied with fighting lawsuits rather than running their business interests. However, on this occasion, I decided to chase down Dan Roan and *Football Focus'* editor to lodge my frustration, in spite of the fact that this would mean clashing swords with my favourite childhood programme. It represented a further twist in the increasingly fraught situation that I found myself in, especially as it jarred with my – albeit vain – expectation that the bond's success would deliver calm and stability to the club.

I soon found myself back in London. After the isolation of Norwich – and having effectively been gagged by the strictures of the bond sale – I knew I that I had to try and restore trust with key journalists in the hope of leveraging the success of the bond to mitigate the supporters' furore. This would be a tall order; especially as even my close friends, whom I hadn't seen since the New Year, seemed genuinely concerned as to whether a Glazer owned United had a future, so pervasive was the negative press. While I felt I did receive a sympathetic hearing from the press pack, I was struck by how much they had been swayed by MUST's campaign (as well as by Keith Harris) who had taken advantage of our weeks of imposed silence to build real momentum. Although there seemed an acceptance that the oversubscribed bond was a success (I was happy to privately admit to reporters a considerable personal relief, too) they seemed more interested in the 'real' story that was also exciting their editors' interests: the apparently growing challenge to the owners' authority at the world's biggest football club.

I felt forced to swallow some humble pie. In fairness to *Football Focus* and Dan Roan – and the legion of journalists now pursuing the hottest story in sport – I was beginning to accept that it was me who was out of step with the pack in a frenzied environment in which the *perception* of Manchester United slipping into inexorable crisis had become reality.

That sense of crisis was to deepen during February as MUST and the nascent Red Knights seized the PR agenda with a stream of press-friendly initiatives. However, inside United the mood was more phlegmatic, the owners and directors resigned to having to weather yet another media storm. At this point, as during the Benfica/Keane/Vodafone crisis of late 2005, I would resume regular communication with Phil Townsend, who was the only person who could share my increasingly surreal journey through uncharted waters. Phil's experience of having worked at the heart of government was also to prove invaluable; indeed, he frequently attested in his no-nonsense tone that the ownership of Manchester United, unlike politics, 'was not a popularity contest, Tes.'

Protests Go Digital

On February 6th, MUST threatened to hijack the 52nd anniversary of the Munich air disaster by stepping up its campaign against the Glazers with tacit calls for a boycott of the next season's games, and by leafleting the 70,000 home supporters at that day's match against Portsmouth. This served to stoke emotions by rekindling the lie that the Glazers had triggered their takeover on the Munich anniversary five years previously. On the pitch, however, it was business as usual as the Reds were restored to the top of the Premier League after cruising to a 5-0 defeat of a football club in real financial dire straits. Rob Draper in the *Mail on Sunday* reported:[115] 'As huge swathes of the stadium sang in unison, they twirled those green-and-gold scarves above their heads, a moving sign of peaceful defiance to the new order

---

[115] Even the gods have it in for Pompey, *The Mail On Sunday*, 7 February 2010

of football club ownership. And here is a curious thing: among the small yet vocal band of Portsmouth followers, there were several green-and-gold scarves being sported by opposition fans. They are supporters who truly know a thing or two about being taken for a ride by greedy or inept owners. Portsmouth last week inherited their fourth owner of the year in Balram Chainrai, another with no interest in the club beyond the financial gain he might be able to extract. And they remain on the verge of extinction, with 112 years of history in jeopardy, because of financial mismanagement. United will merely see their standing diminished if the Glazer family's gamble on their future goes wrong but, despite the chasm in difference between the relative status of these clubs, amply illustrated on the pitch, their cause is a common one.'

Indeed, Portsmouth's plight, brought about by its Leeds United-like profligate spending on players, would see the club plunge to administration and relegation by the end of the season, only two years after lifting the FA Cup. This would serve to drive panic among United supporters who wrongly feared that their club was heading towards a similar fate.

February saw the green-and-gold protest fast becoming a movement which had aroused interest internationally. One rallying cry was the slogan 'Debt is the Road to Ruin', attributed to David Gill in the fog of the takeover battle in 2004, when he had vigorously opposed the Glazers' initial approach (his words were even reprinted onto a banner that was unfurled outside his Cheshire home). David had to run another gauntlet after speaking as an alumnus at his old university; he was involved in an uncomfortable confrontation with some students who challenged him on the spot for selling out to the Glazers.

MUST's impressive propaganda machine – I was even confronted by several 'Love United Hate Glazer' stickers on my ski-lift in the remote French Alps – was to gain further momentum by its clever use of the Internet and social media to mobilise disgruntled supporters and press ahead its agenda. This contrasted with the pre-world wide web era in which protests were largely confined to demonstrations and marches outside the stadium. While these actions would still constitute a colourful and telegenic focal point for supporters' wrath, MUST recognised the value of virtual communications via the Internet and via email-driven campaigns in order to build momentum among supporters and maintain a compelling background noise to sustain press coverage.

MUST was also aided by the emerging influence of online bloggers, in particular by Andy Green, a Mayfair-based partner at a fund manager. He had garnered significant media interest in his own take on United's bond Memorandum, and had produced a well-written running commentary on the club's business model which he dubbed 'Glazernomics'. His purported objectivity was, however, coloured by his avowed hatred of the Glazer family's ownership, symbolised by his signing off each blog with the 'LUHG' acronym. Green's commentary and pithy sound bites would go on to carry substantial weight in the press, especially among those journalists perhaps reluctant to make sense of the accounts for themselves.

The supporters' group received a significant news fillip when it revealed that it was being helped by Blue State Digital, which had advised Barack Obama on his groundbreaking email strategy to supporters during his campaign for the White House. MUST would engage in regular online polling, creating virtual communities of mobilised supporters who were also being cultivated via Facebook and Twitter. Indeed, as the green-and-gold movement grew, MUST would see a sharp rise in the number of subscribers for its e-mail list, from around 30,000 before the bond launch to beyond 150,000 by the end of the season. Regardless of the efficacy of Blue State Digital's advice to MUST, the supporters' group would attract a great deal of publicity for this alliance, so enthralled had the media become in the David versus Goliath battle to oust the Glazers.

Carling Cup Final

With the Glazers maintaining their silence and distance – supported by my steadfast refusal to respond to journalists' invitations to comment on the green-and-gold initiative – it would be Sir Alex

Ferguson's carefully-chosen words that would command the most authority. Ahead of the team's visit to Goodison Park, he achieved a precarious and diplomatic balancing act by declaring satisfaction with the club's hierarchy, while also providing empathy with protesting supporters:[116] 'It's not a concern. It just shows you we have fans who care for the club. Every fan has a right to complain about what they think is right. We also have to run the club the way we think is the right way to do. And I think we are doing the right thing with the club. Obviously there are fans protesting and we understand where it is coming from but we carry on with the football side of it. I've made my point to the supporters, as long as it doesn't interrupt or interfere with the progress of the team, and I think they realise that.'

The following weekend, Manchester United travelled to Wembley to play Aston Villa in the Carling Cup final. One end of the stadium housed the traditional claret and blue of the Villains' supporters, hopeful that they could secure their first domestic silverware in nearly 15 years; the opposite end of the stadium comprised the Red section – albeit mostly clad in green-and-gold – many of whom seemed indifferent to the prospect of winning what had once been dubbed the 'worthless' cup. The Glazers, contrary to press speculation, were in attendance that day. I was sat high in one of the executive boxes, my stomach full from the generous roast beef carvery served in the hospitality dining area, but feeling increasingly queasy as I was forced to witness a passionate demonstration of the potency of the green-and-gold movement. They had even choreographed the release of thousands of yellow and green balloons, many of which stubbornly lingered on the pitch as the match got under way, much to the annoyance of the organisers. Accompanying the cacophony of anti-Glazer chants and banners was a huge green-and-gold satin flag that shimmered serenely over the heads of thousands of supporters. The international newswire Bloomberg reported:[117] 'Banners opposing the club's owners, banned at the team's Old Trafford stadium, appeared in various sections of the

---

[116] Fergie's fine with protest, *The Sun*, 20 February 2010
[117] United's Cup Win Gets Green & Gold Protest Backdrop, Bloomberg, 1 March 2010

crowd of 88,596. One read: "Glazer 4 Ever in Your Debt" and another said "United Against Glazer." There's never been a previous occasion when supporters of one team have turned up in their tens of thousands wearing a different colour to the team,' Malcolm Clarke, chairman of the Football Supporters' Federation, said in an interview. 'This is an unprecedented show of protest at a cup final.'

Absolutely everyone I would encounter at that time would suggest, half-jokingly, whether it was time the team should play in green-and-gold to defy the protests; if I had a pound for every time this idea was suggested I could have perhaps reduced Manchester United's debt myself.

Away from the distraction of the protests, the match proved to be a good one, albeit steeped in controversy as defender Nemanja Vidic avoided a red card for an obvious violation in the third minute that had resulted in a Villa penalty and an early lead for United's opponents. But Aston Villa's lead would be cancelled out by a goal apiece from Michael Owen and Wayne Rooney to provide Sir Alex with his first and only trophy of the season. I left Wembley pleased with the result but also relieved to have exited such a show of strength from the green-and-gold movement, which had become such a prevailing talking point. The *Wall Street Journal* summed it up nicely when it wrote:[118] 'First, sports fans wanted their teams to win. Then they wanted fancy new stadiums with sleek amenities and gourmet food. Now, they want ownership to have a healthier balance sheet. The family of American businessman Malcolm Glazer, owner of the English Premier League's fabled Manchester United club, is locked in a strange battle of wills with part of the soccer club's rabid fan base.'

The Red Knights

The next day I stopped by at United's Pall Mall office to review and

---

[118] In England, a Soccer Tea Party – Manchester United Fans Try to Push Out Their American Owner with a New Color Scheme, *The Wall Street Journal*, 2 March 2010

finalise United's financial results. It was the first time that the club had to post its quarterly results as a condition of the bond, providing investors (and the press) with the most up-to-date guidance on the club's business performance. The numbers were straightforward; all the key metrics had enjoyed strong growth – reflecting particularly robust media and commercial revenues – with a small reduction in the club's debt and confirmation that the Ronaldo transfer money remained as part of the club's £122 million cash war chest.

By around 7:30pm I was leaving the office when my phone rang; it was Oliver Kay from the *Times* newspaper telling me that Sky News was reporting that the Red Knights had been meeting in London that day to discuss a one billion pound bid for Manchester United.

'Tes, what's your reaction?'

'That's news to me Olly. In any case, Manchester United is not for sale.'

'Can I quote you Tes?'

'Sure, as the Glazers' spokesman.'

'By the way, when you say "not for sale" do you mean "not now" or "never"?'

'Nice try Olly. Manchester United is not for sale. That's my statement, I couldn't be clearer.'

So, in that snatched conversation – and confident of not needing to check-in with the Glazers first – I would lay down the owners' unambiguous position, echoing statements I had made since 2006, which I would repeat ad nauseam for the coming momentous days, weeks and months ahead.

Already phone calls were streaming in from other news outlets, also prompted by Sky News' rolling news coverage led by its business editor Mark Kleinman, the same reporter who had broken news of our abortive attempt at a refinancing in 2007. Kleinman had established that a group of self-styled 'Red Knights' – a who's who of City of London finance – had met up earlier that morning in the Fleet Street offices of the lawyers Freshfields Bruckhaus Deringerin (the same firm that had advised the club's PLC board opposing the Glazers' takeover in 2005) hosted by the Mancunian Mark Rawlinson. He was joined by fellow Manchester-born Jim O'Neill Goldman Sachs' high-profile chief economist who had criticised United's bond earlier in the year. The irony wasn't lost on me that the meeting, according to reports, was also attended by Paul Marshall, a boss of a hedge fund, the type of institution so reviled by supporters for having lent money to the Glazers in the first place. Indeed it wouldn't be too long before the cabal's protagonists' credentials would be picked over, especially in relation to how each member had personally enriched himself from transactions during the debt-fuelled boom of recent years. It would later emerge that MUST's hierarchy were at the meeting, too, and that the Red Knights were being advised by the financial public relations agency Finsbury, which, like Freshfields, had also been advisors to the PLC club's board that had resisted the Glazers' takeover.

While initially bristling at the prospect of a tussle with the Red Knights, who had already appeared to have curried a degree of favour among the media, I was also excited that, after more than a month of rumour and innuendo, this group were at last to reveal their hand. This was especially the case as the Glazers (to continue the card analogy) very much held the vital trump card: Manchester United was not for sale.

As it happened, there was barely any information to come out of the Red Knights, merely unattributed talk of a possible one billion pound bid. It struck me as incredibly naïve for them to have gone public with their meeting, given how nascent their talks seemed to have been. Surely it would have been better to have kept their counsel and only move when there was something substantial to say, such as a tangible cash backed offer, pressed home with a series of media interviews?

Late that night, with the first online stories from the UK's newspapers filtering through, I put a call into Joel Glazer. Joel was his measured, good-humoured self, betraying absolutely no stress at the prospect of the Red Knights. 'Understand Tes, the message is simple: Manchester United is absolutely not for sale. We are in it for the long-term, we love owning the club.' While we agreed that we could dismiss the Red Knights, I did suggest to Joel that a number of sensible supporters might be concerned when they read the papers the next morning; perhaps we should consider some form of engagement to assuage their worries? Joel's response was, as ever, diplomatic and noncommittal. 'Sure, let's think on. Send me through some ideas if you like.' So I did, tabling the suggestion of an open letter to fans and/or a media interview.

I would never establish why news of the Red Knights' meeting had leaked; I imagined that the more astute members of the group knew better than to seek publicity for such a half-baked plan, however others might have been excited at the prospect of the media splash, perhaps hoping that the inevitable explosion in news coverage would have galvanised potential investors and pressured Manchester United's owners into considering an offer. I suspected that the leak was just that, someone from within the ranks who acted alone, but perhaps underestimating the impact such a revelation would have. This reflected the inherently dysfunctional nature of the Red Knights; wealthy alpha-males used to calling their own shots rather than having to toe the line to the opinions of others. One thing was for sure: the Red Knights got the publicity, whether intentional or not, in the newspapers the next morning. The potency of a Manchester United takeover story, mixed with an already feverish green-and-gold protest backdrop, produced a level of press coverage rivalling the amount generated during the takeover in May 2005.

I was back in United's Pall Mall office preparing to put out the club's financial results for that day and, fortified by my long telephone conversation with Joel, felt calm about the likely media storm. Ed Woodward was preoccupied with his inaugural investor presentation conference call in the wood-panelled sanctity of the London office's boardroom. It was notable that, ahead of this important call we barely discussed the Red Knights at all as they did not seem relevant to the real business of running a football club. However, we did ready ourselves for the prospect of a question on the Red Knights, our stock response being a simple 'the club is not for sale.' Minutes before the call, however, the connection had gone down, and we all had to scurry around trying to make sense of the spaghetti-like tangle of wires buried underneath the boardroom table. With seconds to spare, the connection was thankfully restored and Ed was able to calmly take Manchester United's bond investors and analysts through a deliberately humdrum PowerPoint presentation, focused on the utility-like reliability of the club's growing cash flow to comfortably service the bond. One reality check to come out of the call – against the media furore evidenced by my BlackBerry vibrating some 30 times during the space of an hour – was that no participant to the conversation had enquired about the Red Knights. Not for the first time there was a chasm between perceptions of 'crisis' and the reality of routine day-to-day business.

'High Net Worth Individuals'

For journalists – especially those on the business desks – the advent of the Red Knights was a dream come true. I had already long realised that the opportunity to speculate about Manchester United being 'in play' would automatically command top news billing. But an extra dimension was added – and media interest was aroused – by the fact that it involved a group of wealthy men spearheaded by the likeable and approachable Jim O'Neill. O'Neill had once been described by an American business magazine as the 'Rock Star' of Goldman Sachs, the investment bank which, post-credit crunch, appeared to evoke as much scrutiny and controversy as Manchester United. Within 24 hours of the Red Knights' London meeting, a short holding statement from the group was released, confirming their meeting as 'a gathering of high net worth individuals, who support Manchester United… looking at the feasibility of putting together a proposal to be put to the Glazer family regarding the ownership of Manchester United.'

The statement was accompanied with further unattributed briefings to the press from the Red Knights and their PR company, which led to saturation coverage and much analysis of a possible takeover. The self-styled 'high net worth individuals' had signalled that they would not be willing to stump up all the cash for the takeover, estimated in need of being north of one billion pounds to tempt the Glazers. Rather, they would need to scour the globe for other wealthy United fans to come on board, with any gap funded – ironically – with debt. There was even speculation that the bond would have to remain in situ given the redemption penalty of paying down investors early. With Manchester

United not for sale in any case, the Red Knights and their advisors can't have been surprised to read rather equivocal press comment, unsure what the group had to offer other than not being 'those ghastly Glazers'. Writing in the *Times*, the business of sport academic Stefan Szymanski wrote:[119] 'There's no doubt that the frontmen for the Red Knights are genuine United loyalists, but are they only the squires? Given that United are known as the Red Devils, it seems appropriate that the Glazers are becoming the most demonised owners in football history. But it is unlikely that getting rid of them will divorce the profit motive from owning Manchester United. What seems surprising about much of the opposition to the Glazers is the presumption that they care less than the fans about the club's success. How could they ever make a profit without it? Perhaps more than any other potential owners the Glazers depend on the team winning. If the Red Knights triumphed it would require a colossal investment. A shrewd supporter should ask this: either the Red Knights are simply altruists, or, if not, how on earth will they get a return on their investment?'

More damning were the opinion pieces written by sports journalists who appreciated the existing stability of the club provided by the Glazers, and lavished scorn on the logic of how City financiers, universally vilified for their role in the financial crisis, could come to United's rescue. The influential Martin Samuel, writing in the *Daily Mail*, astutely cast aspersions on why the club would want to relinquish its status quo for the unknown quantity of the Red Knights:[120] 'O'Neill is the head of the Red Knights, a group of City experts – no, stop giggling at the back – and Manchester United fans who are discussing the overthrow of the Glazers at Old Trafford. The irony is that Sir Alex Ferguson seems content with the current owners. So, on one side, the man who came up with BRIC; on the other, the man who came up with two European Cups, 11 league titles, five FA Cups, four League Cups, one European Cup-Winners Cup, one World Club

---

[119] Stefan Szymanski: Whoever owns it, Man Utd must net a profit, *The Times*, 3 March 2010

[120] Martin Samuel: Who is this Red Knight? *Daily Mail*, 3 March 2010

[121] Ian McGarry: Red Knights? More like the Red Dwarves, *The Sun*, 3 March 2010

Championship, one Intercontinental Cup and a European Super Cup. There is only one Red Knight that needs to be kept happy in Manchester.' In the same vein, the *Sun's* Ian McGarry asked:[121] 'Who will actually run the club if they gain control? Red Knights would boldly put themselves up for that task on the basis that the whole thing was their idea. Let's get this straight. Nine fans want to buy the club with other people's money.'

'Red Herrings'

Personally, I was rather enjoying this latest 'crisis' to land on my plate although I found myself cast adrift from my normal comfort zone of the business journalist community. I suspected they had a fetish for Jim O'Neill and Goldman Sachs and, being so desperate to write about a high-octane takeover story, had ignored the simple truth that the Glazers had no intention of selling their club. To be fair, business journalists are an understandably cynical bunch; for them, it was *de rigueur* to be told with maximum sincerity by a PR man that a company was not for sale, moments before an announcement that a deal to sell it had been done. 'Tes, everyone has a price,' I would be reliably told.

Equally, I was also perturbed at continuing reports that detailed Keith Harris' call for a boycott of season tickets. When I discussed this with the media, I often liked to use an analogy. I would compare it to a group of people wanting to buy the Glazers' mansion, the biggest and most coveted house in the area. Only the Glazers didn't want to sell. So the prospective buyers say, 'Hell, we'll smash down your fences and windows, then. That'll hit you in your pockets, and then you'll *have* to sell.' (In fairness, Joel Glazer didn't like my analogy; he thought that talking in terms of houses didn't do justice to the unique allure of owning Manchester United).

As the Red Knights story took grip I decided to reach as high a profile among journalists as possible, short of providing any on-the-record comment. I needed to project the owners' business-as-usual message, knowing that the 'not for sale' line would be better conveyed to journalists if they could see directly into the whites of my eyes. I travelled up to Manchester for the Soccerex conference, an event held at the city's imposing Manchester Central convention complex and frequented by football administrators and the media. There, BBC 5 Live was hosting a live discussion on the future of football in front of a large audience, with a panel featuring David Gold, the joint owner of West Ham, and Dan Johnson, the spokesperson for the Premier League. I had already spoken on the phone at length to the programme's presenter, Mark Pougatch, briefing him on United's business model and insisting that the Red Knights were superfluous 'red herrings'. The debate was dominated by the desire of supporters – represented on this occasion by an overwhelming majority of middle-aged white males – to have a greater say on the running of their football clubs. I was surprised, though, that the Glazers received less opprobrium than I had expected; rather it was Dan Johnson – whose organisation was preoccupied with sorting out the mess from the meltdown at Portsmouth FC – that seemed to draw the most anger and stinging criticism. On the other hand, had I taken up the BBC's invitation and been up on the platform as the Glazers' spokesperson, I suspect that I too would have felt the full force of resentment in the auditorium that day.

That evening I invited Dan Johnson along to a dinner at Piccolino, an Italian restaurant located a stone's throw away from Manchester's neo-gothic Town Hall. I had also arranged to meet a cross-section of journalists from the *Financial Times*, *Daily Telegraph*, *Wall Street Journal* and Associated Press. At that point, the resonance of the Red Knights story meant that I could enjoy an audience with just about anyone in the press, so anxious were they to glean any insights. For me, having been in the bunker for so long during the bond sale, it provided a rare opportunity, over several bottles of Chianti, to be more bullish about the Glazers' ownership.

The following day I hooked up with David Gill just ahead of his scheduled appearance at the Soccerex conference. It was useful to share what had become such a surreal experience with David; he was one of the few souls who could appreciate the ongoing pressures that took place behind the scenes at Manchester United. He and I were ushered into the green room where Matt Lorenzo, the TV sports presenter, would conduct the interview. As we headed into the packed hall I could sense the grandeur of the occasion; the world's eyes seemed to be on Manchester United and, unusually, its chief executive was scheduled to speak. From the back of the hall I witnessed a bravura performance by David, the stresses of the past few months seeming to drive within him a passionate defence of United's status quo. He proceeded to unleash an unusually unguarded attack on Keith Harris in particular, and the Red Knights in general:[122] 'Keith Harris will go anywhere with some publicity around, that's his modus operandi, but his track record in football isn't anything to write home about. But these are credible people and they do what they think is in the best interests of the club. But it's not going to take them anywhere if the owners have no wish to sell. From our perspective, they are running the club in the right way. Their idea of having 20, 30 or 40 very wealthy people owning and running Manchester United, I just don't know how it would work in practice. The better-run clubs have clear single-decision making that is quick and efficient. I'm not sure what the end game is but the end game is irrelevant because the owners are long-term investors. What the Glazers have done is let me and my team run the business, they've let Sir Alex Ferguson run the football side.'

I had half-hoped that David Gill's unequivocal remarks would draw a line under the Red Knights. Rather, they served to inflame the story, with the Red Knights adamantly responding that they would have the ability to deliver a fair price to force the Glazers to sell. Two days later, Sir Alex Ferguson's weekly press conference was again dominated by questions relating to off-the-field matters, and the manager pressed home the club's frustration with Keith Harris and his calls for a boycott of season tickets:[123] 'Now that is a great idea,' said Ferguson, his voice heavy with sarcasm. 'And that's come from an intelligent guy, has it? There's no chance of that. I don't mind people protesting. I went on an apprentices' march myself when I was younger, so protesting is not a

---

[122] Gill fires broadside at Red Knights, *The Daily Telegraph*, 4 March 2010
[123] Fergie's knight kick-off, *Daily Mirror*, 6 March 2010

problem for me. What is the issue for me, or would be an issue for me, is if it went against the team's performance, if it resulted in the team being affected by it. But I don't think it will. I've no issue with the Red Knights. I'm quite friendly with a couple of them, and don't deny them their right to protest. If they want to try to buy the club, it's entirely up to them.'

'Complete Fantasy'

The Red Knights would infer Ferguson's 'no issue' comments as tacit support for their cause, and would go on to brief the respected *Observer* newspaper:[124] 'Senior City financiers allied to the wealthy consortium planning a takeover of Manchester United claim Sir Alex Ferguson is supporting the controversial bid. Several key sources have told the Observer that they believe that the Old Trafford manager would be prepared to invest his own money in the club if the bid by the group known as the 'Red Knights' were to succeed. "Alex Ferguson is not only supportive of the bid but would be prepared, if successful, to back it," claimed one source who described it as a "killer blow" for the American Glazer family who bought the club in 2005 and who are now facing massive protests from fans because of the club's debts. Another senior City figure, who also requested anonymity, said: "We all know we have his support, that he likes the people involved, but we can't embarrass him."'

The *Observer* splashed the story on its front page, accompanied by a photo of Ferguson with the headline 'Fergie "backing bid to buy United" say City financiers.' Its prominence suggested that the paper had received guidance from a top source within the Red Knights. It was an extraordinary claim which Sir Alex would immediately refute, his denial buried in the fifth paragraph of the story. I sensed that the Red Knights had made a very poor call trying to co-opt the manager who, after all, was an employee of the club. To me, it suggested a degree

---

[124] Fergie 'backing bid to buy United', say City financiers, *The Observer*, 7 March 2010

of desperation on their part.

As soon as I got wind of the story I put a call into Phil Townsend. He told me about Sir Alex's fury at the report, adding that moves had been made to seek a retraction from the newspaper, especially as the *Observer* normally commanded a good reputation for fairness and accuracy. We agreed to coordinate a statement for me to brief in to the inevitable calls from the press. It read: 'There is 100 per cent trust between the manager and the owners and any claims to the contrary are complete fantasy.'

By mid-morning I was inundated with press calls asking me for my response. I was careful to not betray any schadenfreude over the Red Knights' own goal; also, I was keen not to appropriate the loyalty of the manager either. 'I suspect it's completely irrelevant to Sir Alex who owns Manchester United,' I calmly explained to journalists hoping to defuse a story that risked getting out of control. 'His only concern is that he maintains control over the squad to keep on challenging for trophies; he has certainly had this with the Glazers.'

The AC Milan Game

The *Observer* piece would ensure that the Red Knights story would run into the following week. This coincided with Manchester United's home tie against AC Milan, prior to which MUST – by now boasting more than 100,000 subscribers to its email updates, including curious people like me – had called for the biggest demonstration against the Glazers to date.

The blanket daily press coverage at this time meant that I would speak with Joel Glazer at least once a day, sometimes more frequently. Our chats allowed us to take stock of that morning's newspapers, and enabled me to glean any insights from him that could give nuances to the next wave of press calls. Even Joel's unflinching insistence that the club was not for sale (and that, contrary to what the more creative parts of the media alleged, his family's finances were in good health) felt more potent to hear direct from him, and fuelled my confidence at dealing with the ever-challenging calls from journalists. It was just a shame that the media didn't share my access too.

I had tabled a tentative plan for the Glazers to assuage the concerns of the club's silent majority of supporters who, like the manager, didn't care who owned the club provided it was steered towards football success. I argued that these supporters might be owed some reassurance from the owners, given how their club was fast becoming synonymous with green-and-gold tinged protest and dissent.

While the Glazers were willing to listen to my reasoning – which included lengthy telephone discussions with the club's joint chairmen and its chief executive – there was an overriding concern that any statement from the owners, particularly after a five-year vow of silence – could be seen as a knee-jerk response to the Red Knights' and MUST's agenda. This would feel unedifying, especially in light of the *Observer* story. Moreover, after David Gill and Sir Alex Ferguson's business-as-usual responses, asked Joel and Avie, wouldn't any comments by the Glazers risk inflaming an already volatile situation?

I travelled up to Manchester for United's second Champions League leg against AC Milan, arriving early to give me some time to catch up with locally-based journalists. That morning's press had included a prominent *Times* story in its home pages, which appeared willing to do the Red Knights' bidding with the headline 'Financial woes of the ultra-secretive Glazers, owners of Manchester United,' reporting:[125] 'Mr [Malcolm] Glazer attends few matches at Old Trafford – and when he does is jeered by fans. Mr Glazer owns a number of mobile home parks in Florida, which has been hit by America's sub-prime mortgage crisis, and recently sold his Grecian-style mansion in Palm Beach for $24 million (£16 million), adding to speculation about his financial woes.'

In fact Malcolm Glazer had never attended a match at Old Trafford. His two strokes in 2006 had prohibited him from travelling, and he had disposed of his interest in mobile home parks long before his family's acquisition of Manchester United in 2005. Also, Malcolm

---

[125] Financial woes of the ultra-secretive Glazers, owners of Manchester United, *The Times*, 10 March 2010

Glazer had not sold the house that he and his wife had lived in for two decades; they had, however, sold a house that they owned on the same street which had needed major renovations, recouping a $10 million profit. Speaking to Joel, I urged that we consider seeking legal advice to redress the story especially as it appeared in the *Times*, a self-styled newspaper of record. While I could sense a degree of frustration in Joel's voice, he was reluctant to give any further publicity to a spurious story that would only have been magnified by any legal proceedings.

MUST had initially called on supporters to boycott the first ten minutes of the Milan match, only to back down as the game approached, a ploy that risked laying bare the inefficacy of its campaign. Still, the atmosphere outside Old Trafford before the game was charged with anti-Glazer protest, with large swathes of supporters either wearing their green-and-gold scarves or queuing to buy one from the many vendors on Sir Matt Busby Way. As for the match itself, after the interval Manchester United quickly raced to a 2-0 lead, leaving a despondent Milan having to score three goals just to tie the game. With the scoreline seemingly unassailable, the second half proved to be the protest movement's zenith, artfully choreographed by groups of supporters who defied stadium stewards by unfurling huge 'Love United, Hate Glazer' banners at the Stretford End, serenaded by loud and incessant 'Die Glazer Die' chants. Following the Reds' resounding 4-0 victory, United's players must have wondered what was happening to their football club as they exited the pitch to the sight of jubilant supporters holding aloft their Norwich-style scarves.

One of those scarves would eventually find itself wrapped around the tattooed neck of AC Milan substitute David Beckham. The anti-Glazer coalition of Red Knights, MUST et al mustn't have believed their luck to have received what looked like an endorsement from someone as iconic as Golden Balls himself. The *Telegraph*'s Henry Winter elegantly summed up the night's proceedings:[126] 'They came

---

[126] Rampant Rooney rises to the big occasion to destroy Milan, *The Daily Telegraph*, 11 March 2010

to praise Wayne Rooney and bury the Glazers. They came to praise David Beckham and bury AC Milan. This was a surreal as well as starry night, the occasion flitting between testimonial, celebration and revolution… If Beckham's return was a side-show, albeit an emotional one for all parties, the most significant noises involved the extraordinary choruses of dissent towards United's reviled American owners. When Beckham donned an anti-Glazer scarf, becoming Green-and-Goldenballs, two stories elided. As Beckham disappeared down memory lane, United fans loudly voiced their hope that the Glazers could be consigned to history.'

After the match I had a long telephone conversation with Joel Glazer from my hotel room and we ruminated on the significance of that night's protests as well as Beckham's gesture. In truth, had Joel heeded my media engagement advice from a week earlier he would have been at the game in Manchester and would have been preparing for a television interview the following day, its agenda likely to have been dominated by the heat of the green-and-gold movement. I was therefore relieved that the interview would not take place, and that our agreed 'no comment' stance – had I received calls the next day – would help to contain the story. In any event, in a series of mixed zone post-match interviews Beckham went on to distance himself from any protest-related motive behind his act, although that wouldn't stop MUST from milking the gesture for every last drop of publicity. The next morning the photograph of Beckham and the scarf was featured in most papers, the *Times* even carrying it on its front page.

The anti-Glazer movement would get another boost when a national advertising campaign for bookmakers William Hill featured a fan sporting a green-and-gold scarf, with the voice over asserting: 'Show your true colours.' The Red Knights were able to build further momentum with the announcement that it had hired the Japanese investment bank Nomura, where a Red Knight, Guy Dawson, was an employee, to help draw up a bid expected sometime prior to the World Cup in June. While Nomura's role seemed to bolster the Knights' credibility among business journalists, it seemed to me (and the Manchester United hierarchy) to further demonstrate the suitors' increasingly delusional behaviour.

'Nay'

By the end of March we were receiving guidance that the Red Knights were struggling. It was no mean feat to try and raise hundreds of millions of pounds, even a billion plus, from potential investors, especially for them to pledge their hard earned cash on something that was not even for sale. But given the dysfunctional nature of the grouping, and the conflicting visions of what a Red Knights-owned Manchester United would involve, it was only a matter of time before their 'bid' would come to nothing. Significantly, a senior level Knight had approached Robert Leitao, the Rothschild banker who had advised the Glazer family on their acquisition of the club in 2005. Rightly believing that Leitao was still on good terms with Joel Glazer, the Red Knights presumably wanted a categorical yay or nay from Leitao as to whether the Glazers would countenance an offer from them. Leitao's negative response – corroborated by a call to Joel – would be unambiguous.

There were even signs that the green-and-gold movement, just weeks after the pinnacle of the Beckham incident, was beginning to show some strain. From the outset, Manchester-based journalists had told me that splits were starting to form between supporters who resented the politicisation of their football club, and who feared that the green-and-gold movement was threatening to deflect attention from the football. Equally, there were signs of frustration among more militant supporters that the hitherto peaceful protests had been nothing more than a public relations exercise. This manifested itself in strange ways. Even David Gill's 19 year-old son Oliver – who was a reserve player for the club – became the brunt of anti-Glazer fans' protests by being booed loudly whenever his name was announced on the tannoy. In separate developments, an action group targeted the club's 400-or-so corporate box holders by attempting to name and shame them online, and an editorial in the *Red Issue* fanzine sought to up the ante by egging on the lunatic fringe, proposing that 'the chants all tell how the Glazers are gonna die, yet in reality they're free to walk out of the ground unchallenged. Until that changes, nothing will.'

Meanwhile it firmly remained business as usual for those involved in running the club. Sir Alex Ferguson had signed a Mexican centre forward, Javier Hernández (nicknamed Chicharito, Spanish for 'Little Pea') from Chivas de Guadalajara. The signing of an obscure striker, especially for a reportedly frugal £10 million, was greeted with scepticism among those journalists and supporters who were keen to see an older, proven (and substantially more expensive) goal scorer like David Villa come to Old Trafford. Many concluded that the Glazers' post-bond ownership meant that Sir Alex's purse strings had been tightened. The *Independent* commented:[127] 'Conspiracy theorists will say the announcement was choreographed to bolster the impression that United are not a club in reverse; that the Glazer family have the means to spend – but only time will tell whether the 5ft 9in striker will be the new Carlos Tevez, or just another Zoran Tosic.'

There was even a relatively good news story to emerge from the Manchester United board room: prices for the following season's tickets would be frozen. Naturally, MUST's propaganda machine would seek to take the credit for having brought about the pressure on the club to force such a decision. But commercially, the turmoil would have no tangible bearing; potential sponsors may have raised an eyebrow during meetings with United staff regarding the green-and-gold phenomenon, but they seemed pacified by the club's response that it represented a little local difficulty. This was borne out when we launched two new sponsors, Telekom Malaysia and Turkish Airlines, in the space of as many weeks where it was evident that the off-the-pitch turmoil had barely registered in their respective media circles. Reminiscent of the scene in the *Carry On up the Khyber* film, when the Governor persists on entertaining his dinner guests despite an ensuing battle surrounding them, United seemed determined to project a stiff upper lip attitude. That said, some club officials were resigned to the fact that the green-and-gold scarf -which aesthetically, I thought, looked quite striking when accompanied by a red shirt – was here to stay. At one point I mooted to Ed Woodward and Richard

---

[127] United sign 'Little Pea' to fill major squad gap, *The Independent*, 9 April 2010

Arnold that the club could embrace the green-and-gold by reflecting it in the crowd images in the sponsorship presentations, but their joint view was that the movement's momentum would eventually fade.

Still, David Gill, more in his capacity as a fervent United supporter than club official, would vent his frustration at the threatening preponderance of yellow and green inside Old Trafford:[128] 'I've asked the players and they say they are not distracted [by the fans' protests] but if your question is "would I prefer all red and white instead of gold and green" when you have a full stadium and you are playing host to famous opposition, of course I would. If the question is "would I prefer not to look out of my office and see the scarves they are selling on the street," of course I'd prefer that. But as Alex has said, people have a right to protest. Nobody is going to stop that, and in the ground itself we are not going to stop that but I do object to the obstruction of peoples' view by some banner when they have paid good money for their seats. It's not the owners' style to shout from the rooftops, whether United have done well or badly, and while they will continue to review their position on interviews and so forth, I don't see them ever turning into the kind of owners who use the club for their own ego.'

Certainly, the Red Knights and MUST had succeeded in making their campaign a widespread talking point in the UK. Indeed, while playing pool in a north London pub, a group of men at the adjacent table were animatedly debating the merits of the Glazer family's ownership. I kept my counsel, wondering whether an intervention of 'Well actually, I work for the Glazers…' would have worked as well for me as it did for Woody Allen when he managed to call on Marshall McLuhan during the famous cinema queue scene in *Annie Hall*. To my mind the Knights' phoney war threatened to continue to divert the media's attention for the foreseeable future, potentially marring the successes that the team were enjoying on the pitch. By the start of April Manchester United were nicely poised atop the Premier League table

---

[128] David Gill interview to the Manchester United Disabled Supporters Association magazine *Rollin' Reds*, May 2010

and could begin to look forward to a Champions League semi-final, having scored an important away goal in the first leg of the quarter-final against Bayern Munich. In a business where the only true golden rule is that results on the pitch dictate the mood off it, Sir Alex Ferguson's team had achieved the remarkable feat of three successive League title wins despite a backdrop of frequent mutinous turmoil.

An Imminent Bid?

The season would, however, quickly unravel within the space of a few days following defeat to Chelsea at Old Trafford and a subsequent dropping of two points away to Blackburn Rovers. Despite a 3-2 home win against Bayern Munich, United heart-breakingly crashed out of the Champions League on the away goals rule. While another month of fixtures still lay ahead, and the Premier League title was still a possibility, it somehow felt like United's season was as good as over. Facing a period without the prospect of a trophy or two to galvanise them, some United supporters threatened an escalation of anti-Glazer protests. I duly received an email from MUST, having become a 'member' myself under a pseudonym:[129] 'We need to make it clear to the Glazers – we want the final game of this season to be their last in charge of United. We need you to help make this happen. We're planning on flooding Old Trafford with "Glazers Out" flags, cards, and scarves for the match against Stoke so we go into the summer leaving them in no doubt about what will await them if they are still here at the start of next season. So we need to step up the pressure at the Spurs match this Saturday, building towards a climax for Stoke.'

As far as I was concerned, the Red Knights' bid appeared dead in the water, but their public relations machine remained in full swing: this made sense given their only conceivable way of wresting the club from the Glazers would have been by building irresistible pressure

---

[129] MUST email: Want to join the biggest ever Glazers Out protest? 22 April 2010

from a wall of cash rich investors so the appearance of momentum was paramount. Their impetus was also helped by the news that Liverpool's owner Tom Hicks and his advisors were desperately scouring the globe for investors to help cover his and his co-owner George Gillett's spiralling debt costs, while the club's newly-appointed chairman Martin Broughton had been charged by the club's bankers to sell the club. Although developments at Liverpool had no direct bearing on Manchester United, the travails of the Glazers' over-leveraged compatriots were being cited among some quarters as a harbinger for what could befall United without a 'rescue' by the Knights.

By mid-April details began to emerge about the potential contents of the Red Knights bid. A formal bid was likely between the end of the season and early June – around the start of the FIFA World Cup – with around 50 investors being asked to contribute £10 million each, and a further £250 million being obtained by issuing securities to Manchester United supporters in the UK. The Knights planned to retain the outstanding £500 million bond in order to reach a notional valuation of around £1.25 billion for the club. The *Observer* newspaper mooted:[130] 'The Red Knights admit it will be difficult to come up with a deal structure that satisfies the "egos and testosterone" of all the individuals in its investor group. O'Neill's idea is they will only get a small dividend or return on investment as the bid is conceived as an act of altruism. But some investors may be after more than a seat in the directors' box and a small dividend, especially those who have individually approached the owners, the Glazer family, with offers of about £1billion.'

The article led to heightened speculation the following week that a Red Knights bid was imminent. While any bid would not have been entertained by the Glazers, I had frequent discussions with Joel Glazer about how best to handle an approach from the Knights, however unwelcome, were it to materialise. Should we issue a 'thanks, but no

---

[130] Red Knights sign up team of investors for Man Utd bid, *The Observer*, 11 April 2010

thanks statement'? Perhaps invite the Red Knights into Old Trafford for a consolation cup of tea? Or should we aim to stifle any publicity by completely blanking any offer? I was minded that a bid, however perfunctory, would mark a PR coup for the Red Knights, from which they would seek to build renewed momentum. It could also unleash Jim O'Neill, who had wisely shunned any on-the-record media engagement while the bid was gestating, but who might want to lead the charge with a series of interviews. Jim was without doubt the Red Knights' most telegenic talisman and a call to arms from him, delivered in his earthy Salford accent, could have feasibly provoked a further wave of anti-Glazer sentiment among supporters.

Joel Glazer's response was characteristically cautious: he was satisfied that a bid from the struggling Red Knights was, contrary to press hype, not imminent. Intelligence from City circles pointed to their ongoing difficulties in persuading any interested investors to part with their cash. There was even talk that the volcanic ash cloud produced by the eruption of the Eyjafjallajökull mountain in Iceland had hampered the Red Knights' travel plans to the Middle East and Asia.

Reality Check

Joel Glazer was curious as to what the prospect of a Red Knights takeover would mean to Manchester United supporters. As I had been immersed in more than four months of consistently negative press coverage of their ownership I was hardly in the best position to offer an objective overview. In 2007, when the Glazers had wanted to know more about the club's worldwide support, they had commissioned an expensive global market research study. Three years on and, consistent with their technocratic style of management, United's owners sanctioned a stack of fresh market research to investigate supporters' attitudes towards them as well as the Red Knights. The focus groups' findings were intriguing. While there was indeed a suspicion of the Glazers and the debt raised against the club, there was a significant level of acceptance of their ownership and recognition that it had provided the foundation for Sir Alex's remarkable success. Also salient was the high level of suspicion among fans towards the green-and-gold movement, in addition to their hostility to calls for a season ticket boycott. One respondent rounded on the poisonous atmosphere inside Old Trafford, complaining that it was 'splitting the family of supporters.' The focus groups also pointed to the animosity among their respondents towards the Red Knights along with their City credentials.

Armed with the research's insights, Joel Glazer and his family were content to adopt a wait-and-see approach, convinced that the turmoil would die down. There was even the reckoning that the 2010 spring weather had been unseasonably cold – prompting supporters to wear their green-and-gold scarves en masse at Old Trafford – and the suggestion that a significant proportion of fans wore it as a colourful fashion statement rather than out of deep-seated spite towards the owners. Indeed, while attending United's penultimate home game of the season against Tottenham Hotspur, the warmer climes led to fewer fans wearing the scarves and I noticed a distinctly less toxic atmosphere as the Reds rollicked to a 3-1 victory.

However, there was a modicum of uncertainty as to whether the ongoing volatility might impact on season ticket sales (indeed, the Independent Manchester United Supporters' Association had written to its members asking them not to renew their season tickets). The market research, however, had indicated that supporters would be very unlikely to forgo their precious seats at Old Trafford.

Charm Offensive

After so many months of unrelenting bad press – and with the four-week window of optimal season ticket sales approaching – there was a significant need for us to build bridges with the journalist community and to assert the truth that the club continued to be well run, solvent, and forward-looking. Ed Woodward, the Glazers' chief of staff and board director, was the obvious candidate for reporters to meet. Moreover, after years of hearing Ed's name, journalists were genuinely curious to finally meet him and, indeed, to behold the club's 'secretive' London operation. Still, we remained coy about Ed's profile and didn't want any of his insights to go on-the-record lest they inflame the Red Knights story or be viewed as competing with chief executive David Gill's public statements. So David and the owners signed off a series of off-the-record relationship-building meetings between Ed and the press, and I arranged no less than fourteen 45-minute sessions with every influential journalist who wrote about the business of sport, from the *Wall Street Journal* and the *Sun* through to the BBC and Sky News.

The meetings, held in the boardroom at Pall Mall, were condensed into an intense three days, revolving around Ed taking journalists through the same well-versed glossy presentation with which he had regaled potential bond investors earlier in the year. By the second day Ed sounded like a broken record; by the third my boredom threshold had plummeted and I had to prick my index fingertip with the sharp end of my ballpoint pen cap to avoid falling asleep. But, as expected, Ed proved to be a persuasive and sincere communicator in each encounter; for the first time in five long and eventful years – and facilitated by the classified nature of the meetings – Ed was able to speak candidly. He lifted the lid on the American owners' commercial operation and earnestly talked through the club's finances and strategy, revealing the true scale of the Glazers' transformation of running United the Business, which simultaneously allowed Manchester United the Football Club to flourish under Sir Alex Ferguson. In regard to every journalist's most pressing enquiry – the Red Knights, of course – Ed was well drilled to say 'The club is not for sale. No comment on the Red Knights. Next question please...'

Also at the forefront of most reporters' minds was the resilience of ticket sales and whether they would hold up should the Red Knights call for a boycott of season tickets. Ed was bullish, stating that on a match-by-match basis there were only some 7,000 tickets available on the day, which would be balloted among the club's 'One United' scheme, which boasted some 113,000 members. Ed also provided some data on the strength of United's commercial tie-ups; how more than a million Manchester United credit cards had been sold in South

Korea, with the club yielding a handsome royalty for each one. Also, when Saudi Telecom was signed up in 2008 the Arabian telecoms' executives had predicted an activation of 50,000 Manchester United subscribers by the end of the first year; in reality Saudi Telecom had achieved an uplift of 400,000 subscribers – in just the first week.

Judging from the journalists' feedback, and their honouring of the meetings' confidentiality, our 'charm offensive' (as one reporter had called it) seemed to go down well, serving as a useful reality check to counteract the communications initiatives from the Red Knights and MUST.

Fearing that access to Ed Woodward in London may stir resentment in Manchester, I sought to reach out to the regional football correspondents and, alongside Phil Townsend, hosted a couple of lunches in Manchester. A year earlier the meetings might have been tense affairs. But with the bond's disclosure, and realising how sceptical football reporters had been about the Red Knights' advances, I felt more comfortable being with them. The meetings were very convivial and provided further catharsis for all parties involved, although when I reminded one reporter who had challenged the club's ticket price hike that, since 2005, his newspaper's cover price had increased by a larger percentage, I feared for a moment that our friendly breaking of bread would descend into a heated argument. Thankfully it didn't, although I was surprised that a passing remark I made to the reporters about the Glazers once rejecting a Middle East offer of £1.5 billion for the club would excite their interest and would dominate the back pages as a bleary-eyed nation woke up to a hung parliament in the May general election.

Protests Fizzle Out

With the outcome of the Premier League title still open, United's last game of the season pitted them against Stoke City at Old Trafford. During the run-up to the match, the supporters' trust MUST had petitioned its 150,000 or so 'members' hard, asking them to leave the Glazers 'in no doubt about what will await them if they are still here at the start of next season.' Indeed, co-chairman Avie Glazer had intended to be there but his somewhat conspicuous absence was purely due to the lingering ash cloud that continued to scupper transatlantic flights. While I witnessed news journalists scurrying around Old Trafford frantically seeking out any of the threatened disruption, I was struck by how subdued the atmosphere inside the Theatre of Dreams seemed. News of early goals by Chelsea against Wigan quickly permeated among the 70,000 home fans, confirming that United had been pipped to the post for the League title by their west London rivals (in hindsight, the draw against Blackburn in April had proved fatal to United's title hopes).

The Manchester United supporters seemed philosophically resigned to their lot, evidently pleased just to watch their heroes convincingly beat Stoke 4-0 before performing the obligatory last-match lap of honour. Indeed, MUST's much-heralded protests turned out to be a damp squib, the four months of mutinous protest now feeling stale and tired. The *Daily Telegraph* noted:[131] 'According to regular Old Trafford visitors, this was the most vociferous protest yet organised against the Glazer regime, yet although there were reports of fans clashing with police in front of the East Stand, a smoke bomb being set off in the Megastore and stink bombs near the directors' entrance, inside the ground it really felt a pretty low-key, distracted affair, with fans torn between support for their team and heaping odium on the owners. It all made for a weird afternoon. With the spirits of 70,000 effectively crushed after six minutes when the Stoke fans' little dance of celebration informed the stadium of Chelsea's early opener, a perfect platform looked to have been set for a sustained, vociferous protest. Yet it never really materialised. A plane, barely noticed, had flown over the ground trailing a 'Glazers Out' banner before kick-off, bearing a number of support to text. Ah, a very 21st century protest, this. Then, as the second half began, thousands blew whistles and held aloft placards handed out before the game. These were brief explosions of

---

[131] Green and gold protest falls flat at Theatre of Disillusionment, *The Daily Telegraph*, 10 May 2010

defiance, but like the protest chants of 'Glazers Out' which quickly fizzled out whenever the Stretford End tried to rouse the support, it ended up feeling just a bit half-hearted.'

Although the football season was over, and I felt genuinely grateful for respite from the green-and-gold activism that seemed to have marred all the games in 2010, my focus remained on dealing with the ongoing disruption of the mooted Red Knights bid. While we were by now 100 per cent convinced that a meaningful bid was not forthcoming, the only story still fixating the journalist community was the tantalising prospect of an offer. Just one day after the end of the season the Red Knights duly issued a press release pronouncing: 'We have had productive conversations with potential investors in recent weeks which have reinforced our belief that it is wrong to offer above fair value, particularly given the urgent need for the club to reduce debt; and that fair value is likely to be reducing over time given headwinds facing the game of football.' What headwinds? United's business was growing despite the recession; as Ed Woodward had outlined in his press briefings, sponsorship revenues continued to climb and were due to even overtake matchday income in a short time. The Knights' attempt to drive down the value of Manchester United, which they had guided previously to be around £1.25 billion (corroborated by an independent survey by Forbes magazine) seemed desperate, even perverse: not only was the asset the Red Knights so craved not for sale, but they would also sulkily maintain that they wouldn't be willing to cough up the money for it in any case. The end game was near.

More Allegations

Still, I was kept busy with a further stream of news designed to undermine the Glazers' ownership. That summer, while over in Houston, Texas, to promote the club's forthcoming tour to North America, I began to receive a stream of press calls from the UK on the prospect of a hike in the interest rate on the payment-in-kind note, something that the *Financial Times* and other outlets had reported when the bond was being marketed earlier in the year. The *Times* speculated:[132] 'The 2 per cent rise will strengthen fears that the Glazer family, United's unpopular owners, will try to pay off the high-interest loans rather than spend money on the team, a move that would infuriate supporters.' The *Times* was half-right: by this time Joel Glazer and Ed Woodward were locked in negotiations with advisors to redeem the controversial PIK, hopefully making the interest rate rise academic, so their – and my press – response was a phlegmatic one.

Of more potential damage were allegations dug up and circulated by the 'andersred' blogger Andrew Green. He supplied MUST with an aggregated estimate of some £433 million being the total interest costs and fees paid out during the Glazers' ownership, which the Supporters' Trust regurgitated in a colourful press release:[133] 'Without the Glazers' takeover, every supporter could have attended Old Trafford free of charge for the last 5 years and in addition the club could have paid every season ticket holder £700 cash lump sum each and the club would still have been no worse off if it wasn't for the tax the Glazers have avoided paying!'

Logically, there's an opportunity cost for *everything*. Forget football; that money could have provided each Salford citizen with a near £2,000 windfall! Such a line of attack seemed to me to be vacuous, given that supporters were willing to pay for their tickets – priced favourably compared with other top clubs – and given that Old Trafford was routinely full to capacity.

More forensically, Andrew Green claimed that the Glazer family were enduring financial difficulties in the US – in particular with their shopping mall property portfolio traded under the umbrella of their First Allied Corporation – and that this could negatively impact on their ownership of Manchester United. Green would contact the BBC's *Panorama* programme, the corporation's flagship investigative news strand, with publicly available information that he had researched,

---

[132] Interest rate rise increases fans' fears over Glazer debt at United, *The Times*, 19 May 2010
[133] MUST press release: Glazers wasted millions of united fans' money, 18 May 2010

detailing a number of Glazer owned assets reputed to be in financial distress.

At the same time, to complete the pincer movement on my charges, I was approached by the *Guardian's* investigative reporter, David Conn, with an identical list of allegations to those passed onto *Panorama*. To both sets of enquiries my response was 'None of your damn business.' I was adamant that the Glazers maintained their right to privacy over their financial affairs; while the reporters presumed the publicly available documents on some of their assets to be the last word on their wealth, they of course were not, and we would not assist them with guidance or by divulging any private information.

Panorama had approached me in mid-April, failing to disclose that it had Green's research but claiming that it wanted to make a programme about football ownership in light of a possible Red Knights bid and, as such, wanted our side of the story. My response was guardedly positive as I was happy to provide off-the-record guidance on the family's ownership of Manchester United to a high-profile television programme. From the outset, though, we would not be willing to cooperate with the programme on-the-record as we hardly wanted to dignify the Red Knights' agenda with an aired response. My dealings with the *Panorama* producers were initially friendly; however by the start of May I could feel their exasperation at our refusal to fully engage against a backdrop of a faltering Red Knights' bid, which had delayed the original transmission date. So the increasingly terse conversations began to focus on a central issue: my refusal to discount any of the £100-odd million on the club's balance sheet, including the Ronaldo money, from being carved out as stipulated in the bond Memorandum to pay down the PIK directly (which *Panorama* claimed was contradicted by David Gill's assertion back in January in a BBC radio interview that the PIK had nothing to do with the club). To be fair to *Panorama*, there was an apparent contradiction but it was nuanced by the reality that the cash remained, as ever, fungible. Phil Townsend emailed the producers with a pithy statement authorised by David Gill and the Glazers: 'The Club stands by everything in David's interview with Garry Richardson on 31 January 2010. The PIK loans have no recourse to the Club's assets.'

Eureka!

Despite the football season having ended, the ongoing media pressure led me to the conclusion that we had to curb speculation over a Red Knights bid. I lobbied Joel Glazer hard that we should put out a defining statement. Joel warmed to the idea, but was apprehensive about putting out a statement, as it could be seen as a response by the ownership to the flagging Red Knights' agenda. While conceding that an interview would not be appropriate, it would have been inevitably interpreted as a measure of desperation by the ownership, I was convinced that we needed to put out something official in writing and asserting – beyond my tape-looped spokesman-speak – that the club was not for sale. However, agreeing with Joel that any statement should not be seen as 'extraordinary' I was stuck as to how we could execute it.

Towards the end of May we were scheduled to release the club's third-quarter results to the end of March to comply with the financial disclosure meted out by the bond offer. The results would show a steady growth in total revenues and, significantly, would confirm that the Ronaldo money remained in the club and had not, contrary to expectations, been leached by the Glazers. Working on the press release, I had a 'Eureka!' moment: we could put out the 'not for sale' statement in it, which could be seen as a routine official line to address those bond investors who had seen speculation of a sale having a material impact on its price (the price had risen on speculation that a Red Knights takeover would precipitate an early redemption of the bond and penalty pay-out).

I put a call into Joel Glazer who immediately liked the idea although I would, as always, have to wait for his official stamp of approval once he had run it past his family members and advisors. The decision to make a statement happily coincided with news that the Red Knights, if not officially dead, were on a life support machine, with the *Guardian* reporting:[134] 'The Red Knights' attempt to take control of Manchester United looks increasingly doomed to failure after it

---

[134] Red Knights bid to buy United looks doomed, *The Guardian*, 20 May 2010

emerged that key players within the consortium have become disaffected and are losing hope of persuading the Glazer family to relinquish power at Old Trafford. Senior figures involved with the Red Knights have told the Guardian there are internal divisions and that they suspect they are fighting a losing battle when it comes to putting together a takeover bid of sufficient value to end the Glazers' unpopular regime. Although the consortium is rigidly maintaining its public stance that it is confident of being in power for the start of next season, one of the businessmen prominently involved has lost confidence to the point that he believes they might not even submit a bid were it not for the criticism they would attract after such a highly publicised campaign.'

While there was talk of the Red Knights putting a bid in to save face, I counselled that we should seek to avoid that development if we could. I was minded that the Knights, like their Black Knight counterpart in *Monty Python and the Holy Grail*, would stubbornly refuse to ever give up, despite having all their limbs dismembered.

On the eve of the release, Joel agreed to the statement, which we crafted together to create as unambiguous a message as possible: 'The Board notes recent press speculation regarding a possible bid for Manchester United. The owners remain fully committed to their long-term ownership of the club. Manchester United is not for sale and the owners will not entertain any offers.'

Given that the financial results were a non-event, especially as the press had already got wind that the Ronaldo cash was in situ, I was keen that the main story should be the statement, and rang around the main news outlets including the BBC and international newswires alerting them to expect a 'significant' announcement.

The morning of the results and statement release coincided with the publication of a rare in-depth interview with David Gill in the *Independent*, where David affirmed his belief that the green-and-gold movement would fade, like its Red Knight counterparts:[135] 'I think that [green and gold] minority will go away. I see people from Asia walking

---

[135] Gill hits back at Green and Gold, *The Independent*, 28 May 2010

out of the [Old Trafford] megastore with a red and white scarf on and they just assume they [green and gold] are official scarves and go and buy one. I think there is an element of that. A lot of people understand what it means but a lot of them don't. They [fans protesting] are not going to change their opinion even if we win three Champions League titles in a row. We couldn't have been much more successful in the last three years: we won the league [2007-2009], we were Champions League winners and runners-up and we won the Carling Cup. But they are never going to be happy.'

When we went live with United's results, which included the board's statement, I felt a strong sense of relief; finally we could put the distraction of the Red Knights to rest. Indeed, I was instantly pleased that the first online news stories led with our 'not for sale' line. Yet I also felt emotionally drained by this time too, having lived and breathed the bond document and the subsequent furore and protests for six whole months. My stress was to manifest itself in my barking at a mild-mannered BBC correspondent who responded to seeing the not for sale statement by saying, 'Yes Tes, the club's not for sale but everyone's got a price.' His remark got my hackles rising. 'Listen, the club's not for f**king sale. Period,' I hissed, much to the surprise of my Pall Mall colleagues who seemed genuinely taken aback by my rare show of temper. My festering anger was also meted out later that afternoon to a newspaper journalist who insisted on enquiring about the PIK which I was refusing to comment upon. Exasperated, I ended up fulfilling my threat to drop the call. The resulting headline and article the following morning was as hostile to the Glazers as could be imaginable; a tangible insight into the value of fostering good media relations to ensure positive coverage or, rather, what happens when they break down.

Newspapers reported the obvious that weekend: that a bid would be abandoned. But by the start of the new week the Red Knights, clearly with nothing to lose except pride, still managed to put out a mealy-mouthed statement maintaining that their bid had merely been put on hold. 'We will only attempt to purchase the club at a sensible price,' was code, I reckoned, for 'we were never near to raising the funds in the first place.'

Seeing off the Red Knights provided some satisfaction. Notwithstanding the unprecedented pressures placed on it, the club remained strong and in unison, with the upheaval even serving to forge an even closer bond between the owners, David Gill and Sir Alex.

While the Red Knights had calculated they could push through a sale by parking their public relations tank on Old Trafford's lawn they had, of course, underestimated the Glazers' thick-skinned resolve to resist their reputational attacks. Personally, I felt proud that I did not succumb to the temptation to fight in the phoney war. I was always careful to avoid publicly criticising the Red Knights, by implication suggesting that they were an unwanted nuisance rather than meaningful threat.

Panorama

Still, with the Red Knights gone, I wasn't able to look forward to any respite. The following week my focus returned to the BBC *Panorama* programme which was now set for broadcast at the start of June. After some thought, Joel Glazer agreed with my suggestion that Ed Woodward and I should meet the programme's producers for an off-the-record briefing identical to those that we had done with the press in May. We duly arranged a meeting in Pall Mall on the Friday prior to broadcast.

The producer was accompanied by the show's presenter John Sweeney, an award-winning investigative journalist renowned for a furious tirade aimed at a Scientology spokesman that went viral on the Internet. Minutes into the meeting it became apparent that the *Panorama* team had little interest in the detail of United's business model that Ed was hoping to talk them through. Their restless and agitated demeanour suggested they had an entirely different agenda. As it transpired, the meeting soon turned to questions about the Glazers' private wealth, or alleged lack of it. This led to a tense stand-off as I, as their spokesman, refused to enter into a speculative debate about how much the Glazers may or may not have, especially after Ed had clarified that Manchester United continued to be run and funded as a stand-alone business entity. At one point I put it to Sweeney whether he would be fronting a documentary about a private American family with alleged ailing property interests had they not owned Manchester United? Clearly not, but given our protests that United's operations were separate from the vagaries of the Glazers' wealth portfolio, there did not seem to be, in our view, justification to the programme. A brooding Sweeney glared back at me. For a fleeting moment I feared the prospect of his Scientologist-aimed wrath, but the ever-positive Ed Woodward looked sideways at me, raised his hand a few centimetres before patting it down again. 'Calm down Tes,' was the signal.

The bruising encounter ended after about an hour, with a resumption of fake cordiality, but Ed and I were in no doubt that the *Panorama* programme would, regardless of our attempts at mollification, be another hatchet job on the Glazers' ownership. I later reported back to Joel Glazer who seemed entirely indifferent to *Panorama's* output especially as its premise had become nullified by the previous week's felling of the Red Knights. The programme would also be shifted from its prime time slot to a more obscure one following a lone gunman's shooting spree in Cumbria, a tragic incident which was to dominate the UK news agenda.

Still the BBC promotions department were to go into overdrive, hoping to drum up as much interest as possible in the *Panorama* investigation ahead of the World Cup. The programme's producers even penned an article for the *Daily Mail* on the morning of broadcast, an 'exclusive' outlining their supposedly dire findings:[136] 'The Glazer family's ability to keep control of Manchester United is in doubt again after it emerged the American owners are struggling with debts of £1.1 billion. The revelations, to be made by BBC's Panorama programme on Tuesday night, expose £400 million of previously unknown debt and cast more uncertainty over how much money manager Sir Alex Ferguson will be given to strengthen his squad this summer. The programme *Man Utd – Into the Red* centres on the Glazers' ailing

---

[136] Revealed: the Glazers' staggering £1.1bn debt, *Daily Mail*, 7 June 2010

shopping-mall empire, run by their company First Allied Corporation, and is based on the findings of City analyst Andy Green, a United supporter who has joined the anti-Glazer green-and-gold campaign.'

The coordinated campaign was completed by David Conn of the *Guardian* who alleged[137] on the one hand that the Glazers' property empire had been hit hard by the recession, while on the other conceding (buried in the bowels of a 1,000 word article) that it was actually returning a multi-million dollar profit.

The tactic of seeking to drum up interest in the programme via two sensationalist articles in the *Mail* and the *Guardian* – both with headlines beginning with 'Revealed...' – smacked of desperation, although it did prompt many phone calls from other news outlets, which I refused to take knowing that our interests were best served by starving the *Panorama* of any comment or attention. Indeed, I didn't bother watching the programme when it was broadcast. I also kept my phone off, diverting it to voicemail in order to avoid the inevitable wave of press calls the following day, all seeking out the Glazers' response.

It was only a few days later – amid the now satisfyingly muted press coverage of the programme – that I could bring myself to watch it on the BBC's iPlayer. John Sweeney topped his report with his watching his own team from the stands – the third tier Tranmere Rovers – and pronouncing that, because his club didn't have debt and Manchester United did, his club was richer. This ludicrously perverse analysis permeated throughout a bitter, one-sided report on the Glazers, whom the producers deigned appropriate to depict as garden gnomes. At least the Glazers' US property portfolio allowed for Sweeney to squeeze in some transatlantic travel (presumably funded by fellow BBC license fee payers, I mused) as he fronted several pieces to camera from outside their shopping malls, rehashing the allegations dug out by blogger Andrew Green.

With the start of the World Cup just days away, and *Panorama* having seriously lacked in editorial balance, I was pleased to see it

---

[137] Revealed: truth about Glazers' business empire, *The Guardian,* 7 June 2010

disappear without trace; I never even asked Joel Glazer whether he or his family had managed to see the programme and what he may have thought of his gnome portrayal. A few weeks' later the BBC World Service called me to ask for my input into a recast version of *Panorama*. I delivered a diatribe about the tasteless and insulting depiction of the Glazers. The programme was not re-broadcast.

North America Tour

The club was looking forward to its North America tour. The facilities promised to be first-class and the United States represented one of the few places on earth where players could freely leave their hotels and enjoy the relative anonymity of being able to walk around without being accosted by over-zealous supporters.

We met up in Manchester Airport's Terminal One, adhering to a meticulous military style operation similar to the previous year's tour. That year, Turkish Airlines had become the club's new airline sponsor, so we were treated to a whole Boeing 777 plane to ourselves, providing a very spacious environment for our 80-odd entourage. Sir Alex Ferguson and some of the club's veteran players like Paul Scholes, Ryan Giggs and Edwin van der Sar were treated to first-class accommodation with compartmentalised sleeping areas in the front of the plane (the chief executive and other directors would fly out separately later that week). The business class, also with flat beds, was occupied with the rest of the squad and the coaching staff. The rest of us – the club executives, the large posse of security staff and the MUTV crew – were directed to the economy sections, which was no hardship, as we each enjoyed huge amounts of space in the wide-aisled plane.

The first port of call was Chicago, which was wilting in a summer heatwave. Our arrival was met by a small army of dedicated and enthusiastic fans rather than the frenzied crowds of Asia, but we still enjoyed the full VIP trappings that had made the previous year's trip so wondrous: being sped through bemused customs, police escorted motorcades and our luggage delivered straight to our luxurious hotel rooms. No game was scheduled, but Chicago happened to be the city in which the club's new shirt sponsor, Aon, had its headquarters. Aon had already benefited for a (cost free) association with the club after announcing the deal in the spring of 2009. The official unveiling took place that evening at Nike's principal store on North Michigan Avenue, Chicago's main shopping drag. The huge retail space was transformed into a temple devoted to Nike-swooshed Manchester United merchandise, and for one night housed a lavish champagne and canapé party attended by corporate bigwigs including Chicago resident Bryan Glazer. There we witnessed the hotly anticipated – and intricately choreographed – reveal of the new white-collared shirt, sported by five United players perched upon a stage alongside their beaming manager.

The following morning, club ambassadors Bryan Robson and Denis Irwin, both in their spanking new Aon branded football shirts, joined commercial director Richard Arnold to ring the bell to mark the opening of Wall Street trading; quite a publicity coup that had been arranged by Aon's PR team. Aon would launch its sponsorship to its Chicago stakeholders with equal panache; each and every one of its thousands of Chicago employees (plus many worldwide) were kitted out in the new shirt as they streamed out of the company's 80-storey skyscraper and crossed over to the Millennium Park in a vision straight out of Fritz Lang's *Metropolis*. A huge rally celebrated the new partnership with customary American razzmatazz and evangelical fervour. This included a tub-thumping address by the city's mayor, Richard M. Daley, that seemed appropriate in the Windy City but would, I'm sure, have jarred with more cynical sensibilities had it happened in England.

After Chicago it was up to Toronto. Security was tight throughout the tour; even though we enjoyed the privilege of being able to bypass the usual check-in rituals before driving onto the airport's flight apron and straight to the plane's steps, before actually boarding the flight we were all (manager and players included) subjected to vigorous and time consuming security checks, often under the intense heat of a blazing sun. One of the courteous but unsmiling security guards told me that 'Only the President of the United States of America is not subject to security. No other exceptions.'

Toronto's Staples Center played host to the club's first game of five; a friendly against Glasgow Celtic. Walking around the city centre earlier in the afternoon I was astonished to see so many Manchester United shirts and scarves being sported by pedestrians on the bustling streets, but was also dispirited to see some green-and-gold, too. However, the stadium itself was not full, perhaps reflecting the long flight delay getting to Toronto which had forced the club to cancel its press conference and promotional interviews. Also, the game clashed with a free Indy motorcar race that weekend.

Sir Alex Keeps us all Waiting

Just before kick-off I ventured into the press lounge. I introduced myself to a local journalist who said there was an email that he would like to forward me. It had been sent to him by a woman – an ex-pat Scot living in Toronto – who was attending the game. She purported to be the daughter of a close friend of Sir Alex and, if possible, wanted to meet the United boss afterwards.

The email enquiry could have been from a crank, of course, but I sensed it to be genuine and forwarded it to Phil Townsend, who would have been able to quickly check with Sir Alex. Phil shot back a response: 'SAF would like to meet her.' Not having her telephone number, and banking on the sender having an email device with her, I sent her a line suggesting we hook up after the game. But I still needed proof that she was genuine before arranging anything concrete. Sometime later, just as the match was coming to a close, I began to wonder whether she had indeed got my email. The woman, called Elaine, emailed me back to inform me of her whereabouts in the stadium. I hurried down to the pitch side and ran towards her section of the stand, which had a phalanx of security surrounding it. Unable to phone her, I sent her an email telling her that I was standing next to the red bucket of players' drinks. Confronted by a swarm of supporters and autograph hunters who had stayed behind to await the exiting players, somehow I was able to pinpoint Elaine as she frantically waved at me. I ushered her towards the pitch side where I asked her to wait for Sir Alex to finish his post-match press conference. While doing so, a composed Elaine explained to me that her late father had worked with Alex Ferguson – and had become firm friends with him – during his formative years in Glasgow.

With his post-match press duties over, and having chatted briefly with Celtic chairman John Reid, Sir Alex came back into the stadium bowl whereupon I introduced him to Elaine and her teenage son, who was clearly dumbfounded by the occasion. After volunteering to take some ad hoc photos of the trio I stepped away and savoured one of my proudest public relations achievements, watching Sir Alex conduct a warm and animated conversation with Elaine for 15 minutes-or-so. The Manchester United manager clearly enjoyed reminiscing with the fellow Scot, who must have been her son's age when she and her father had left Scotland before emigrating to Canada.

Sir Alex's generosity with his time with Elaine meant that the two tour buses, ready and waiting in the tunnel filled with the players and United staff (together with a convoy of limousines carrying the Glazers and their guests) were made to wait. This was highly unusual given the clockwork precision of the tour itinerary.

For me, those moments inside the Toronto stadium symbolised two things: Sir Alex Ferguson had, uniquely in the club, earned the right to keep everyone waiting, regardless. But, more importantly, it brought home to me how grounded a man he was, despite his success, wealth and fame.

During my six years with the club I was, of course, asked frequently what sort of person Sir Alex was. In truth, we probably didn't exchange more than an hour's-worth of conversation during my entire time, although our paths crossed frequently at club events. Aside from his technical and tactical expertise as a football boss, I thought that Sir Alex was one of the most exceptional people managers I had come across; while he was absolutely driven by his love for Manchester United and football in general, he was also very easy to talk to and was an attentive listener. I witnessed this in particular in his dealings with youngsters. At the launch of new commercial sponsorships the manager would do his usual glad-handing and photo opportunities with the VIP 'grown-ups,' but as soon as Sir Alex clocked any star-struck children accompanying their chief executive fathers he would immediately engage them in football conversation, feeding off their energy and enthusiasm. Sir Alex could also be very warm and funny and, during the dead time while hanging about a hotel lobby or inside an aeroplane, would regale those lucky to share his company with a variety of anecdotes. As for his infamous 'hair dryer'-style rages, I can fortunately say that I never saw them. Judging from YouTube footage of his early days at United – when he seemed to inspire as much fear as respect – I was conscious that I was now witnessing someone in his late sixties who seemed considerably mellow, and who appeared comfortable in his own skin.

Sir Alex could also be very caring. At the end of the North America tour when we were huddled, jet-lagged, around the luggage carousel in Manchester Airport, there was a junior United colleague who was leaving the club to pursue another role. She was clearly feeling bereft. Noticing her sadness, Sir Alex bounded up to her before putting his arms round her to console her and wish her farewell. Sir Alex acted as the patriarch of a tight-knit 'family' club, shaped around his success and work ethic, and he dispatched his responsibilities with an intense dedication coupled with a down-to-earth humility.

Bored in the USA

From Toronto we flew down to Philadelphia. Here, we could look forward to the stability of a week's stay, sufficient time for the squad and coaching staff to take root and to benefit from the city's excellent training camp facilities.

Earlier, in Toronto, I had managed to snatch a few conversations with Joel Glazer. It became evident to me that he and his family continued to have no desire to engage with the press, even on his North American backyard. This sentiment was echoed by United's chief executive David Gill who realised that any observations on the previous season's extraordinary events would have risked rekindling past controversies. Mindful of my unguarded comments during the previous year's Asia tour, I too had taken a vow of silence and skirted away from providing off-the-record insight to journalists.

This meant, though, that I would feel largely redundant during the remaining two weeks' long trip. Since there was so little for me to do, I could have simply regarded the tour as a glamorous, all-expenses paid gig. However, while my United colleagues frantically went about their business, my boredom and frustration – together with the mental and emotional exhaustion from the previous six months – reinforced my growing belief that my role as the Glazers' gatekeeper was coming to a natural end.

By the time our entourage had arrived in Philadelphia, I would have to continue fobbing off numerous enquiries from both UK and US journalists. An exception to this saw me and Phil Townsend inviting a group of British football writers – including those from the *Telegraph*, *Guardian*, *Mirror*, *Daily Mail* and the *Sun* – to an informal steak and ribs dinner. We hoped that, by being thousands of miles away from our usual workplace, this would provide some welcome relief to the previous season's stresses. And so it proved, as the meal was as relaxed and as congenial an occasion as we could have hoped for. It was also an opportunity for me and Phil to project some optimism about the club's immediate future, in particular the prospect for season ticket sales which we knew to be the yardstick with which the club's off-the-pitch fortunes would be judged.

The match in Philadelphia, played against the local MLS Union team in the still sweltering heat of the evening, proved to be a good competitive game, determined by a single goal by United's Gabriel Obertan. The next day I travelled by train to New York, where I hooked up with journalists from the *New York Times* and the *Sports Business Journal* who seemed to have a genuine interest in the English Premier League, in particular the reason why so many Americans had piled in as owners.

After the week long sojourn in Philadelphia, the tour resumed a more hurried feel as we visited three cities in less than a week. Kansas City, in the heart of America's Midwest, offered the club its wholesome folksy hospitality. Our hotel, the Intercontinental, was conveniently situated for players' shopping jaunts next to an upmarket mall and was unusually busy as it was also playing host to Sir Paul McCartney's touring entourage. This ensured that the number of the ex-Beatle's fans outside the hotel managed to compete with the small vigil of local Manchester United supporters. Having arguably three of Britain's most celebrated knights – Sir Paul, Sir Alex Ferguson and Sir Bobby Charlton – all staying in the same hotel (in Kansas City of all places!) proved irresistible to the awestruck local press. Moreover, I managed to secure a cherished claim to fame by having my name cited in the same article alongside Paul McCartney, one of my all-time music heroes.[138]

Manchester United played a friendly against the Kansas City Wizards in front of a record crowd of more than 50,000 spectators in the Arrowhead stadium, which replicated every other American NFL stadium I had visited in terms of its scale and superlative facilities. The result – a 2-1 defeat to the local hosts – was a touch embarrassing, not least since the Wizards were a man down for the entire second half. This shock outcome, however, helped to propel the story to the front page of the *Kansas City Star* the following morning, further embellishing Manchester United's brand recognition in the States.

Houston, Texas, was the penultimate stop off. From a previous visit I knew that its large Hispanic population would provide feverish interest in United's presence, especially as the match versus the MLS All Stars – a collection of the American soccer league's best players – was billed as a competitive game. On the eve of the match, the sponsor and media appearances having been dispensed with, the tour entourage was treated to a VIP tour of NASA's Johnson Space Center. This included privileged access to the floor of the Mission Control, a boon to the more middle-aged among the tour party who were reminded of the vicarious thrill of watching blurred television images of NASA's Apollo voyages from our childhoods. Shortly afterwards, Avie Glazer's wife Jill hosted a cocktail party at the team hotel, attended by the manager and the players as well as a number of her charity fundraising friends. It was the first time that I met Javier Hernández – aka Chicharito – who had joined the squad for the first time in Houston having turned out for Mexico in the previous month's World

---

[138] Manchester United's knight out, *Kansas City Star*, 24 July 2010

Cup. Hernández proved delightful company, speaking perfect English and possessing a winsome combination of intelligence and genuine humility. When Sir Alex came over and embraced him it was immediately apparent how much he warmly valued his new striker.

Come the match day, Phil Townsend and I hooked up with the *Houston Chronicle's* sports correspondent, Jose de Jesus Ortiz, who had taken a close interest in soccer for his newspaper. After chewing the fat over an authentic tasty Tex-Mex lunch, Jose walked us over to the home of the city's Major League Baseball team, the Houston Astros. There we received a VIP tour of the ballpark before witnessing a rare procession of home runs by the Astros who went on to resoundingly beat the visiting Chicago Cubs. Jose introduced us to the Astros' owner, Drayton McLane, who offered to host us in the most coveted seats inside Minute Maid Park. Located directly behind the home plate, the seats were in full sight of the batsman and pitcher and, McLane explained to us, were normally reserved for the franchise's most distinguished fan, the former President George Bush Sr. In truth I felt embarrassed by the level of access we were given, especially as I knew near-to-nothing about baseball and realised that every one of the 30,000 spectators that day would have pounced at the opportunity of having our vantage point. It was also striking how smoothly the *Houston Chronicle's* journalist went about his business and schmoozed with the Astros' senior personnel; it was impossible to imagine an equivalent *Manchester Evening News* reporter enjoying similarly unfettered access within Old Trafford.

Later that evening the atmosphere inside Houston's Reliant Stadium – packed with more than 70,000 fans – felt close to a full blooded competitive match, with a strongly partisan crowd cheering America's best, but perhaps not appreciating how little training time the disparately assembled players had spent with each other in contrast with their illustrious visitors. The All-Stars' tactical naivety would be punished by United as they romped to a 5-2 victory, the icing on the cake being a sublime lob by Javier Hernández, his first goal for the Reds scored in front of an ecstatic Hispanic contingent.

Hernández Hysteria

The rousing reception in America for Hernández, complimented that day by a noticeable vigil of young fans outside the team's Houston headquarters, proved to be a small foretaste of the mass hysteria that we were to witness on the last leg of the summer tour in Guadalajara, Mexico. Upon arrival at the hotel we nervously navigated the underground car park that had been besieged by hordes of screaming fans desperate for a glimpse of their local hero. Minutes later, at the press conference packed with the country's football journalists, Chicharito – flanked by Sir Alex Ferguson and David Gill – made his first official press appearance as a Manchester United player. It was the only time that I would witness Sir Alex and David Gill's presence at the top table seem largely irrelevant; they were simply usurped by the smiling, diminutive Mexican as 50-or-so reporters desperately sought comment from this most affable and forthcoming of superstars.

Moments later I was in the back seat of a blacked out 4x4 with chief executive David Gill. Our driver, with horn honking and tyres screeching, was in high-speed pursuit of an identical vehicle in front of us carrying its very special passenger. As we neared our destination – the Nike store in one of Guadalajara's upmarket suburbs – it was evident that the place had come to a complete standstill, surrounded as it was by thousands of football crazy, red-clad Chicharito fans. Our small convoy pushed its way impatiently towards the store where, shielded by security guards, we all quickly alighted before being guided into the store's basement. There, we took stock for a few minutes, allowing for some dramatic tension before the appearance of Mexico's favourite player.

Finally emerging into the store upstairs, we were able to experience at first-hand the decibel-busting cacophony from the screaming fans, every one of them desperate to catch a glimpse of their idol. Through another set of doors we followed Chicharito outside the store as he climbed up onto a specially made platform, decked with Nike and Manchester United liveries, where – armed with a marker pen – he proceeded to meet and greet fans and sign hundreds of autographs on every conceivable type of merchandise. He emitted that rare star quality of being able to make every fan (mostly female, in this case) feel special during those fleeting seconds spent with him. Just one year after I'd accompanied Ji-Sung Park in his native South Korea, the intensity of supporters in Guadalajara seemed to even eclipse the mania that I'd witnessed in Seoul. This carried over into the following evening at an occasion to mark the grand opening of a brand new stadium belonging to Club Deportivo Guadalajara (also known as Chivas). Manchester United had been invited to take part in the inaugural match, in effect a game that had formed part of the transfer deal which saw Hernández moving from Mexico to Manchester. He would diplomatically start one half for Chivas, and the other for his new club.

After two hours of theatrical fireworks, thunderously pounding music through the Estadio Omnilife's brand new PA system, and an enjoyable game won 3-2 by the Mexicans, the final whistle marked the end of Manchester United's summer tour. Along with the familiar 'job done' feelings of fatigue and relief came some pangs of sadness, compounded by the sense that my involvement with the club was perhaps coming to a natural close. The post-match dinner, a rushed but surprisingly tasty three-course affair in a large, freshly-painted lounge inside the stadium, would be the last time I would be assembled with the club's personnel; the owners, the executives, the coaches, the players and the tour executives. A short time later we were spirited out of the stadium and, bypassing normal security and customs protocols, headed straight onto our chartered Turkish Airlines plane. The jet would skilfully navigate its way through a stunning but frightening lightning storm, flying us safely back to Manchester where a new season awaited.

Epilogue

My Last Visit

My first visit to Old Trafford at the start of the new 2010/11 season would turn out to be the last in my role. I attended the launch of yet another new sponsor; on this occasion the Hong Kong based PCCW. We hosted the telecoms company's senior executives over a buffet dinner in one of the South Stand's bustling hospitality suites, before moving outside to the rows of reserved seats adjacent to the press box. There we witnessed United cruising to a 3-0 victory against Newcastle United; a satisfyingly auspicious start to a new commercial partnership.

That night there was a conspicuous absence of green-and-gold livery inside and outside Old Trafford; admittedly it was still summer and most supporters' scarves may have lain in hibernation deep inside their owners' chests of drawers, but the hiatus after the end of the previous season seemed to provide a bookend to the active protests against the Glazers. Simmering resentment would persist, of course, in negative press coverage which focused on the fact that season tickets hadn't completely sold out. That said, the early September sales of 52,000 – just 2,000 short of the target – were greeted with relief by the club, especially given the stiffening economic conditions.

By early October, the team had clocked up a relatively inauspicious three wins and four draws from its first seven games (although a home victory against Liverpool had helped to assuage neurotic concerns). I was also sitting on a mixed bag of news to be revealed by the full year accounts which, while showing that strong media and commercial revenues had helped power operating profits beyond £100 million for the first time, would also reveal an annual pre-tax loss of some £80 million, largely a £67 million legacy of the bond refinancing charges and a substantial hit from the ill-fated interest rate swap. Mindful of the loss – which would likely excite press coverage – I was keen that we should try to lodge the positive operating profit figure ahead of the official publication of the results, while also managing expectations that financing costs had pushed the club back into the red. I duly approached a few journalists with the £100 million figure, also confirming that Ronaldo's transfer income had lain untouched. I also outlined that pre-tax losses had widened to ensure against angry comeback when the figure was eventually divulged. The resulting coverage the following morning was mixed: the *Daily Telegraph* ran the headline 'Operating profits at Old Trafford top £100m' while the *Times* went with 'Anti-Glazer protests set to be revived by £67m loss for United.'

When we eventually published the figures, my leak had seemed to dampen the resonance of the large loss. Chief executive David Gill was in robust form when speaking to journalists in telephone interviews, insisting in particular that the club's £165 million cash pile meant there was no pressure at all to sell any star player. The *Telegraph's* Paul Kelso commented:[139] 'The accounts published yesterday demonstrate once again that, despite the objections of the supporters ranged against them, the massively leveraged business model they imposed on the club is doing what they intended. A debt burden of £700 million may make some of us queasy but not apparently the Glazers.'

Wayne Rooney Dumbfounds

The fortunes of the Glazers' Manchester United were in marked contrast by now with those of Liverpool owners, Tom Hicks and George Gillett, who were reported to be consumed with feuding, financial meltdown and – more urgently – with an unedifying legal

---

[139] All going to plan for Glazers, *The Daily Telegraph*, 9 October 2010

tussle with their board who desperately wanted to sell the club to another set of Americans.

But if I – or anyone at Manchester United – were tempted to revel in the travails at the club's traditionally most vehement rival, we could not have foreseen that United would itself become suddenly convulsed by crisis. Within days of Boston Red Sox owner John W Henry II taking the helm at Liverpool, the *Sunday Mirror* splashed the headline 'Screw Roo, Fergie,' claiming:[140] 'Wayne Rooney will quit Manchester United following a series of explosive rows with manager Sir Alex Ferguson. Talks over a new contract that would keep Rooney at Old Trafford for the peak years of his career have broken down – paving the way for the 24-year-old England international to leave United in a £50 million deal.' The story was initially dismissed as 'nonsense' by the club, but intense briefing by Rooney's entourage that Sunday would ensure that the story commanded prominent coverage across the media by Monday. There were allegations that the Glazer family, saddled with the debt and those widening accounting losses, would want to cash in on Rooney's departure, not least as there was only a year-and-a-half to run on his contract. A shrewd tactic by Rooney's camp, I thought, to deflect United fans' opprobrium away from the striker towards the club's unpopular American owners.

It was inconceivable to me that the Glazers would welcome Rooney's exit. On countless occasions they had stressed in private conversations that he was absolutely integral to the club and, as understood by press and fans alike, they would never interfere with Sir Alex's team selection. But it appeared from the many calls from journalists at the start of the week that Rooney's aides – together with United supporters group MUST – were seeking to blame any potential move on the perceived lack of ambition and investment by the Glazers, citing the recent disclosure of the £80 million loss. But despite my off-the-record protestations to journalists that the club had substantial cash reserves and had no desire to see Rooney go, by the start of the new week there seemed a growing resignation among the club's hierarchy that Wayne

---

[140] Screw Roo, Fergie, *Sunday Mirror*, 17 October 2010

Rooney could be on his way out to join Abu Dhabi-owned Manchester City. This was a fate acknowledged by Sir Alex Ferguson, who gave an emotionally-charged address at the end of a routine Champions League press conference where he admitted he been 'dumbfounded' by the striker's request to leave the club. Henry Winter of the *Daily Telegraph* darkly warned:[141] 'The Glazers will dispute the allegation they are 'leeching' off United but the recent annual accounts, with interest repayments gorging on profits, makes grim reading for United fans... To lose one star like Cristiano Ronaldo could be considered a misfortune. To lose another, in Rooney, looks more than carelessness; it looks like the dreaded hand of debt holding United and Ferguson back. The shame of the Glazers' regime is now fully exposed.'

The following day Manchester were to host Turkish side Bursaspor at Old Trafford in the Champions League but the media focus remained firmly on Wayne Rooney's future. I continued to speak extensively to the press – on condition of not being cited – reminding them that the club was bigger than any individual, especially one that may no longer want to continue playing in a Manchester United shirt. I even had to beg one journalist eager to foretell the demise of United to show a little more respect, reminding him of the club's illustrious tradition of conquering setbacks. As the match approached there was growing speculation that Rooney, who was injured and would not be playing that night, would nevertheless be making a statement. Just two hours before kick-off a short statement from Rooney was released saying: 'I met with David Gill last week and he did not give me any of the assurances I was seeking about the future squad...about the continued ability of the club to attract the top players in the world.' It was a crudely-disguised dig at the Glazers' ownership. I was duly barraged with calls from reporters demanding a response. I felt like coming back with a sarcastic riposte, reflecting my frustration at being roped in to such a self-serving spectacle. However, I knew that the only retort amid such a fevered atmosphere – which had extended to

---

[141] Henry Winter: Shame of Glazers' reign fully exposed, *The Daily Telegraph*, 20 October 2010

television pictures of a supporter holding up a banner reading 'Who's the whore now?' – was not to dignify the statement with a response and was instead to say absolutely nothing. The *Daily Mirror* noted:[142] 'If [Rooney's] camp hoped that the anti-Glazer sentiment would keep supporters on his side they were wrong. One season ticket holder added: 'As much as I detest the Glazers, to blame them over the petulance of a spoilt footballer is plain nonsense.'

By Thursday – after four days of a most unedifying public relations battle between Rooney and Manchester United – the club confirmed that it had entered into intensive talks with the player's representatives, suggesting that a rapprochement was possible. I, like everyone else not privy to such discussions, waited for the conclusion. On Friday afternoon I received a call from an excited James Cooper from Sky Sports News asking for my reaction to the big news. 'What news?' I replied. 'Rooney's staying with the club; he's signed a contract after speaking with the Glazers.' Clearly, and not without some embarrassment before Cooper I found myself out of the loop, ignorant of the fast moving developments up in both Manchester and the States. It transpired that Joel Glazer had spoken to Wayne Rooney by telephone reassuring him about his ambitions for the club, demonstrated amply by a reported offer of a new £200,000 a week deal.

With Rooney renewing his contract, I appreciated how my spokesman role might have fanned the controversy by providing journalists' speculation with a refuge. I began to have the irrevocable feeling that my job was done; indeed, ever since we had lifted the drawbridge to the Red Knights at the start of June I had sensed that I was a spent force at Manchester United. I had even drafted an email upon my return from the North America tour to Joel Glazer and Ed Woodward with the suggestion that his family dispense with the spokesman role altogether; if they didn't want the attention, why retain a proxy that still attracted constant media attention? But self-interest dictated otherwise and I never sent the email. I mean, who in their right mind would willingly forgo working for Manchester United?

---

[142] Get Lost, *Daily Mirror*, 21 October 2010

Lame Duck

On a crisp autumnal afternoon in late October, with the lime trees glistening gold in Green Park, I made my way to the club's Pall Mall office. Ed was unusually tense but also seemed more focused than normal on the task ahead. We sat down around the boardroom table. 'Tes, this is going to be difficult...' Immediately, I knew what was coming, my adrenalin kicking in at the final reality of leaving my role; half excitement, half dread. Ed explained the decision to reassess the owners' communication management strategy, acknowledging my growing frustrations with the job and relayed Joel Glazer's offer of a generous golden handshake. I felt assured that I would be leaving my spokesman role at Manchester United on the best possible terms.

Although the announcement of my exit would come some weeks later, I was with immediate effect a lame duck, no longer privy to the inner workings of the club, which I marked by recording an 'away on annual leave' voicemail message on my phone. The calls didn't stop, however, but I felt relieved at not having to answer them anymore. With one foot out of the door I could see more objectively the occasional absurdity of my role; while Ed Woodward's London office was seeking to close a new sponsorship deal with office equipment provider Epson, rumours abounded (inflamed by the wildfire-like Twitter) that Manchester United's owners were in *takeover* talks with Epson. It felt liberating to no longer have to deal with such spurious speculation.

Swan Song

Joel Glazer would offer me an opportunity of a satisfying swan song. During my exit meeting Ed Woodward had hinted that something significant was afoot and suggested that my last assignment could be to steer it past the press, thus enabling me to leave on a high. I guessed it revolved around news concerning the removal of the PIK note, the loan instrument that the Glazers had originally used in their takeover, and which continued to accrue interest of around 16 per cent a year, well in excess of the 9 per cent that the bond cost. It was an issue that I knew Joel Glazer and Ed had been grappling with throughout that summer.

The early redemption of the £220 million PIK would provide me with a logical reason to bow out of my role. As long as the PIK existed, a spokesman for the Glazers was necessary to assuage fears that it could compromise their ownership of Manchester United. With the PIK gone, the post of a spokesman for the owners, separate to the club, was rendered obsolete.

When the call came from Ed to see him in his office in mid-November I sensed that, finally, he had good news on the PIK front. His broad grin upon greeting me confirmed that this was the case, although it would transpire that a multitude of fine detail was still being worked on with advisors. However, as my role was effectively over I would not be privy to Ed's discussions with Joel relating to just how the PIK had been removed, and that suited me just fine.

I advised Ed and Joel that the media would dwell on two obvious questions: was any of the Ronaldo cash used to pay off the PIK, and how was it paid down? To my relief the answer to the first question was a simple 'no'; the second would prompt a well-versed and unequivocal 'no comment / mind your own business' message, consistent with the jealously-guarded privacy the Glazers continued to, understandably, wield over their financial affairs. Not for the first time in my role – but now for the last – my ignorance would prove bliss as I would feel no pressure having to withhold any sensitive information when I eventually spoke to the media.

But I did strongly advise that we should go hard with the positive message that the club's cash reserves had not been plundered, and should release an official statement from the Manchester United board to this effect in order to coincide with the publication of first quarter financial results. I nevertheless warned internally that this assurance would inevitably be spun by supporters' groups as vindication of their public campaign throughout 2010 that had called for the Glazers to leave the club cash alone, theoretically made available to the owners by the fine print in the bond prospectus at the start of the year.

By late afternoon, confirmation arrived that the PIK had been paid down. Given the large circle of investors who had owned the very lucrative, high-yielding instrument – some of whom would no doubt be peeved to have been bought out – it was only a matter of time, perhaps as little as a few hours, before the news would leak into the market. So it felt ironic that I had been invited that evening to a Sports News Lobby annual drinks reception with every sport business journalist in attendance, while sitting on the closure of a story that had exercised so many of them for five long years.

I had arranged to meet Phil Townsend ahead of the function to convey news in person of my exit. As we traipsed around the streets of Knightsbridge I was able to divulge two significant developments: that the PIK had gone (to his immediate relief and delight) and that I was going too, which seemed to prompt shock and apprehension on his part. The end of our close working relationship was near.

We entered the reception inside the Royal Thames Yacht Club which was populated with a who's who in UK sport: heads of organisations, politicians, fellow PR people and, of course, senior reporters sipping complimentary wine in a friendly, strictly Chatham House rules environment. But my imminent departure meant that I was feeling withdrawn, coupled with feeling nervous about the prospect of any leaked PIK revelation while I was inside a lion's den of journalists. After an hour or so I sneaked out of the bustling room, ruminating wryly to myself that I would probably be speaking to many of the journalists again the following day. My satisfaction would, however, be short lived. As I headed home and emerged out of the underground train tunnel, I discovered that my BlackBerry phone was clogged with some 20 voicemails and text messages. News of the PIK's redemption had broken via Tariq Panja from the Bloomberg newswire. Tariq, it transpired, had disseminated his scoop via Twitter, immediately alerting his fellow reporters at the reception, something that I only wished I'd witnessed myself.

The next morning, with the publication of the official press release clarifying that club cash had not been used to pay down the PIK, journalists, as expected, focused their enquiries on the second question; if the Glazers didn't use club cash, where did they get the

£220 million from to redeem it? I was surprised how many even speculated that the Americans may have already sold off a chunk of the club to raise the cash; a suggestion that I had anticipated and was under strict orders from Ed Woodward to straight bat with a neither-confirm-nor-deny reply. It was no surprise, then, that some reporters' incredulity boiled over into frustration upon being stonewalled by my 'no comment.' One senior journalist erupted, telling me what a PR disaster the announcement had been and how pointless my job had become; that reporter probably didn't appreciate how close to the truth his anger had taken him. Indeed the good news that the PIK had disappeared fell on largely deaf ears among the media, typified by the *Daily Telegraph's* headline the next morning: 'Glazers repayment of £220m payment-in-kind loans at Manchester United leaves more questions than answers.'

Questions I was relieved to no longer be charged with fielding; answers I would miss the challenge of providing.

A week later I publicly announced my exit and Joel Glazer telephoned me for the last time:

'Hi Tes, well, what can I say, it's been one hell of a ride. I'm only sorry that you had one arm tied behind your back during your time, given our reluctance to engage.'

'Listen Joel, I have loved every moment of it and feel very privileged that you and your family gave me the chance. It's been life changing.'

'You'll always be a friend to us and the club. Thanks again, Tes.'